SUPERMAN ON TELEVISION

TENTH ANNIVERSARY EDITION

your friend
George Reeves

SUPERMAN ON TELEVISION

TENTH ANNIVERSARY EDITION

WRITTEN & COMPILED BY
MICHAEL BIFULCO

MICHAEL BIFULCO
GRAND RAPIDS, MICHIGAN

SUPERMAN ON TELEVISION: TENTH ANNIVERSARY EDITION

Library of Congress Catalog Card Number: 98-92686

This book was designed, edited, hyphenated, justified, illustrated, paginated, and typeset on an IBM-PC, utilizing the professional capabilities of MagnaPage software developed by Magna Computer Systems, Inc. The author never touched a Mac.

Cover designed and produced by Robert McKeon Design, Grand Rapids, Michigan

ISBN 0-9619596-3-0

Printed in the United States of America

March 1998

10 9 8 7 6 5 4 3 2 1

this book is dedicated
to the lasting memory of
George Reeves

Contents

Author's Note
1988

THIS BOOK BEGAN AS AN EPISODE LISTING WITH BRIEF COMMENTS ON EACH OF THE SHOWS IN the television series to assist my collecting activities. Eventually, I sort of found myself getting carried away by all of it. What developed you will find on the following pages.

The project was fast becoming an obsession that had me running all over town in search of photographs, lobby cards, posters, and copies of past interviews and review material. I literally spent hundreds of hours in front of television sets and movie screens watching and rewatching the *Adventures of Superman* in an effort to capture as much insight and influence as possible. I must confess, it made me feel like a kid again.

The production quality of the series is certainly inferior by today's standards, but to judge the work fairly, one must consider the period in which it was made. Even today, one cannot help but be impressed with the spirit and charm of the performances. I hope you enjoy reading about the *Adventures of Superman* half as much as I did writing about it.

—MJB
August 1987

Introduction
1988

EVERY GENERATION HAS HEROES. THEY HAVE APPEARED IN THE NEWSPAPERS, BOOKS, magazines, radio, television, and motion pictures. To list all of them would be a monumental task in itself, but since 1938, one heroic figure has made his way into every media format—SUPERMAN.

He was born in the comic book illustrations of Jerry Siegel and Joe Shuster. He was animated in the studios of Max Fleischer, assuming the voice of Bud Collyer both in the cartoons and on the Mutual radio network. Toward the end of the 1940s, he materialized in the body of a dedicated actor named Kirk Alyn in thirty episodes of two theatrical serials. In recent years, Christopher Reeve has given life to the Superman character in four feature motion pictures *(through 1987)*. Today, the Man of Steel continues to do battle against the forces of evil as always in a thriving collection of comic magazines, and on Saturday mornings in more modern, but less sophisticated cartoon stories than the adventures presented in the Fleischer series.

However, to those of us who grew up in the fifties, GEORGE REEVES will always be the *real* Superman. As a child, no matter where I was or what I was doing, I somehow knew when it was time to plant myself in front of any available television to watch the *Adventures of Superman.* My understanding mother always knew it was time to start preparing dinner when she heard the sound of my crashing through the kitchen doorway immediately followed by the familiar theme music emanating from the living room.

As I distinctly recall, the style of the opening title would indicate which of the two actresses that I loved equally would appear as LOIS LANE. Certain familiar background music was characteristic of the better episodes in the second season, and even as a youngster, I remember noting that as Superman's hair became thinner and Clark Kent's glasses became thicker, the storylines seemed to get less violent and more amusing. But all of them were enjoyable if for no other reason than to watch how the bad guys would react when they encountered this strange visitor from another planet who came to Earth with powers and abilities far beyond those of mortal men to fight a never ending battle for truth, justice, and the American way.

In the summer of 1951, the back lot of a movie studio in Culver City, California became the location for the filming of a low budget movie entitled *Superman and the Mole Men,* starring George Reeves and Phyllis Coates. The project was produced by Barney Sarecky and directed by Lee Sholem, and the feature picture was designed to be the first of a series of television episodes made specifically for syndication. This procedure was not at all like how series television shows are introduced today by a major network during prime-time viewing hours.

Within six months, the feature version of Superman was released to the theatres and became an immediate success. Another twenty-four, half-hour episodes were completed before the end of 1951. The project was produced under the guiding hand of Robert Maxwell, who had in recent years been responsible for the Superman series on the Mutual Radio network. These shows along with the feature film edited into a two-part episode represented the first full season, but it wasn't until early in 1953 that any were broadcast over the air.

Following a successful television debut, the series went back into production in the summer of 1953, but now it was under the leadership of a new producer. Robert Maxwell and his team were replaced by Whitney Ellsworth from National Comics, the Superman Inc. parent organization. They felt that although Maxwell had generated a solid show, it was a little too serious and hard hitting for their taste. Whitney Ellsworth was brought in to tone it down by underplaying the violence and injecting more humor and wholesome entertainment. Some critics feel he may have gone too far.

From 1953 through 1957, Whitney Ellsworth produced seventy-eight half-hour *Adventures of Superman,* fifty-two of which were originally photographed in color, but initially released in black and white. Ellsworth continued with all of the original cast members except Phyllis Coates, who was not available at the time production started up again in 1953. Noel Neill was brought in to fill the role of *Lois Lane,* the same part she portrayed in the 1948 and 1950 Superman serials made over at Columbia Studios with Kirk Alyn. Ellsworth also made more frequent use of the appearances by Jimmy Olsen and Inspector Bill Henderson in his episodes of the show.

On the following pages, you will find the impressions of this author with regard to each of the 104 filmed episodes of the series. Whether you agree with them, some of them, or none of them, I certainly hope they will at least remind you of the experience you had as a kid when these shows first lit up your television screen. I'm guessing it is a memory of wonder and excitement, or you would not have bothered to crack the cover of this book.

Since this book is intended to celebrate what we hope were the best years of George Reeves' life, I will not dwell on the macabre details of his untimely death other than to say he passed away in June of 1959 from a gunshot wound. Fate is not always kind, but in this case at least, we have 104 episodes of the *Adventures of Superman* and one segment of *I Love Lucy* with which he will always be remembered. Collecting and documenting his career as the Man of Steel for my children and perhaps their children is my way of saying thanks to him for being a part of my growing up. From all the material written or said about him, it seems he was a very kind and generous human being. No child or adult could do better than pick George Reeves as a role model for a way to live their life.

Introduction
1998

IT IS HARD TO BELIEVE THAT TEN YEARS HAVE PASSED SINCE THIS BOOK WAS FIRST PUBLISHED. A multitude of fond memories fill those ten years and I am constantly reminded of many of them everytime I look at my kids. Gracie *(now thirteen years old)* was just a toddler and wondering what I was doing when I was watching and rewatching every one of the 104 episodes in preparation for the original writing of this book, and Andrew *(now eleven and with aspirations to become a comic illustrator)* was merely a baby and somehow trusted that I knew what I was doing.

It would be easy to fill an entire book on all that has happened to me in the last decade, but that would be of little interest to many of you, seem a bit self-serving to most of you, and quite boring to all of you. However, if you would please indulge me for a few paragraphs, I would like to chronicle three important events regarding the publication of this book.

It was sometime in 1987, during the last stretch of prepress work to get the original edition of this book ready to release, I received an unpretentious telephone call from Jim Hambrick. Thankfully, I had by then heard of him from viewing a television piece showcasing his collecting activities, and I knew he was most likely the world's tallest Superman collector in the field. He was interested in the book and invited me to attend the Summer of 1988 celebration in Cleveland, Ohio.

The second important event was indeed the visit to Cleveland that Summer where I introduced the book to a crowd of enthusiastic fans. Not just Superman fans, but George Reeves fans. I was utterly amazed and pleasantly surprised at the number of people my age that still retained memories of the same television show with which I grew up. The best word to describe the experience is euphoria. I was allowed the opportunity to meet in person both Jack Larson and Noel Neill as well as a fine group of their admirers, many of whom I have kept in touch with over the years. I would love to list the names, but I would undoubtedly omit quite by accident a name or two and regret it until the next edition of the book. You all know who you are, and I hope to see you all in Metropolis sometime.

The third important event was my marriage to the lovely and gracious Carol. I know, I promised not to burden you with personal happenings, but being very happily married was and still is a critical ingredient in the production of this book. Without Carol's encouragement, patience for the long hours, and understanding of my obsession with George, this new edition would never have been published.

In the decade since the first edition was published, there have been at least a hundred interviews and articles written by many qualified researchers regarding various behind-the-scenes aspects of the *Adventures of Superman*. Many people have called to my attention what have proven to be omissions and inaccuracies in the first edition of this book. Their input is greatly appreciated, and I have attempted to correct all of the mistakes. But after ten years of letters, telephone calls, and meetings with hundreds of George Reeves fans, I must hold to my original intention for writing this book. That is, I hope to present this work again as a celebration of what I believe we all hope were the best years of Reeve's life.

However, for those of you who indeed share an interest in the circumstances of his death, I would recommend you read the most scholarly written and thoroughly researched piece on the subject, *George Reeves: The Man, The Myth, The Mystery,* by Jan Alan Henderson. It was published in a magazine called *Speeding Bullet* in 1995 by Cult Movies in Hollywood, California. I understand an expanded book version of this project is currently in the works.

Finally, I would like to thank Robert McKeon for his kind cooperation in the design and production of the cover for this new edition, and his patience with my insistence on a color scheme that pays tribute to the classic black & white costume is greatly appreciated. Any acknowledgment must also include my wife, Carol, and my daughter, Gracie, for their vigorous attempts to catch all of my grammar and spelling errors. However, any mistakes that remain are entirely my fault. And I would like to thank everyone who supported the first edition of this book. I have a file cabinet full of wonderful letters, and I have spent many enjoyable hours on the telephone over the last ten years talking to more George Reeves fans than I ever imagined who still share fond memories of the *Adventures of Superman*.

Michael Bifulco
1998
email: BIF35FILM@AOL.COM

TENTH ANNIVERSARY EDITION

The Episodes of
1951

NATIONAL COMICS HAD ALREADY GIVEN LIFE TO ITS MOST POPULAR HERO IN A SERIES OF lavishly produced animated cartoons, two action packed movie serials, and a long-running radio series produced by Robert Maxwell. Television was young and hungry for new programming to fill the broadcast day. The next logical step in the evolution of the Superman character was obvious—a collection of half hour episodes, packaged for the small screen.

Robert Maxwell was given the reigns as head of the production. National also drafted Whitney Ellsworth from the New York offices to prepare what we might today call a "pilot" script which was entitled *"Nightmare"* by the time it went before the cameras in Culver City. Although the budget was ordered to be very conservative, to further protect their investment, the producers decided to kick off the project with a motion picture in the event that television failed to catch on. It certainly did catch on, and the rest is history. When the series hit the airwaves early in 1953, it was an instant success.

The motion picture was called *Superman and the Mole Men,* and it was filmed within a whirlwind twelve-day schedule in the heat of July. In addition to George Reeves in the lead role, only Phyllis Coates as *Lois Lane* was along for the ride on this first adventure as Producer Maxwell was still in the process of finalizing the rest of the cast for the series. But it was a good beginning, a nice blend of science-fiction and social commentary, and it provided plenty of opportunities for Superman to establish himself as the unltimate action-hero.

After filming was completed by director *Lee Sholem* for the feature movie introduction of Superman, *Tommy Carr* joined the production team. He directed fifteen of the first season's offerings, with Sholem picking up the balance of nine. The feature film was edited into a two-part show which completed the first set of twenty-six episodes.

Time and budget dictated the procedures for filming the *Adventures of Superman.* Each of the two directors was given his assigned scripts and each would plan the filming schedule for photographing a handful of shows at one time. As it happened, either by luck or design, approximately one third of the scenes unfolded in or around the offices of the Daily Planet. A set such as Clark Kent's office would be assembled, decorated, and lighted with the camera and crew positioned a few feet away.

For several days, each of the key players would be given script pages. When the director called for "action!" they would enter, exit, sit, stand, and speak their dialog as if

Superman faces off against the mob led by "Luke Benson" *(Jeff Corey)* with "Matt" *(John Phillips, left)* and "Eddie" *(Steve Carr, center)* looking on in amazement.

they really knew what story was being dramatized or how it would all be pulled together on the moviola by film editor *Al Joseph*.

Of course, every film actor was accustomed to this condition of performing sequences by order of convenience to set requirements, a practice created early in the history of Hollywood movie making. But unlike working on a feature motion picture with a single story, the Superman Family of characters was usually playing out several individual plots at one time.

Fortunately, the task of insuring continuity was made a little easier by the costume requirements of the principal cast members. Jimmy's sweater and bowtie, the career clothing outfit worn by Lois, and Kent's blue-gray suit rarely changed except for an occasional location visit to a jungle or gym, and it appears as if Perry White wore the same striped tie from the black & white episodes right into the color seasons long before *Rush Limbaugh* provided us with a greater variety of options.

Another contribution to scene continuity were similarities in the basic story of each adventure. In order to begin and end neatly within twenty five or so minutes of screen time, the plots usually revolved around simple ideas like solving a mystery or stopping the evil use of some scientific discovery. Most often, the villains' only deadly miscalculation was getting either willingly or unwillingly involved with one of the lead characters which ultimately demanded the attention of Superman.

It wasn't really important for actress *Phyllis Coates* to know why Superman's appearance was required in order for her to conjure up the proper motivation for an insulting lecture to Clark Kent for his display of timidity or his hasty retreat in the face of adversity. Likewise, it wasn't necessary for *Jack Larson* to understand why he was being kidnapped or threatened by a villain for him to give a proper performance as the eager and naive junior reporter. And it probably worked out better this way for *John Hamilton's* portrayal as the angry editor because his character usually didn't know why his employees were always running off without warning anyway. All that mattered was the completion of the scene and a move to the next one.

What separated the *Adventures of Superman* from the westerns, comedies, and crime dramas of television was obviously the amazing talents of the title hero, especially his ability to fly. For his take off and flight sequences, *George Reeves* was initially photographed while suspended by wires that were not intended to show in the final print. Subsequently, his lift from the ground was filmed from a much wider angle than those later using the springboard. This technique required Reeves to get a running start and then leap over the cameraman's head and hopefully tumble to safety. It also required a tighter camera shot to allow enough room for his feet to clear the top of the picture.

During the production of the *Ghost Wolf* episode, filmed near the end of the shooting schedule, one of the wires snapped and Reeves came crashing to the floor of the set. Luckily, he was not seriously hurt, and Reeves has often been quoted to have said, "That's enough of that! Peter Pan can fly with wires, but not Superman!"

Unlike today, there were no strong rules against actors doing their own stunt work. Reeves preferred it because more realism was added to his performance in what some must have felt was a very silly costume. Anyway, with a nice assortment of techniques for take off and flying sequences, the television audience was certainly allowed to believe this strange visitor from another world could defy the natural laws of gravity.

A characteristic mostly attributed to the first season episodes under the leadership of Robert Maxwell was the profusion of violence. It was evident in every show with fist fights, kidnappings, shootings, murders, postwar nazi activities, and suicide. In *The Evil Three* episode, an elderly lady in a wheel chair is pushed down a flight of stairs. And there is even a touch of child abuse as demonstrated toward little Cathy Williams in *The Birthday Letter*.

Violence on the screen is one thing, but when it carries over into real life, it usually takes its toll from the cast and crew. One such incident occurred on the set of *Night of Terror* when Phyllis Coates accidently took a live punch to the face from actor *Frank Richards*. Apparently, he was only to give her a light brush of wind, but as with so many productions where there is never enough time for rehearsal, a performer would sometimes miss a mark and the unexpected would happen. Legend has it that director Sholem insisted the scene be completed before her face began to swell.

Superman *(George Reeves)* and Lois Lane *(Phyllis Coates)* in the closing scene of *Superman and the Mole Men.*

It seems that no one on the Superman set was immune to the hazards of making an action series. Director Tommy Carr came close to breaking his neck when he first demonstrated the springboard for George Reeves. In *The Stolen Costume* episode, the rigid support frame was not removed from a fake apartment door before Reeves was to come running through it. And Jack Larson often found himself almost completely submerged in water which at the very least resulted in his catching a cold.

In two and a half months, which would be considered a record today, the cast and crew completed their work for what would amount to twenty-six, action packed half hour programs. The feature version of the series *Superman and the Mole Men* was released theatrically in November of 1951 by Lippert Pictures, Inc. Meanwhile, the television episodes were edited, special effects elements were added, and the now familiar moody themes were merged with the sound track from a generic library of background music. The series was finally introduced to the airwaves beginning in the Fall of 1952, and by the

Spring of 1953, the show could be seen across the country as it was sponsored by Kellogg, the greatest name in cereal.

Though its popularity certainly grew from word-of-mouth, the show was frequently promoted in the print media to maintain momentum. For example, Superman was proudly featured on the cover of *Radio and Television NEWS,* a complimentary program guide offered by RCA Victor sales and service outlets in March of 1953. Alongside a striking akimbo pose of the live-action hero was the following blurb:

IT'S "SUPERMAN"—With the physique of an American All-Star football player, George Reeves brings an astounding believability to the role of "Superman," now seen each Monday on KECA-TV.

A glowing review occupied an entire page within this publication carrying the following headline: *"SUPERMAN," THRILLING ACTION-PACKED SCIENCE-FICTION SERIAL, ON KECA-TV.* The article went on to say:

Monday nights are thrilling nights on channel 7, with famed "Superman" and his unequaled feats of daring bringing to TV viewers entertainment of the highest order. Bows go to George Reeves, who won the stellar role after more than 200 candidates were auditioned and interviewed. Reeves brings to the character of "Superman" an absolute believability that at first glance would seem to be beyond the powers of a young actor. Reeves completely fulfills the conception of the fabulous character known to millions of cartoon and radio fans. . .

"Superman" is sustained TV excitement from the moment when the planet Krypton's leading man of science, fearing the planet's destruction, places his infant son in a small space ship and sends it hurtling to earth. . .

EYES ON "SUPERMAN"—Attractive Phyllis Coates, in the role of Lois Lane, reporter and pal of "Superman," lends exciting charm to the famed science-fiction series now seen each Monday on KECA-TV.

Each episode is complete in itself. . . but the viewer's curiosity is such that each succeeding chapter is eagerly awaited.

Superman was clearly a no nonsense crime fighter with no tolerance for the hardened criminal types that attempted to operate in Metropolis. Unlike the later episodes under Ellsworth's control, Superman usually wrapped up the case with a violent confrontation. However, in spite of the criticism, Robert Maxwell's collection of first season episodes rightfully deserves and holds a place in television history.

PRODUCTION CREDITS

producers .... Robert Maxwell, Bernard Luber
associate producer .... Barney A. Sarecky*
assistant director .... Nate Barragar, Art Hammond*
cameraman .... William Whitley, Clark Ramsey*
sound engineer .... Harry Smith
art director .... Ralph Berger, Ernst Fegté*
wardrobe .... Izzy Berne
casting .... Harold Chiles
props .... George Bahr
special effects .... Danny Hayes
dialog director .... Steve Carr
make-up .... Harry Thomas
sound editor .... Barton Hayes
film editor .... Al Joseph

*For the production of *Superman and the Mole Men*

The 1951 feature film *Superman and the Mole Men* is available from Warner Home Video.

EPISODE 1

SUPERMAN ON EARTH

directed by TOMMY CARR
written by RICHARD FIELDING

The premiere episode of the series retells the origin of Superman based upon the story as it appeared in the comic book edition of *Superman #53*, and it details his arrival on Earth as an infant from the planet Krypton. Although it was numbered in the release package to television as the first episode, it was actually one of the last shows to be filmed in October of 1951.

It opens with a narration establishing a distant solar system with a planet called *Krypton* where a meeting of the High Council has been called to order by **ROZAN** *(Herbert Rawlinson)*, the majority leader. Speaking before the august body is one of the planet's chief scientists, **JOREL** *(Robert Rockwell)*. Based on his research, he announces the pending destruction of their world.

Faced with objections and hostility, Jorel outlines his plan for survival, the rapid construction of a fleet of rocketships to carry the people of Krypton to safety on a far away world similar to their own. He further explains that he has a model ready to test, when **KOGAN** *(Stuart Randall)* demands to know where Jorel plans to send it. As he names *Earth* to be the destination, the room begins to rumble because of a tremor beneath the surface of the planet. Claiming the disturbance to be only thunder, the members of the Council drive Jorel out of the chamber with laughter and disbelief.

In his hilltop home, which looks very much like the observatory overlooking Hollywood, Jorel continues to work in his laboratory, unwilling to admit defeat. As his wife, **LARA** *(Aline Towne)* enters, more quakes announce that Krypton's doom is nearer than expected. Jorel and Lara agree their baby boy should be saved. He is placed inside the model rocketship and blasted into space.

Parents of Krypton,
Jorel *(Robert Rockwell)* and Lara *(Aline Towne)*.

Jorel *(Robert Rockwell)* and Lara *(Aline Towne)* moments before the rocket will blast off and carry their son to Earth.

On Earth, **SARA** *(Frances Morris)* and **EBEN KENT** *(Tom Fadden)* are driving down a country road in their jalopy when they hear a high pitched ringing in their ears. Within seconds, they stop at the crash site of a burning rocketship. Hearing the cries of a baby, Eben rushes to save the young visitor from Krypton and they decide to keep the child as their own.

More narration tells how they named the boy Clark and raised him on their farm. One day, he begins to wonder why he seems to have powers beyond those of his friends. Sara explains to the twelve year old **BOY** *(Joel Nestler)* how he was saved from the burning wreckage.

The years roll by. **CLARK** *(George Reeves)* keeps his heritage a secret and grows to manhood. On the 25th anniversary of his arrival, Eben has a stroke and the family **PHYSICIAN** *(Sam Flint)* sadly announces that he has died. Sara says goodbye to Clark at the Smallville transit depot where he is about to depart for Metropolis. Sara reminds him of his great responsibility to use his powers for good. With a special costume woven from the red and blue blankets of his native world packed away in his suitcase, he nods a sad good-bye and gets on the bus.

Following a skyline shot of Metropolis, a narration explains how Clark Kent is taking his first step toward dedicating his amazing powers to the cause of justice. He has resolved to keep his Superman identity a secret by adopting a behavior of mild-mannered timidity. So he may be where he will learn immediately of any emergency requiring his help, he seeks employment at a great metropolitan newspaper, *The Daily Planet.*

After waiting for hours outside the office of Editor, **PERRY WHITE** *(John Hamilton)*, Kent thanks the **RECEPTIONIST** *(Dani Nolan)* for her kindness. She suggests that he return the following day when Mr. White will hopefully be in a better mood. Then Kent decides to steer his fate by climbing out a storage room window and walking the outside ledge of the building to find another way into the office of the editor.

Perry is talking to reporter **LOIS LANE** *(Phyllis Coates)* when Kent enters the office through the window. As Perry tells Kent to get out of his office, blaming his secretary for letting him in, **JIMMY OLSEN** *(Jack Larson)* barges into the office with a news flash! Lois grabs it away and reads aloud how an oil company dirigible was

Parents of Earth,
Sara *(Frances Morris)* and Eben *(Tom Fadden)*.

attempting to dock in high winds when it suddenly pulled eleven men aloft on a landing rope. All but one has dropped to safety and is clinging for life a thousand feet up in the air.

After Lois and Jimmy rush away to cover the event, Clark strikes a deal with the editor. If Kent can get an exclusive, he will get a job as a reporter. White agrees only to rid himself of the crazy man who walks building ledges twenty eight stories above the sidewalk.

Kent runs to the storage room and leaps out the window as Superman in what was to become stock footage for the other twenty five episodes of the first season. As the man hanging from the rope lets go, he drops into the extended arms of this strange visitor from another world.

The final scene in Perry's office has the **RESCUED MAN** *(Dabbs Greer)* telling how a superguy in a red and blue costume came flying through the air to save his life. After setting him down behind an airplane hanger, he passed out.

The next thing he remembers is Clark Kent giving him a taxi ride to the Daily Planet.

Of course, Perry White makes good on his deal and gives Kent the job. However, Lois has a couple of critical questions.

How did he get to the airport before she did?

And how was he so lucky to find the man before every other experienced reporter in the business?

As Lois waits for an answer, Kent smiles and then says, "Maybe I'm a *superman*, Miss Lane."

EPISODE 2

THE HAUNTED LIGHTHOUSE

directed by TOMMY CARR
written by EUGENE SOLOW

Unlike most of the later episodes, many of the first season shows featured only one or two of the main series characters. This show belongs to Jack Larson, with George Reeves arriving later to bring it to the predictable conclusion where Superman saves the day.

The story begins with a view of a seaside cottage surrounded by a mist blowing in from the ocean. Clark Kent establishes the dreary setting and the macabre story in a narration telling how Jimmy has come to Moose Island to visit his Aunt Louisa and his cousin Chris.

Watch for the shadow of the opening door and Aunt Louisa against what should be the distant sky background as she comes out of the cottage to greet Jimmy's arrival.

Television historians will note that at least one passage of Reeves' narration would be excised if the *politically correct police* of modern society had their way. The reference to *Alice* being "deaf and dumb" would no doubt be replaced with "audibly and verbally impaired" to quiet the liberals. Of course, we could take this exercise to the extreme by considering how the entire first season would fare by today's standards. The censors would certainly be displeased with regard to how Superman and the authorities were so predisposed to use what might be labelled excessive force when confronting the criminal element long before they bother to take a breath and read them their rights.

Anyway, Jimmy soon discovers himself in the midst of a mystery. He hears an eerie voice crying for help, claiming to be drowning, a voice that

Jimmy *(Jack Larson)* and Clark Kent discuss recent events on Moose Island.

Jimmy cannot seem to locate. While out exploring the surrounding woods, Jimmy stumbles upon a sailor named **MACK** *(William Challee)*, who mistakes him for Chris. When Jimmy later reports the meeting to his relatives, **CHRIS** *(Jimmy Ogg)* accuses Jimmy of spying on him and warns him to mind his own business.

Rumors surface from the nearby village that the lighthouse on the bluff has been seen some nights casting a guiding light out across the foggy ocean, yet **AUNT LOUISA** *(Sara Padden)* insists that it has been shut down and dark for years. His cousin Chris never quite seems to warm up to Jimmy's presence in spite of the fact that they must've been boyhood buddies. The fact that Jimmy hasn't actually seen Aunt Louisa and Chris in many years gives the viewer reason to suspect that something is not quite right, but of course, it will require Superman to shed any light on the mystery.

Late one night, Jimmy observes a bright beam of light coming from the lighthouse. When he goes to investigate, he is warned away by a knife thrown by Chris.

Another strange development occurs when a note is left on Jimmy's bed claiming to be from Aunt Louisa. It says she is in trouble. **ALICE** *(Allene Roberts)*, the mute housekeeper, meets Jimmy in the hallway and offers to lead the way. When Aunt Louisa stops their departure in the kitchen, Jimmy figures everything is okay.

With the assistance of Clark Kent, Jimmy sets out to solve the puzzle of the sometimes working lighthouse. Jimmy finds his way into a cave where he is eventually knocked out and left caged within the cave as the tidal waters begin to rise. Just when all seems lost for the young reporter, Superman arrives to save the day. They discover the old lighthouse is being used to guide coastal smugglers to the safety of the hidden port near the caves and Aunt Louisa and Chris are party to the scheme.

But Jimmy's disappointment in his relatives is quickly lifted when Superman finds the *real* Aunt Louisa has been kept under lock and key and the real cousin Chris is off serving his country.

Superman flies out to a Coast Guard vessel and alerts the **COMMANDER** *(Steve Carr)* of the smuggling operation and returns to the cottage as Clark Kent in time for the family reunion and

an almost too revealing wrap up scene. The real **AUNT LOUISA** *(Effie Laird)* is explaining that the eerie voice crying for help is actually her talking bird that escaped during her capture, and she is remarking how happy she was to see the very handsome Superman. Then Kent walks in for an introduction. The resemblance Kent has to Superman is too obvious for Aunt Louisa, but before she has a chance to voice her theory, Kent skillfully changes the subject just before the final fade out.

Fans of *Maude Prickett*, after noting her name listed in the closing credits, have no doubt experienced disappointment when subsequent viewings of this episode revealed the absence of this fine character actress. However, she does make an appearance in a key role for the *Deserted Village* episode later in this first season. My thanks go to Ronald Vivian for pointing out this rather embarrassing error in the original edition of this book.

EPISODE 3

THE CASE OF
THE TALKATIVE DUMMY

directed by TOMMY CARR
written by DENNIS COOPER
& LEE BACKMAN

For a surprise on his birthday, Kent and Lois take Jimmy to the theatre to see a show featuring a new ventriloquist act.

"A guy's birthday only comes once a year," explains Kent.

"Now there's a sharp observation," remarks Lois, never passing up an opportunity to give Kent a little jab.

MARCO *(Syd Saylor)*, the ventriloquist, comes out on stage and begins his act with Freddie, the dummy. After a few stale jokes, Lois notices that the dummy seems to have a second voice speaking at the same time as Marco. To further the mystery, Marco seems visibly upset with the unplanned phrases and excuses himself from the stage before the act is over. Lois and Kent decide to investigate.

Backstage, the eccentric Marco explains that Freddie has misbehaved like this once before,

The "Daily Planet" building as it appeared on the corner of LaBrea and Wilshire in 1988.

about a month ago. It is suggested that another jealous performer was in the audience trying to ruin the act. Kent asks Marco to call them if it happens again.

Later, Perry White assigns Lois and Kent to get details from an armored car company regarding future plans to beef up security after the half million dollar robbery they had last month.

At the office of *HARRY GREEN (Pierre Watkin)*, the president of the Green Armored Car Company, Lois is getting pictures of him and his assistant, *DAVIS (Tris Coffin)*. Davis is obviously camera shy, but Kent and Lois don't seem to notice.

Green goes on to explain how the armored car routes are planned by himself and Davis the night before each trip. Then the plans are locked up in a sealed envelope. The drivers get their assigned orders just as they are to start their journey. A fool proof operation.

The next day, when Kent arrives at the office, he is greeted by Lois and Jimmy to discuss the

recent armored car robbery that has just made the headlines. They both make the connection between the robbery location and the words spoken by the dummy of the ventriloquist.

At police headquarters, Lois and Kent present their theory to a skeptical Inspector *HENDERSON (Robert Shayne)*. He insists their idea is a long shot, but it may be enough to get the complaining Mr. Green off his back for a while.

Jimmy stops at Green's office to pick up his approved pictures for the feature story. Jimmy tells Green not to worry too much about robberies because he and his associates have just given the police a solid lead on the crimes. Green humors the eager young lad with his gratitude for the encouraging news.

In the hallway outside Green's office, Jimmy notices the theatre *USHER (Phil Pine)* going into the office of Davis. He moves to listen as the usher tells Davis that he recognizes him from prison. Davis must be the one giving out the armored car routes to the usher by telephone, which he in turn passes on by throwing his own voice to the dummy on stage. The usher demands more money for his services, but Davis tells him to get out and leave him alone.

Jimmy finds an empty office and puts through a call to the Daily Planet. As he is explaining to Perry that he may have the key to the entire scheme, an unknown assailant knocks him out and hangs up the phone. Perry sends Kent and Lois to Green's office to find out how Jimmy has gotten himself into trouble again.

Meanwhile, Jimmy is unconscious and stuffed into a safe by the unknown assailant. When the *SAFE MOVER (Robert Kent)* arrives with his assistant, Davis and Green meet them in the hallway to sign the papers.

As Kent and Lois arrive within two blocks of the Green Company, Kent sees Jimmy in the safe being lowered out the window several stories above the street. Before Lois can question him, Kent slips out of the car and into a nearby alley. Within seconds, Superman is on the scene in time to catch the falling safe when the ropes break on the block and tackle assembly.

If you watch the top of the picture carefully, you can see the stalled shadow of the suspended safe against the building until stuntman George Fisher executes his landing on the sidewalk. Then you can see the shadow begin to move just before the safe falls into view.

"How do you always manage to show up at the right time?" Lois asks.

"Why, it's my job, Miss Lane," Superman calmly replies.

Kent and Lois bring Henderson to the theatre in hopes of witnessing another disclosure. Kent sees the usher and follows him to a phone booth where he overhears plans for another armored car robbery.

When Marco comes out on stage to do his act, the usher puts new words in the dummy's mouth. Two thugs in the audience hear the disclosure and quickly exit. Lois has noted the location given and Henderson agrees to set a trap. Kent tells them that Green is the ringleader and he'll prove it. After he runs off, Lois looks to Henderson.

"Where does he go all the time?"

Henderson replies, "Maybe he runs into an alley, takes off his glasses and changes into Superman."

Lois laughs it off as a bad joke.

At Green's office, Superman arrives in time to break up a confrontation between Davis and Green. Davis has figured out he's been framed when Green is apprehended.

In Henderson's office, Lois and Kent are told how the operation has been uncovered and all the guilty parties are caught. Lois wants to know how Kent knew Green was on the other end of the phone conversation with the theatre usher. As he is about to make up an explanation, Henderson gets a telephone call.

"If you're so smart, Mr. Kent, who's on the phone now?" asks Lois.

"It's the chief and he wants us back in the office in ten seconds!" replies Kent as he hustles Lois out of the police station.

EPISODE 4

THE MYSTERY OF THE BROKEN STATUES

directed by TOMMY CARR
written by WILLIAM JOYCE

This episode begins when **PAUL MARTIN** *(Tris Coffin)* and his **PARTNER** *(Phil Pine)* enter the artcraft shop of **MR. BONELLI** *(Michael Vallon)*, pay him for ten plaster statues, and then smash each one on the floor. After fingering the debris and finding nothing, they make a quiet exit just as Lois enters the shop. Bonelli tells Lois what has just happened.

When Lois arrives at Edward's gift shop, she finds the **SHOPKEEPER** *(Steve Carr)* sweeping up a mess of broken plaster. She can easily guess what must have happened.

At her office, Lois begins to tell Kent what she has discovered, but he already knows. Seven shops have been hit so far. Obviously, Kent says, the men are looking for something and they are not breaking any laws in doing so. But Lois can feel a story and convinces Kent to help her investigate by going to other shops and buying plaster statues to see what might be inside.

Martin and his partner watch from a parked car as Lois comes out of a shop carrying an armful of little statues. When she drives away, they follow after her.

In her apartment, Lois begins to smash the little figures until she finds a key inside one of them. She quickly calls to report her find to Kent. Martin and his partner are listening outside her door as she tells Kent that some men had already visited most of the shops. She also tells that so far, they have collected an acorn, a toy automobile, a safety pin, and an onion. Kent has also learned of a found dollar bill and a little plastic cow. When Kent hangs up, the two thugs crash into Lois' apartment. She lets out a scream!

Another **SHOP OWNER** *(Maurice Cass)* is watching **PETE** *(Wayde Crosby)* and another thug smash several statues when Kent telephones him. The shop owner is more interested in counting his cash than calling the police.

Superman flies across the city skyline. The thug at the shop finds three pennies on the floor among the pieces of broken plaster. As Pete and the thug attempt to exit, they are strong armed by Kent, acting very much like Superman as he insists they answer a few questions.

At police headquarters, Henderson tells Kent he cannot hold the two men on any charges, even though he knows they are working for the notorious Paul Martin. When Kent goes to visit Lois, he finds her apartment in a mess, indicating that a struggle has taken place.

Lois Lane *(Phyllis Coates)* is bound and gagged by a gangster *(Phillip Pine)* and his boss, Paul Martin *(Tris Coffin)* just before they load her onto a plane.

Meanwhile, Martin and his partner have Lois confined in the National Import warehouse and insist that she turn over to them the key she found. Lois replies by smashing Martin in the head. After his partner drags her away, Martin finds the key hidden in her purse.

Without a clue to act on, Henderson begins to roll up his sleeves as he threatens Pete in the interrogation chair while Kent watches nearby. When Pete finally tells them about Martin's airplane parked out at the Ramsey airport, Kent makes a quick exit.

Lois is bound and gagged, and loaded into an airplane by Martin and his men, but Martin does not get on board. As the plane rolls down the runway for a takeoff, Superman arrives and grabs hold of the tail section, forcing it to stop.

At Henderson's office, Kent has assembled the clues on a blackboard. The Inspector and Lois watch as he adds and subtracts items until he arrives at the answer to the rebus, *PO97M*. It's a post office box at the main branch, and Martin has the key!

The next morning, Martin is met at the post office with handcuffs by a **POLICE OFFICER** *(Joey Ray)* and placed under arrest by Inspector Henderson. The package found in the post office box is opened at Henderson's office under the watchful eyes of Kent and Lois. Inside the package is a ceramic pig figure which contains a famous missing gemstone ruby. Lois credits Superman with an assist in the mystery and Kent confesses that two heads are always better than one. His exit brings a strange expression to Lois' face as the show goes to fade out.

EPISODE 5

THE MONKEY MYSTERY

directed by TOMMY CARR
written by BEN PETER FREEMAM
& DORIS GILBERT

Superman enters into the cold war in this episode when he assists in the recovery of a formula for defense against atomic weapons. The story begins in Central Europe as a scientist named **JAN MOLESKA** *(Fred Essler)* is running from the police with his daughter, **MARIA** *(Allene Roberts)*. While hiding in a cave, Moleska confesses that he is too old and weak to run anymore. He gives a locket to Maria and instructs her to escape with new hope for humanity. She is to deliver the secret formula contained in the locket to the President of the United States so his life's work may be used for the good of mankind. With the pursuit dogs and the secret police fast approaching, Maria says goodbye to her father and runs away.

Publicity photo from 1951.

A montage shows Maria making the journey across the continent and the ocean to America, but it is no secret to the enemy forces. A message is sent to foreign agents waiting in Metropolis through a courier in the person of **TONY** *(Michael Vallon)*, an organ grinder. He has with him a little monkey dressed in a superman costume.

Clark and Lois are on their way to cover a story when they stop to watch the organ grinder's monkey. In exchange for a small donation, the little monkey hands out fortune-telling slips of paper. When Lois reads her fortune, she quickly realizes it is a message telling of Maria Moleska's arrival and how she will be traveling by train to Washington. Without allowing Kent to see the note, Lois rushes away in a taxi.

In the office, Lois is scrambling to make travel arrangements when Jimmy asks why she is taking a plane to Baltimore to get a train to Washington? She confesses to Jimmy how she accidently learned of Maria's arrival and plans to get an exclusive interview.

Meanwhile, Tony arrives at the drop for the message he was to deliver. He sends the monkey up the drain pipe to a room where the boss named **CRANE** *(Harry Lewis)* is waiting. **MAX** *(Bill Challee)*, his accomplice, arrives with news that the buyer for the secret formula is anxiously waiting for a delivery. Crane tells him of the break in security, and that he is to get rid of the organ grinder before he blows everything.

When Jimmy tells Perry White about Lois and her wild discovery she received from a monkey, he throws a fit. Kent remembers the fortune she was reading and rushes out of the office to try and catch up with her.

On a speeding passenger train, Lois finds the compartment of Maria Moleska. When she enters and finds Maria unconscious. A man quickly comes up behind her and knocks her out.

Superman lands on top of the moving train, a scene that would later appear in the *Double Trouble* episode. After discovering Lois and Maria, he calls in a **DOCTOR** *(Steve Carr)* to examine them. Lois is okay, but Maria is still unconscious, suffering from a more serious head wound. When she awakens, she recognizes Superman as the symbol of justice. She wishes for him to take her father's formula to the President, but the locket is gone.

Kent telephones Perry to let him know that Lois and Maria are okay, but he must have Inspector Henderson locate the organ grinder to learn the identity of the enemy agents. Then Jimmy rushes in with news that Tony's dead body has turned up in the river.

Max returns to the Boss with the locket. Now they can deliver the microfilm with the secret formula and collect $200,000 for their trouble. However, when they hear Kent on the radio requesting help from anyone who may know of a monkey wearing a superman costume, the Boss orders Max to find the monkey.

Jimmy calls in to report he has located the missing monkey in an alley. Kent and Perry are on their way, but Max arrives first. When the monkey gets away, Max clobbers Jimmy and takes him back to the hideout. Jimmy is tied up as the two villains watch out the window to see police assembling on the street below.

Kent and Perry have the monkey. Kent gives him a piece of paper and lets him go. They watch as he climbs up a drain pipe. Kent quickly excuses himself and within seconds, Superman emerges from a nearby alley.

Superman arrives through the window just as Max is about to shoot the monkey. After deflecting bullets and beating the two villains in a fist fight, he moves over to untie Jimmy. The secret formula is recovered and the world is safe for yet another episode in the *Adventures of Superman*.

EPISODE 6

NIGHT OF TERROR

directed by LEE SHOLEM
written by BEN PETER FREEMAN

In this bleak episode, Lois Lane arrives at the scene of a recent crime. The *Restwell Tourist Camp* is in the Blue Mountains, just a few miles from the Canadian border. A threatening situation is immediately introduced when the unconscious body of a woman is discovered behind the front desk. As Lois is about to search for a telephone to summon the authorities, she is intercepted by a tough looking gangland thug named **SOLLEY,** *(Frank Richards)*.

It was while filming this confrontation that Phyllis Coates was actually knocked out cold quite accidently by Richards. Shortly after Lois hits the deck, the other member of the dastardly duo, **MITCH** *(John Kellogg)*, walks in to find they now have two unconscious women sprawled out on the floor. Mitch orders Solley to lock the ladies up until he can figure out what to do with them. This requires that he get in touch with the boss who never appears before the cameras.

The plot is furthered along when Lois extracts the details that have created this grizzly predicament from the now revived **MRS. KING** *(Ann Doran)*. When her late husband and co-owner of the tourist camp discovered that the mob was using their premises as a haven for fleeing criminals, they brutally murdered him and proceeded to beat up Mrs. King. Lois suggests to her that she forget all that and concentrate on more positive things like how they might escape. Lois concludes that her immediate duty is to get to a telephone in a pay booth outside and call for help.

Meanwhile, back in Metropolis, Superman has returned to his office and manages to change into his Clark Kent disguise just as young Olsen comes eagerly knocking at the door. Jimmy has tickets for a baseball game. Kent tells Jimmy that he has a pressing appointment with Inspector Henderson regarding the *Ellsworth Jewel Robbery,* but agrees to meet him back at the office in time to go see the ball game.

By now, Lois has made her way out to the telephone booth that is situated dangerously within eyesight of Solley. Being careful not to catch his attention, she puts through a call to the Daily Planet. Anyway, Jimmy takes the call that lasts only long enough for Lois to tell where she is before Solley grabs her away from the phone.

Unable to reach Kent at the police station, Jimmy elects to rush off on his own to rescue Miss Lane after quickly scribbling a message for **MISS BACHARACH** *(Almira Sessions)*, the receptionist, to forward onto Kent upon his return. Miss Bacharach decides to leave the message on Kent's desk and go on her dinner break. Of course, the message inevitably ends up on the floor when she slams the door closed, and it ultimately is picked up as trash by **OSCAR** *(Joel Friedkin)*, the janitor.

The cheap construction of the interiors is apparent in the scene where Oscar enters Kent's office and leans the broom handle up against what is obviously just a piece of fabric stretched over a wood frame rather than a solid wall. Oscar collects Kent's trash. He notices the folded note on the floor, and without bothering to read it, he stuffs it into the bag and exits. This one scene must have had a lasting impression on me since childhood because I never leave my highrise office without first scotch taping down everything left on my desk at night.

Once again, Lois is locked up with Mrs. King and Solley repeats the question to Mitch, why can't they just knock off the two dames and beat it? Mitch says the boss likes his jobs done neat and clean and he's sending out a special torpedo named Baby Face Stevens. Solley is so excited that he is going to meet an underworld celebrity, he totally forgets the most intelligent question his mind has ever formulated. The boss must know these guys better than we ever will.

A car pulls up to the motor camp. Jimmy Olsen steps out of the car and approaches the two gangsters. He innocently asks where he might find Lois Lane because he heard that she might be in trouble. Solley takes it as a joke from the comedian killer, Baby Face Stevens, and immediately offers over his gun after discovering that Olsen has not thought enough to pack a rod.

Jimmy finally figures out that his identity has been mistaken, and Mitch is too much in a hurry to blow this place to realize the mistake. Armed only with a gun carrying two bullets, *one* more than Barney Fife ever had, Olsen is shoved into the locked room to do away with Lois and Mrs. King. Lois wishes Jimmy was Kent, Jimmy undoubtedly wishes he were Superman, and with her husband lying dead in the gully behind the camp, Mrs. King probably doesn't care one way or the other. Although he is holding the loaded gun, Jimmy impatiently waits for Lois to think up what they should do next.

And meanwhile, back in Metropolis, Kent learns from Miss Bacharach of the missing note. She can remember nothing other than Jimmy blurting something about Miss Lane being in trouble at some place with 'well' in the name. Kent gets on the phone with **MR. QUINN** *(Steve Carr)*, a clerk at the Tourist Camp Association.

Fortunately, he manages to locate three vacation spots with the word 'well' in the name.

Kent rudely hustles Miss Bacharach off the set, changes into Superman and leaps out the window. If you watch carefully, you will notice a flying shot that runs a little too long. Superman's cape stops flapping in freeze frame before the clouds stop zooming by in the background.

As Superman swoops down on the first of the three possible locations for this episode's night of terror, the real *BABY FACE STEVENS* (Richard Benedict) arrives. After slapping Mitch and Solley around instead of producing more formal identification, Stevens manages to trick gun-toting Olsen into harmlessly discharging the only two bullets he has on hand.

Superman touches down at the Sleepwell Cabins resort where he is greeted by the *MANAGER* (Paul Bryer). No Lois Lane here.

Just as smiling Stevens is about to put an end to the entire affair, Superman crashes through the ceiling. He quickly fells the three villains with several pulled punches, and then tells Lois and Jimmy that Clark Kent said he might find them here before the final fade out leads into the closing credits.

It is interesting to note the similarities between Clark Kent's character and Superman's character when it is evident that he is running out of time. Kent is quick to shed his mild mannered attitude and risk exposure when he needs answers in a hurry. Fortunately, he has the good sense to only drop his timid disguise around people like Oscar, the janitor, and Miss Bacharach, the dizzy receptionist. And this is only episode number six, so no one has yet enough cause to start wondering about the connection between Clark Kent and Superman.

EPISODE 7

THE BIRTHDAY LETTER

directed by LEE SHOLEM
written by DENNIS COOPER

This episode is producer Robert Maxwell's best attempt at a human interest story. It begins in Perry White's office as Lois reads aloud a letter that has been submitted and addressed to

Superman by a handicapped child. In it is a request that he escort her to the local fair so that she may have fun like other children. Perry is touched and assigns Lois to represent the paper, to take the young girl to the fair, and to do a story about it.

CATHY WILLIAMS (Isa Ashdown) is sitting at home with her favorite singing doll when she takes a phone call from a gangster named *CUSAK* (Paul Marion). From a phone booth, he quickly rattles off the time, the day, and the place before he is shot to death by an unknown assailant.

MARCEL DUVAL (Maurice Marsac) and *MARIE* (Nan Boardman) enter their apartment to meet with *SLUGGER* (John Doucette), their gangster assistant, who seems to be all muscle and no brains. They were supposed to have received a message from Cusak, but he apparently dialed the wrong number. They soon establish that the telephone Cusak made contact with is that of the little girl whose story about wanting a visit from Superman appears in the newspaper. Slugger is ordered to dress up like Superman and bring in the little girl.

The part of Slugger is played to the hilt by Doucette with a heavy accent typically reserved for this standard brain-drained prize fighter role. The broad difference between this character and the one he portrays in the second season episode *Lady in Black* is a graphic demonstration of John Doucette's wide range of acting talent. The interplay between Slugger and innocent Cathy Williams is fun to watch.

Back at the Daily Planet, Kent visits with Lois in her office. Lois wonders if Superman will respond to the Cathy Williams story in the paper. Kent reminds her that Superman hasn't disappointed her yet as he makes a hasty exit.

Kent moves quickly down the hall, into the storage room, and then out the open window as Superman. He zooms across the city in a very good flying sequence and then enters the Williams apartment through a conveniently open window to meet with *MRS. WILLIAMS* (Virginia Carroll). She is reading a note that indicates Cathy has been taken away by Superman and she immediately begins insisting that he bring her home or she will summon the police. Superman is certainly confused by her hostile attitude.

Inspector Henderson *(Robert Shayne)* is ready to take Marie *(Nan Boardman)* and Marcel *(Maurice Marsac)* into custody.

Meanwhile, Slugger brings little Cathy into the Duval apartment through a window from the fire escape while listening to her question his credentials as the Man of Steel. Marcel and Marie soon arrive and pretend to be Cathy's aunt and uncle in an effort to gain her confidence and learn the message she has intercepted from Cusak. She remembers the time and the day *(tomorrow)*, but cannot recall the place he mentioned.

In Kent's office, Lois is disgusted with a rival newspaper's account of how Superman has kidnapped the little girl. **PERKINS** *(Jack Daly)* enters the office to claim the reward money offered for information on Cathy Williams' disappearance. He tells that he is the owner of the tobacco store where Cusak was gunned down and that he found a phone number written on a piece of paper that was in Cusak's possession.

Recognizing the number as being the same as the Williams residence is what brought Perkins to the Daily Planet. Perkins also tells Kent that a plain and ordinary looking couple with a French accent recently appeared at his store and inquired about Cusak and the telephone number.

Kent telephones a friend at the FBI for some information. Lois decides to go and investigate at the Williams home and perhaps give some positive news to Cathy's mother.

At the Duval apartment, they are still trying to coax the location out of Cathy by bribing her with gifts. But she is getting homesick for her favorite singing doll and begins to cry.

The Duvals go to the Williams home to get the doll. While they are rummaging through the apartment, Lois arrives. When the Duvals decide to make a getaway, Lois follows after them.

Back at the office, Kent now has a positive

identification based on Mr. Perkins' description. They are international phoney money experts and Kent figures out what must have happened with the mix up of telephone numbers. When Lois reports her encounter with the Duvals and their escape in a taxi, Kent gets on the phone with the cab company to have them tracked.

Slugger is caught by the Duvals trying to take Cathy home. They tie him up and get ready to force the message out of the little girl when the song from her favorite doll, *Mary Had a Little Lamb,* reminds her of the place mentioned on the phone, *The Lambert Company.*

Here follows a bit of cruelty that upset the critics of the day. Little Cathy's leg braces are torn from her so she will not be able to walk and ultimately give away the location of the Duvals meeting.

At the Daily Planet, Kent receives the report from the cab company indicating the location of the Duval apartment. He tells Lois to summon Henderson right away as he rushes toward the door. Lois yells for him to wait for her, but he hastily replies, "This is a job for Superman. . . I mean, I've got to find him!"

Superman leaps into the sky above Metropolis as the Duvals arrive at the meeting place. A gun battle begins as Superman enters through an open window to put an end to the shooting. In an attempt to destroy the evidence, Marie tosses the counterfeit printing plates into a vat of acid, but Superman easily retrieves them.

Cathy is back at home, reading a Superman comic book when the real Superman enters through the window. The final scene has Cathy flying high over Metropolis with her birthday wish complete.

EPISODE 8

THE MIND MACHINE

directed by LEE SHOLEM
written by DENNIS COOPER
& LEE BACKMAN

This is an episode that definitely belongs among the top ten. It's a fast paced, hard hitting, crime busting drama that pits Superman against the forces of evil when a scientific invention is taken over by an underworld syndicate leader.

The story begins as **DR. STANTON** (Griff Barnett) is working in his vacuum tube and chemistry laboratory with his assistant, **DR. HADLEY** (Steve Carr). Three masked men rush in and kidnap Stanton along with his latest invention, a machine that looks very much like a television set. When Hadley attempts to stop the abduction, he is knocked to the floor and instructed not to call the police or he may never see Stanton alive.

At the Daily Planet, Kent and Lois are huddled around Perry White at his desk looking over a headline in the morning edition regarding the State Crime Committee hearings. Senator Taylor has rallied an investigation into the affairs of syndicate leader, Lou Cranek, and Lois is scheduled to be a key witness.

Hadley is found by Kent waiting in his office. He tells Kent that his employer, Dr. Stanton, has been kidnapped along with his hypnotherapy machine. He explains to Kent that the device was created to allow a skilled therapist to make mental suggestions directly into a patient's mind to help him overcome behavioral disorders. He further warns that in the wrong hands, the device could prove to be very dangerous.

The next day, in Cranek's mountain hideaway just outside Metropolis, **CURLEY** (Ben Welden) is reading the classifieds when he calls to the attention of **CRANEK** (Dan Seymour) an advertisement requesting information about the disappearance of Dr. Stanton. Cranek tells another of his henchmen, **AL** (Harold Kruger), to bring Dr. Stanton into the room. With his unwilling assistance, the mind machine is activated, and the gangsters tune in on the crime committee hearings.

As an ex-syndicate accountant named **WAGNER** (Harry Hayden) is about to spill his guts about Cranek's illegal activities to **SENATOR TAYLOR** (James Seay), the machine takes over his mind. Wagner suddenly refuses to expose any evidence. He is dismissed with charges of contempt and quickly leaves the hearing chambers. Kent and Lois attempt to get his statement, but he refuses and runs into the street.

Kent and Lois are following Wagner until he realizes he is being watched. He hijacks a woman's car and drives off quickly. Kent and Lois follow him into the country until he is forced to stop when a tire blows out. He then takes control of a school bus and drives away, headed down a mountain road. Lois and Kent arrive to learn from the **BUS DRIVER** (Lester Dorr), who had been under the bus attending to the brakes, that the vehicle will never hold up to the speed.

Lois and the driver go after the bus while Kent pretends to stay and help the hijacked woman. He quickly changes to Superman and leaps into the air. Superman catches the runaway school bus. Lois and the driver arrive to find out the kids are okay, but Wagner is dead. Superman reports that his brain has been destroyed.

Later, Lois insists on testifying in spite of the possible dangers. Kent and Hadley make use of Dr. Stanton's private plane to comb the nearby area in hopes of detecting the location of the mind machine on a radar scope. When they finally make contact, Kent telephones the office from the plane only to find out that Lois is about to testify. Out of desperation, Kent knocks Hadley out cold, puts the plane on autopilot, and exits as Superman.

When he arrives at the hideout just before Lois is about to have her brains scrambled, a fist fight begins with Cranek and his two thugs. While Superman cleans up the room, Stanton smashes his machine. He tells Superman it is just too dangerous to have around.

Meanwhile, the plane has run out of gasoline. Superman tells Stanton to call the police. Then he leaps into the sky to rescue the falling airplane.

Back at the office, Kent explains to a confused Hadley how he managed to safely land the airplane, but Hadley cannot remember anything. When Perry tells Kent how Superman saved the day while he was out roaming the countryside, he defends himself by saying he was trying to help Lois. She smiles and says she has no need for Kent as long as Superman is on duty.

EPISODE 9

RESCUE

directed by TOMMY CARR
written by MONROE MANNING

In a mining community called Carbide, the stage is set for a disaster when **POP POLGASE** (Housely Stevenson) is unwillingly barred from working in his unstable mine. Inspector **D.K. SIMS** (Fred Sherman) declares the tunnel unsafe and posts a warning that it is a death trap. He further informs Polgase he will be locked up if he continues to operate before improvements are made.

Kent and Lois arrive in Carbide. Lois is to stay and observe Sims on his appointed rounds in order to collect information for a mining story. Kent is off to Washington to get an interview with some unnamed newsworthy subject. The plan is for him to pick up Lois on the way back to Metropolis.

Meanwhile, Polgase is trying to pursuade another worker, **STAN** (Ray Bennett), to help him in the condemned tunnel. When Stan refuses, claiming the timber is rotten and will no longer support the roof, Polgase resolves to go it alone.

Inevitably, Polgase miscalculates the swing of a pick axe and brings the roof down around him. Stan alerts the nearby miners, calls for the rescue squad, and sounds the alarm. Lois is about to get a comment from Sims on how the city is safe in spite of the network of tunnels beneath them when they hear the disaster signal and rush to the scene. Lois quickly dials up the Daily Planet and tells them to stand by for further details.

Someone confirms that Polgase is still alive from the sound of his voice behind the rubble, but it is decided that a rescue attempt through the existing tunnel is far too dangerous. An alternate plan of sinking a new shaft from above is put into operation. In the confusion, Lois sneaks away and gets into a miner's outfit.

In Washington, Kent declares to **HARRY** (Milt Kibbee) that his assignment is a bust, and he decides to go back home. Figuring Lois has not yet completed her fact finding tour, he leisurely begins the drive back to Carbide.

Relentless as always, Lois goes into the unsafe tunnel before Sims can stop her. She winds her way through the fallen debris until she reaches Polgase. He has been pinned down by a heavy piece of timber. In a weak attempt to free him, Lois ends up making matters worse by causing the collapse of her only escape route.

While Sims and his men are trying to dig a new rescue shaft, Kent is slowly driving back to Carbide. As luck would have it, the car decides to act up. When Kent lifts the hood to tinker with the accelerator mechanism, the noise of the engine prevents his notice of a news bulletin announcing the recent mining accident.

Lois never gives up, but while attempting to offer some encouraging words to Polgase, she notices a strange odor in the air. Polgase sadly informs her that they will both soon be overcome by the presence of coal gas.

As the rescue team is about to break through the roof, the coal gas is detected and the order is given to abandon the operation. While they are clearing the area, Kent casually arrives with his hands in his pockets. When he learns about how Lois and Polgase are trapped, he's gone. Within seconds, Superman runs toward the camera for the first of the great springboard takeoffs.

Superman arrives on the scene, runs into the tunnel, and quickly clears a path through rock and timber to reach Lois and Polgase. At the top of the hill, a stray piece of trash has been ignited by the sun's reflection off a miner's helmit left behind during the evacuation. The wind blows it into the rescue shaft where it sets off an explosion when it hits the coal gas. Below, Superman holds up the roof until Lois can get Polgase out of the tunnel to safety.

Like the Lone Ranger, his work is done, and Superman makes a quiet retreat. Shortly, Kent makes an appearance to discover that Lois and Polgase will recover very soon. Lois tells Kent how she is very happy that Superman has finally taken her out. Kent smiles at the pun as the episode fades out to the closing credits.

EPISODE 10

THE SECRET OF SUPERMAN

directed by TOMMY CARR
written by WELLS ROOT

Clark Kent is home asleep when he gets a telephone call from Jimmy's mother at the beginning of the episode. **MRS. OLSEN** (*Helen Wallace*) is very concerned at one o'clock in the morning that her son is not yet home from work. Kent does his best to convince Mrs. Olsen not to worry by suggesting that Jimmy is probably out somewhere trying to be a good reporter, and to

further soothe her unrest, Kent promises to investigate. This was the first and last appearance of Jimmy's mom in this or any of the other 104 episodes of the series.

On a hunch, Kent telephones the office of Perry White. There we see a hand lift the receiver, and then another hand forces it back down. Suspicious of foul play, Kent quickly changes into Superman and leaps out into the night sky.

At Perry's office, a **HENCHMAN** (*Larry Blake*) is shining a flashlight in Jimmy's face. Jimmy seems to be in some sort of hypnotic trance. After Jimmy obediently points out the editor's private file cabinet, the Henchman moves to pick the lock. He opens a drawer and removes one of the file folders.

After the Henchman leaves, Superman arrives through the window. He quickly changes into Kent. When Jimmy wakes from the trance, he remembers nothing except earlier talking with a stranger at the diner. They soon discover the file folder on Superman is missing.

Meanwhile, at the Metropolis News Club, the **COOK** (*Steve Carr*) summons **HERMAN** (*Joel Friedkin*) the waiter to the night service window for a tray of food.

"Take this up to room 322, and don't fall asleep on the way, Mr. White is waiting," says the cook.

But on his way to deliver the order, Herman is ambushed by **DR. H.L. ORT** (*Peter Brocco*) and his henchman. Then Dr. Ort delivers the food order to an anxious Perry White. After dropping a drug into Perry's coffee, he begins to question Perry repeatedly regarding Superman's secret identity.

When Herman recovers from the ambush and arrives to warn Perry, he collapses on the floor and is soon surrounded by several arriving newsmen. Dr. Ort suggests that someone call for help, and in the confusion, he escapes. Kent arrives to find Perry in the same condition as he found Jimmy. Perry remembers nothing except being served coffee by an unknown waiter.

When Henderson arrives later to investigate, a telephone call from the police lab reports there were traces of a truth serum in Perry's coffee. It is a very new drug similar to one used by espionage agents to paralyze a subject's brain cells and extract secret information.

Perry is now fully conscious and demands to know why anyone would want to use such a drug on him? Kent suggests that someone is trying to learn Superman's secret identity. Since it has been rumored that Superman might indeed work for the Daily Planet, Kent remarks, "Say, Chief. Maybe you're Superman?" Perry barks back, "Me? In that outfit?"

From a document left behind by the unknown waiter, they discover that Kent and Lois are next on the list for a test of the truth drug. The plan is for Perry to publicly fire Kent from his job and allow him to go undercover.

Kent continues the rest of the episode without a necktie. After leaving the unemployment office and aimlessly wandering the streets, he is approached at a diner by the Henchman. Jimmy is watching from across the street with a detective that has been following him.

Jimmy sees the Henchman drop something into Kent's coffee. Jimmy rushes to save Kent. There is a struggle and when the Henchman tries to escape, the detective shoots him in the back after first taking a bullet in the leg. Kent tells Jimmy to call for help. Then Kent runs to assist the Henchman.

Kent is led to the office of Dr. Ort by the Henchman, who is struggling to stay on his feet. Jimmy has followed them and puts a call through to Lois. Inside, Dr. Ort offers Kent a drink and laces it with his truth drug. Kent takes a drink and pretends to be hypnotized. Dr. Ort instructs him to take the dead Henchman's body away and drop it into the river. Then he is to return immediately. Kent nods an agreement and leaves.

Lois has arrived to meet Jimmy across the street from Dr. Ort's house. Lois tells Jimmy to stand by while she goes in to find out what happened to Kent. Inside, she confronts Dr. Ort. She insists that he drop the double talk and confess to having Kent locked up somewhere. After sipping a drugged cup of tea, Lois goes into a trance. After a series of questions, Dr. Ort determines that if Lois is not Superman, then Kent must be Superman. Lois agrees.

Kent is in Henderson's office telling him about the dead Henchman and how he has pretended to be drugged in order to fool Dr. Ort. Jimmy calls in to speak with Kent, but Lois has arrived to force Jimmy to hang up the telephone. She then tells Jimmy to follow her back to the house. Kent suspects trouble.

Superman arrives just in time to prevent Dr. Ort from shooting Lois and Jimmy. Lois, still in the hypnotic trance, addresses Superman as Clark Kent. Dr. Ort has escaped but is confronted by the police outside. Superman tells Jimmy to stay with Lois when gunshots are fired outside. Dr. Ort is killed by the police. When Kent returns to Lois and Jimmy, she has snapped out of her trance. When Kent asks her about what has happened, she replies with not being able to remember anything. Kent sighs with relief as the picture fades out.

EPISODE 11

NO HOLDS BARRED

directed by LEE SHOLEM
written by PETER DIXON

An announcer's voice speaking over stock footage of championship wrestling establishes the background for this episode. **BAD LUCK BRANNIGAN** (Dick Reeves) has used his mysterious paralyzer grip to put seven of his opponents in the hospital. Perry White, a devoted wrestling fan, suspects foul play and decides to investigate.

Kent is called into the office to hear the plan. Wayne Winchester, last year's intercollegiate wrestling champion, is going to be hired by the Daily Planet as an expert observer for tonight's match between Brannigan and Simmons. Perry is convinced that Brannigan is somehow cheating because his manager named Murray is a known crook. Perry is hoping Wayne will detect any illegal holds used by Brannigan and expose the fraud.

Later, all the regular Daily Planet cast members are gathered in Perry's office to watch the wrestling match on television. With them is their newly hired expert, **WAYNE** (Malcolm Mealey). After watching another Brannigan victory, Wayne reports how the fight appeared more like attempted murder than professional wrestling, and he wants to help prove it.

Meanwhile, fight manager **MURRAY** (Herb Vigran) is meeting with his own wrestling expert, a Indian named **RAMM** (Tito Renaldo), who is very upset to learn that his ancient body secrets are being used for evil purposes. Murray calls

Brannigan and *CRUSHER* (Henry Kulky) into the room to back up his threat to Ramm. If he refuses to help them, he will be deported from the country. Murray orders Crusher to escort Ramm back to his room. When Brannigan expresses concern for Ramm's refusal to teach him more tricks, Murray says not to worry. After the match Friday night with a contender named Adonis, Ramm's services will no longer be necessary.

Friday night, Wayne and Lois are watching the match from ringside while Perry and Kent watch on the television in the office. After Brannigan quickly finishes *ADONIS* (Karl Davis), he puts out a boastful challenge to the crowd that he is the new champion and that no one can stop him. Wayne jumps up to the ring and accepts the challenge while accusing Brannigan of being a cheat.

Later, Wayne and Lois return to Perry's office. Wayne is convinced that Brannigan is not a good wrestler and he wants to expose his deadly tricks. Kent believes Wayne can defeat the crooked wrestler and in spite of objections from Lois, Perry assigns Kent to assist Wayne and also be responsible for his safety. As Kent explains that he may have some ideas, Lois tells Kent she never wants to see him again. She storms away.

Kent makes an uninvited visit to Murray's office and listens from outside as Murray and Brannigan are discussing the new development. With Ramm's assistance, Brannigan will easily put this college wrestler away for good and discourage any other attempts to defeat him.

Kent changes into Superman and leaps up to Ramm's window. He bends the security bars and steps inside to visit with the meditating swami. Superman assures him that Murray is deceiving him with talk of deportation. He promises to help Ramm if he will teach him the secret body tricks being used by Brannigan. Ramm agrees.

Later, Kent is in his apartment with Wayne. He explains to the college champion about how he has learned of secret pressure points on the body that are used to weaken an opponent. Wayne is to get into shape by building up a resistance to the deadly paralyzer grip. Wayne is not sure why, but he confesses to believe Kent may know all the right answers.

The following Friday night, Lois enters Perry's office and says she just couldn't bring herself to watch the fight. Perry says Kent is pretty confident that Wayne will be okay— Kent is usually right.

"Maybe so," says Lois, "but there comes a time when he's got to be wrong. It's human nature."

As Perry moves to turn on the television, he replies, "Sometimes I wonder if Kent *is* human."

Of course, Kent proves to be right. Brannigan attempts to use the paralyzer grip, and Wayne merely smiles at him. After Wayne successfully finishes the match, Kent and Jimmy accompany him to the locker room. Kent listens through the wall and overhears Murray talking to Brannigan. Murray realizes they have been betrayed and gives the word to rub out Ramm.

As Kent is about to exit, he is confronted by *SAM BLEAKER* (Richard Elliott), a fight promoter. He wants Kent to help him start a new trend: *honest wrestling.* Kent finally manages to get away by telling Bleaker to discuss his plan with Wayne's new manager, Jimmy Olsen.

At Murray's training facility, his men are torturing Ramm when Superman arrives.

"All right, boys! The party's over!"

Superman leaps down the stairs and single handedly cleans up the room full of wrestling thugs and gangsters. By the time Perry, Lois, and Jimmy arrive, Superman has changed back into Clark Kent. He tells how Ramm was innocently victimized by Murray. He is also pleased to announce that Ramm has agreed to use his talent to heal all the hospitalized wrestlers.

"Like magic," remarks Lois.

"Like the only real magic," Kent replies. "The magic of knowledge."

EPISODE 12

THE DESERTED VILLAGE

directed by TOMMY CARR
written by DICK HAMILTON
& BEN PETER FREEMAN

Another moody tale begins in a hazy mist through which we see a road sign identifying *Cliffton by the Sea, population 525.* A hand slowly crosses out the first two numerals in a mysterious jesture to indicate the remaining residents now number only five. In the village, a slow moving figure wearing a radioactivity protection suit walks the deserted street.

At the Daily Planet, Lois is unsuccessful in her attempts to telephone her childhood friend, Mrs. Taisey, and she soon learns that no one in Cliffton can be reached. When Kent enters, Lois explains how every year, Mrs. Taisey sends her a ginger bread man for her birthday, and how she has been trying to call and thank her. The switchboard **OPERATOR** (*Ann Tyrrell*) has informed Lois that the telephone lines appear to be fully functional, yet no one in Cliffton is answering the ringing telephones. Lois is obviously worried, so Kent suggests they make the one hour trip to Cliffton and investigate.

As Lois and Kent arrive in Cliffton, the strange man in the radioactivity suit throws a rock through a house window. While Lois and Kent are trying to figure out why the road sign has been altered, a dog runs up to the rock throwing stranger, and then falls over dead. When the two reporters enter the village, Kent sees some activity a few blocks away and takes off running with Lois following close behind him.

They find the dead dog when they reach the house, but the strange man is gone. Lois recognizes the house of the town doctor. Inside, they find **DR. JESSUP** (*Fred Sherman*) on the floor near the broken window. When he moans and points toward the nearby desk, Kent opens the drawer to notice a gas mask and a gun before taking a capsule of smelling salts.

Jessup takes a breath and quickly recovers to recognize Lois as a reporter from Metropolis. He passes off the recent event as merely a fainting spell and immediately questions Lois about her arrival. Lois explains her concern about not being able to reach anyone by telephone. Jessup strongly advises they leave Cliffton at once.

"Is that a warning or a threat?" asks Kent.

Jessup insists it is only good advice, and there is nothing of interest to any newspaper. Jessup then excuses himself abruptly because he must rush to see a patient, Matilda Taisey. Lois asks if she is alright, and Jessup suggests ominously that she may in fact be. . . dead.

The three hurry down the street where they find **MATILDA TAISEY** (*Maude Prickett*) working in her garden. She recognizes Lois with a noticeably cold welcome hug as Lois expresses her relief to see that she is okay. When Jessup reminds Taisey that these two visitors are newspaper reporters,

she questions Lois about her arrival. She politely suggests that they stay only long enough for a social visit before departing on a return trip to Metropolis. Lois finally insists on knowing what is going on and why there doesn't seem to be anyone left in town? This fact of missing people and the dead dog is obviously down played by Taisey and Jessup.

Jessup walks away, and as Lois is about to go inside with Taisey, Kent notices a gas mask carefully hidden under some flowers in a basket. He quietly tells Lois to gather what ever information she can while he takes a look around. He also insists that she refrain from drinking anything. Before Lois can inquire about his suspicions, he moves away.

When Kent discovers the dog is missing, Jessup arrives. Kent pointedly tells how he knows the dog died from the presence of a poison gas and that Jessup himself fell victim to it from the broken window before he could get to his gas mask hidden in the desk drawer. Jessup responds by again advising that he and Lois should leave Cliffton, and then he walks away.

When Kent discovers a set of large footprints near the broken window, **PETER GODFREY** (*Ed Cobb*) appears to introduce himself as the town druggist. Kent asks him why only a few people remain in town? Godfrey replies with a story of how the oyster beds have dried up putting many people out of work. Kent is also introduced to Godfrey's son, **ALVIN** (*Malcolm Mealey*). Neither of them knows anything about the dead dog or why it might have been carried away.

A short time later, the radioactivity suit man is walking the streets. When Kent hears a gunshot, he goes running back to find Taisey claiming to have been shooting at a rabbit in her garden. Kent insists that he knows the town has been plagued with a poison gas and a grotesque figure who leaves large footprints. Realizing that Lois has wandered off in the direction of the sea, Kent quickly runs after her.

Watching through a telescope, Godfrey sees Superman appear in the rocks near the sea. Superman finds and follows footprints leading into a cave. Inside, Lois is digging with a shovel when Kent startles her by his arrival. She has discovered some drill core samples and Kent wants to have them analyzed. He insists that it is dangerous to stay around here and makes her promise to wait for him in nearby Havenhurst. Then he slips away as Superman for a quick visit to a nearby laboratory.

Lois will not be ordered around, especially by whimpy Clark Kent, so she returns to the cave. Soon, the suited man arrives to give Lois a whiff of canned gas. Lois screams before falling faint, and as the suited man is about to bury her, Jessup arrives. The suited man knocks out Jessup with the shovel. Taisey arrives with a gun pointed at the suited man. Godfrey arrives behind Taisey and attempts to overpower her. Then finally, it is Superman to the rescue.

After bringing Lois out of the cave for fresh air, he unmasks the suited man to reveal Alvin as the mysterious stranger. Godfrey and his son discovered deposits of a rare element called hydrozite and they were using Alvin's frightening disguise and the poison gas to scare all the townspeople away so they would be free to reap the profits of the mining venture. Taisey and Jessup had hoped to solve the problem themselves, but are certainly thankful for the assistance of Superman.

On their way out of Cliffton, Kent stops to correct the road sign. He tells Lois he knows the whole story. Lois had hoped for a scoop and when she inquires about Kent's unknown source of information, he calmly replies that a little bird told him everything. Someday he may even reveal the little bird's identity.

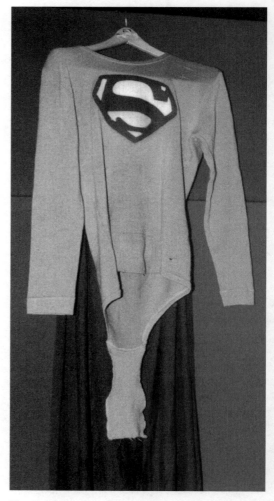

The "stolen costume" is eventually recovered. It currently resides and is on display at Jim Hambrick's *Super Museum* in Metropolis, Illinois.

EPISODE 13

THE STOLEN COSTUME

directed by LEE SHOLEM
written by BEN PETER FREEMAN

George Reeves is the only familiar face from the regular cast of characters in this adventure. It begins as a burglar named *SIMMS* (Norman Budd) is being chased by the police. He enters the window of Clark Kent's apartment in an effort to hide from capture when he accidently discovers the secret closet. There he sees Superman's costume draped on a hanger. Simms takes the costume and quickly makes his way back out into the alley where he is shot in the back by a

POLICEMAN (Bob Williams), before he somehow manages to get away.

ACE (Dan Seymour) and *CONNIE* (Veda Ann Borg) are relaxing in their apartment when the door bell rings. Connie answers it to find Simms. He staggers into the room and falls on the sofa. He is making a difficult attempt to talk about a big deal and Superman when they notice the costume.

Kent greets the arrival at his own apartment of his private detective friend, *CANDY* (Frank Jenks). He has been invited over to investigate the robbery. Kent starts to explain how a new insurance plan at work required he take a physical examination and that is why. . . he decides not to tell Candy what has been stolen. He shows the detective the empty secret closet and instructs him to dust for finger prints. The only way to recover the stolen item is to discover the identity of the thief.

Back at Ace's apartment, Connie is trying to cut Superman's costume with a pair of scissors without success. It must be the genuine article. But why isn't Superman wearing it? Connie suggests he has taken it off on account he wants to be the other guy. She decides to go and find out who lives in the apartment that Simms burglarized.

Candy returns to tell Kent about how a small time crook's body has been found in a vacant lot with a bullet in it's back. Nothing of value was found with him, but Kent decides to go to the morgue and check for himself. He tells Candy to wait for him at his apartment.

Pretending to visit the wrong apartment, Connie meets Candy in a staged purse dropping accident in the hallway. She assumes he is Kent. Later, she reports to Ace that Kent is a news reporter who works for the Daily Planet. Ace is sure they have the right man because every time Superman does something sensational, it is first reported in the Daily Planet.

A telephone call from Kent at the morgue tells Candy he found nothing. They decide to meet later. After Candy leaves the apartment, Ace and Connie break in and plant a bomb inside. Now all they need do is wait to see if Kent survives the explosion when he returns.

Later, Ace and Connie are sitting in their car outside of Kent's apartment building when Candy arrives. Connie points him out as being Kent. Ace remarks how he doesn't look at all like a superman, but Connie figures he must look better when he is wearing the costume.

Inside, Kent is waiting for Candy as he enters the apartment. Seeing how depressed Kent appears, he once more offers to help if only Kent will confide in him. Kent tells him not to worry and they decide to go get some dinner. As Candy goes to wash up, he notices the partially open closet and calls Kent. He quickly rushes in to save Candy from the explosion. The test is complete, and Ace and Connie quickly drive away.

When they return to their apartment, Ace telephones Kent to see if he's still alive. He offers to return the missing item if a meeting can be arranged. They agree to meet at Kent's apartment in fifteen minutes. Kent then asks Candy to leave. He agrees, but tells Kent he is no longer responsible for what might happen to him.

Outside the apartment building, Candy is standing around when Ace and Connie arrive. They mistake Candy for Kent and he agrees to go with them. Kent looks outside the window to see the three driving away. He quickly begins to loosen his tie, but he realizes he is wearing no costume. Then he runs out of the apartment.

Back at Ace's place, he begins to question Candy. Why does he carry a gun? He answers that a reporter often gets into dangerous situations. This doesn't add up, and when Ace asks him what was stolen from the secret closet, he has no answer. As Ace is about to put his theory to the test by pointing a gun at the detective, Kent rushes up the stairs and crashes through the door. He quickly knocks Candy unconscious before Ace takes a few shots at the intruder. It is obvious that Kent is the real Clark Kent and the real Superman.

Ace proposes they make a deal, but Superman doesn't make deals with would be murderers and criminals. Then Ace threatens to tell the world that Clark Kent is Superman.

"Yeah, and that'll put the whammi on your Superman racket, but good!" says Connie.

Kent insists they will tell no one.

"How you gonna stop us?" they sneer. "Everyone knows Superman doesn't kill people."

Kent replies by telling them to gather up some warm clothing.

A flight to the frozen north lands Ace and Connie on the top of a snow capped mountain. Superman informs them of a warm shelter and that he will return with plenty of food to keep them alive until he can figure out a way to guarantee their silence. After he flies away, Ace convinces Connie that Superman has no intentions of returning. Their only hope is to attempt a climb down the icy slopes of the mountain. Within a few moments, they fall to their death.

Later, Candy is trying to get a report from Kent. He never learns what was stolen, only that

Kent recovered the missing item from a man and a woman before they died falling off a cliff.

EPISODE 14

MYSTERY IN WAX

directed by LEE SHOLEM
written by BEN PETER FREEMAN

This episode begins when **DR. JOHN HURLEY** (Steve Carr) receives an invitation to attend a private exhibition at Madame Selena's museum of wax art. The highlight will be the unveiling of her latest sculpture portrait of a person she predicts will die.

Later, a group of spectators are assembled in the small auditorium at the museum. It appears to be a normal gathering of the socially elite until the presence of the somber **MADAME SELENA** (Myra McKinney) brings a hush over the crowd. Commanding their undivided attention, Selena steps up on the stage and slowly recites her opening presentation.

"It now becomes my unhappy duty to reveal to you the person who within the next six months will dieeeee!" Then, her whimpy husband, **ANDREW** (Lester Sharpe), raises a curtain to reveal a life-like figure of Dr. Hurley. He is in the audience and is suddenly frightened as everyone else focuses their attention on him with an obvious sigh of relief.

In the next scene, Dr. Hurley is walking like a zombie through the city streets. He approaches the end of a pier, methodically removes his shoes, and then jumps into the harbor just before a running policeman tries to catch him.

The next day, Kent and Lois are in Perry White's office discussing last night's apparent suicide of Dr. Hurley. Perry knew the doctor to be a happy and successful man. He is certain that a clever trick is being perpetrated by a lucky guess from Madame Selena and he doesn't like it. Kent and Lois are assigned to investigate.

At the museum, Kent and Lois request an audience with Selena when they are greeted by Andrew. While they wait as if expecting a meeting with royalty, they visit a wing of the museum called the *Hall of Death*. It is a collection of life-like wax images of former suicide victims

predicted by Madame Selena. Each display is accompanied by a voice recording of the wax image, telling how they died. Lois is disgusted with the exploitation of these unfortunate souls and she expresses her feelings with sarcasm when Madame Selena finally grants them an interview.

Selena all but ignores Lois as she answers questions from Kent. When she claims that her uncanny predictions are the result of hearing voices from another world, Lois rolls her eyes and Kent signals her to keep quiet. The interview concludes without revealing anything except a mutual dislike between Madame Selena and Lois Lane, finally expressed by Selena's refusal to shake hands.

Of course, Kent, Lois, and Perry are invited to attend the next unveiling of a suicide figure. We are sure it will be of Lois, but Kent sees through the curtain just before it is raised to reveal a life-like figure of Perry White.

"What kind of nonsense is this! I don't like practical jokes!" exclaims the outraged editor of the Daily Planet.

Madame Selena seems to be enjoying the reaction. A guarantee of publicity is expressed in Perry's closing remark as he storms away.

"This is a farce, and you Madame are a fraud!" says Perry. "I'll see you run out of town!"

A meeting in Perry's office has Kent and Lois insisting that he retain a body guard, but he refuses. Later, Henderson wakes Kent up from a sound sleep with a telephone call telling him to pick up Lois and come down to police headquarters. When they arrive, the Inspector informs them that a police officer found Perry's shoes at the end of the pier, the same as with the other predicted suicides.

At the office, Lois is finding it very difficult to write Perry's obituary notice. Kent is trying to figure everything out. He comments on how all the victims managed to carry out their suicides by dropping off the same pier, and always with a witness nearby. A telephone call from Henderson takes Kent away after he suggests that Lois stay put until he gets back.

Of course, Lois decides to do her own investigating, and just before closing time, she slips in unnoticed to hide in the wax museum. When Selena comes up from a secret doorway in the floor, Lois overhears her tell Andrew that

Perry White *(John Hamilton)* is the last in a series of Metropolis citizens victimized by Madame Selena.

there is room for three more subjects in the private museum. When the coast is clear, Lois goes down into the basement where she discovers Perry White and the other suicide victims alive and held captive in a bank of cages.

Perry orders her to escape and call the police, but Madame Selena and Andrew prevent her departure. Lois is rendered unconscious with a whiff of chloriform and locked up in another cage. The sharp viewer will notice as Perry watches the struggle helplessly from his cage, he inadvertently reveals the rubber bars on the cage door that will later be bent out of shape by Superman. Selena delivers a speech to a nonexistent audience about how everyone fears her power of prediction in a great impersonation of the Gloria Swanson character from *Sunset Boulevard.*

Upstairs, Kent and Henderson arrive and demand to see the private living quarters of Selena and Andrew. Kent stays behind, using the old shoe tying ploy, and when all are out of sight, he quickly changes into Superman.

The disturbance caused by Superman crashing down the secret stairs to free the captured people brings Selena running. She attempts to attack Superman and Andrew pulls a gun to shoot at the caped intruder. When Superman is busy apprehending Andrew, Selena makes a rush for the gun and screams out how her death predictions will now come true. Superman grabs away the gun and tosses her, kicking and screaming, over to Henderson while he quickly tends to Lois.

The next Daily Planet headline tells how all the previous suicides have been found alive, and Perry comments on how all is well that ends well. Selena's predictions were fulfilled when her husband impersonated the abducted targets and faked their deaths.

When Kent cheerfully enters the office, Henderson asks where he had disappeared to just before Superman arrived to solve the mystery?

"Hiding behind a wax figure?" says Perry.

"No," replies Kent, smiling. "Behind Superman, Chief."

EPISODE 15

TREASURE OF THE INCAS

directed by TOMMY CARR
written by HOWARD GREEN

This adventure begins on a familiar exterior street location in Metropolis, **PROF. LAVERRA** (*Hal Gerard*) is pacing the sidewalk in front of an auction house. A collection of South American art objects and antiques is about to be put on the block and LaVerra is ready to buy. When Lois arrives, he comments on her honest face and introduces himself as a nameless visitor from Peru. He offers her $1,000 to bid for him on a tapestry, explaining that it would not be wise for him to be seen inside. Lois sizes him up as a harmless eccentric and agrees to honor his request.

After Lois goes inside, a sinister looking man named **MENDOSA** (*Leonard Penn*) with a scar on his face forces LaVerra into an alley at gunpoint. They disappear around the corner, we hear a dull thud, see LaVerra's arm fall to the ground, and then escaping feet.

Later, when Lois emerges from the auction house with the rolled tapestry in hand, she is approached by Mendosa. He claims to be an amigo of LaVerra and requests the tapestry. Lois politely refuses and insists that he tell LaVerra to contact her at the Daily Planet.

In the office, Lois displays her purchase to Kent and Jimmy. Noticing a hole in the upper corner of the ragged tapestry, Jimmy remarks how it doesn't appear to be worth ten cents. Lois points out the hole is actually a cut out shape of a star. They have no idea what it means, and it has not yet been claimed by the eccentric professor.

Perry White sends Kent down to the morgue on a routine investigation. From there, he contacts Lois and tells her that the body of Professor LaVerra has been found in an alley behind the auction house. He tells her to come down right away to make an identification and suggests she bring the tapestry. As she is about to leave, Mendosa arrives with a gun. He insists on having the tapestry and when she refuses again, he attacks her.

Kent is pacing the sidewalk, watching for Lois to arrive. By chance, he looks with his telescopic x-ray super vision across the city to see Lois lying on the floor of her office. Quickly, he runs across the street and down into an alley. As a policeman is about to give chase, he sees Superman come out of the alley and leap into the sky. Who was that running man?

Superman arrives to find that Lois is merely shaken up. She explains how the man who approached her earlier claiming to be LaVerra's friend has taken the tapestry. Superman tells her that LaVerra was a professor at the University in Peru and he suggests that she allow Kent to handle the story. We know Lois has other plans.

When she goes to Perry White for approval to investigate, he emphatically says no because he is the boss. She agrees and tells him that is why she already told Pan Am he would approve her airline reservations for a flight to Peru. Realizing a losing battle, he insists she take Olsen along for protection. She gives him an unexpected thank you kiss and then rushes off to pack her bags.

Stock footage of a commercial airliner is followed by an arrival in Lima, Peru. Lois and Jimmy finally get settled at the El Mirado hotel in spite of Jimmy's weak attempt at the Spanish language.

The next order of business is a ride with the taxi **DRIVER** (*Julian Rivero*) to visit the local police, where Lois and Jimmy learn from the police **CAPTAIN** (*Martin Garralaga*) that an investigation is under way.

When they arrive at the University to meet Dr. Cuesta, they are greeted in the hallway by **ANSELMO** (*Steve Carr*). He claims to have been LaVerra's assistant and leads them into meet **DR. CUESTA** (*Juan Duval*), only to find that Clark Kent has already arrived.

"How did you get here so fast?" asks Jimmy.

"When I'm in a hurry to get someplace, I really fly," replies Kent, smiling.

Cuesta explains how Professor LaVerra had hoped to return from America with the tapestry that would help unlock the secret location of an ancient Inca treasure. It would have been used to help many poor and needy people of their country. Anselmo watches with keen interest as Cuesta removes another tapestry from the safe and explains how it would reveal the site of the buried treasure by the location of the cutout star in the missing tapestry.

Publicity shot of Clark Kent *(George Reeves)* that was apparently taken as he was studying his script.

and Jimmy. With a smile, Superman gives credit to Kent for telling him about their trip to Madira.

Later, as Lois and Jimmy are leaving the hotel, she tells Kent how sorry she is about having only two return airline reservations. Kent smiles and says not to worry about him, there's always more than one way to get back to Metropolis. Lois returns the smile and jokingly suggests that if he had wings, he could fly.

"Come to think of it," replies Kent, "that's not a bad idea."

Another closing pun at the risk of exposing his closely guarded secret. Analysis would probably have proved that Kent had a subconscious desire to betray his own identity, a theory that would be demonstrated in many episodes to come.

EPISODE 16

DOUBLE TROUBLE

directed by TOMMY CARR
written by EUGENE SOLOW

Later, Anselmo returns to the office. He breaks into the safe to steal the tapestry, and then he telephones Mendosa.

The next day, Anselmo offers to take Lois and Jimmy for a sightseeing drive in the country. Kent has just come from the library where he was reading up on the ancient Incas. He suggests they visit the area near Madira as a possible treasure site. Leaving Kent behind, Anselmo drives Lois and Jimmy to a secluded desert location and then forces them out of the car with a gun. After a struggle with Jimmy, Anselmo gets away in the car, leaving Lois and Jimmy to die in the wilderness.

After a long walk in the hot sun, they catch up to the car, now parked just outside a cave in the hillside. When they enter the tunnel, they are confronted by Mendosa and Anselmo. Confined with shackles and chains, the two nosey reporters are left with a lit stick of dynamite. Ironically, we see the fuse to the explosive forms the shape of an 'S' as we hear the rapid approach of Superman.

Superman enters the tunnel by crashing through a wall of rock. He quickly tosses the stick of dynamite in the direction of the fleeing crooks. The explosion causes a landslide to trap the bad guys as he breaks the chains to free Lois

The story opens aboard a ship docked in the Metropolis harbor that has apparently been placed under quarantine. Disguised as an official health inspector, **FISCHER** *(Howland Chamberlin)* enters a stateroom. A robed character, who is later discovered to be **OTTO VON KLABEN** *(Steve Carr)*, greets him from behind the door while pointing a gun. Fischer explains that he has been sent to accompany the visitor to the rendezvous. As he moves to the porthole to point out the waiting ambulance that will serve as the getaway car, Von Klaben knocks him out cold. In order to escape unnoticed, he begins to disguise himself as a woman.

Lois and Jimmy arrive and wait near the Customs check point to get an interview with a celebrity expected to come ashore. Von Klaben, now appearing as a woman, makes his way past the customs inspectors, and just before getting into a waiting taxi, he manages to get Jimmy's attention. Under the pretense of being in a hurry, Von Klaben uses a French accent to convince gullible Jimmy that he is really a lady with a twisted ankle. He asks if Jimmy would be so kind to take a small package over to the men waiting near the ambulance.

Superman *(George Reeves)* with Inspector Henderson *(Robert Shayne)* in a publicity still from 1951.

In true boy scout tradition, Olsen innocently takes the package to the men in white uniforms. As *HEAVY (Ross Ford)* shoves Jimmy into the back of the ambulance, Lois manages to catch a glimpse of his kidnapping. This is her last appearance in this episode.

Jimmy is escorted into an office where he hands the package over to *DR. ALBRECHT (Rudolph Anders)* sitting behind a desk. As Jimmy explains how he was recruited by a French lady to deliver the little parcel, Albrecht puts on a pair of heavy oven mittens to open and discover that the package is empty. He is obviously disturbed.

Then Albrecht learns from a telephone call that Fischer's dead body has been discovered in the stateroom of a certain Madame Charpentine. Albrecht gives the order to lock the young reporter in a secret closet until he can figure out what is happening to his perfectly planned smuggling operation. Albrecht tries to put through an overseas telephone call to *U.S. Base Hospital 991*, but he is informed it will be at least three hours before he can get a clear connection.

Meanwhile, Kent pays a visit to Henderson at police headquarters to inquire about Jimmy's mysterious disappearance. After failing to convince Kent that Jimmy is probably off doing some clever ambulance chasing to get a scoop, Henderson decides to let him in on everything he knows so far. The murdered man has been identified as a known criminal named Fischer with ties to Germany, the passport of the woman who occupied the stateroom is a phoney, and the gun they found at the scene was covered with male fingerprints that did not belong to the victim.

After cleverly concluding the woman was really a man and that a double cross has taken place in some smuggling operation, Kent requests a copy of the fingerprints. Henderson is hoping to have them checked out through connections to Germany, but atmospheric disturbances are preventing a clear transmission. We all know that Kent has some other means of transmission in mind.

In the police lab, *JAKE (played by Mickey Mouse Club leader, Jimmy Dodd)* provides Kent with a set of fingerprints. When Jake leaves the room, Kent changes to Superman and executes a takeoff out the window that sounds very much like a landing, followed by a nice close-up flying shot of Superman over the ocean.

Kent arrives to meet with **COLONEL REDDING** *(Selmer Jackson)* of Army Intelligence at the U.S. Base Hospital 991 in Frankfort, Germany. Yes, it's the same place that Albrecht was attempting to contact when he discovered the betrayal by Von Klaben. Almost immediately, Col. Redding finds a match to the set of fingerprints brought in by Kent. They also learn that Von Klaben works as an orderly within the hospital.

When **DR. SCHUMANN** *(Howland Chamberlin again)* enters, Kent gives him a blank stare and Col. Redding remarks that he looks as if he's just seen a ghost. In reply to questions, Schumann reports that one Otto Von Klaben was discharged from service two weeks ago and that he knows nothing of a reputed Nazi espionage agent named Fischer.

After Schumann leaves, Kent informs Col. Redding of his remarkable resemblance to the deceased Fischer and is convinced there is some connection between the two of them. Col. Redding introduces **MAJOR LEE** *(Tom Keene)*, the chief of medical supplies. He tells Kent about the million dollars worth of radium the size of a peanut that is locked up securely in the walk-in safe. When the three of them go into the lead lined safe, Schumann rushes into the room, slams the heavy door shut and makes a hasty

escape. His attempt to lock up our hero is easily foiled as Kent, under cover of darkness, forces the door open.

Although the lead lining has prevented Superman's x-ray vision from making a positive identification, Redding is sure it was Schumann. When the two army officers go chasing after him, Kent changes into Superman and flies back to Metropolis.

Kent returns to Inspector Henderson's office. The Inspector tells him the taxi that picked up the French lady at the pier has been located. They have learned that she escaped on one of three passenger trains. He also says that a report from Col. Redding in Germany says Schumann was captured and that Kent should be credited for the double play. Kent replies smiling that Superman should be given credit for an assist. When Henderson invites Kent to the planned arrest of Albrecht, he promises to be there and then exits.

From an alley, Superman leaps into the air. After landing on a moving passenger train, he captures the escaping Von Klaben with the stolen radium and informs the steward that this passenger will be returning East by air.

Meanwhile, every police car on the force has gathered around the office building of Albrecht who claims that he will never be taken alive. Superman throws open the double doors and tells Albrecht to drop his gun or he will make him eat his words! Albrecht responds by uttering a few words of German dribble and wastes several rounds of ammo on the costumed figure.

Henderson arrives with his troops to clean up and Superman rescues Jimmy from the secret closet. Jimmy tells Superman how all this got started just because he wanted an interview with a very pretty French movie actress. Jimmy confesses that Superman looks prettier to him than all the movie stars in the world. Golly.

EPISODE 17

THE RUNAWAY ROBOT

directed by TOMMY CARR
written by DICK HAMILTON

When two simple-minded crooks, who we later know as **ROCCO** *(Dan Seymour)* and **MOUSIE**

Clark Kent *(George Reeves)*, Horatio Hinkle *(Lucien Littlefield)*, Lois Lane *(Phyllis Coates)*, Jimmy Olsen *(Jack Larson)*, and Inspector Henderson *(Robert Shayne)*.

(John Harmon), are hurriedly emptying the contents of a jewelry store, they are interrupted by the arrival of the Runaway Robot. Although the rather slow moving, crudely constructed tin man poses no real threat, walking very much like the mummy of the Universal horror pictures, its mechanical voice causes enough of a distraction to allow an alarm switch to be activated by the store's clerk tied up on the floor. "Put up your hands, you are under arrest!" Actually, the voice is that of the robot's inventor, *HORATIO HINKLE (Lucien Littlefield)*, who is remotely directing the automaton from a control box equipped with a joy stick and television monitor.

The crooks manage to escape easily, and the robot begins to move wildly out of control. After dumping the reclaimed loot out on the floor, it begins to crush most of it in a mechanical dance, and Horatio enters the shop just in time to stop the robot before it can stomp down on the store clerk's head.

Horatio's bungled attempt to prevent the robbery is justly rewarded by a trip to jail. Just before the *JAIL KEEPER (Herman Cantor)* throws away the key, Horatio claims to be the rural correspondent of the Daily Planet, and he is rescued by the arrival of Kent, Lois, and Jimmy. When Horatio demands the release of *Hero*, his mechanical invention they have locked up in the police garage, Kent explains that he is being held responsible for the $60,000 in missing jewelry. To further complicate the situation, they discover that Hero has been stolen from police custody. Horatio then explains that the tin man could be very dangerous in the wrong hands. Jimmy is assigned the duty of escorting Horatio back to Kent's apartment while he and Lois investigate.

Meanwhile, the two crooks have returned to their hideout. Apparently empty-handed, they report to the boss, *CHOPPER (Russell Johnson)*. The story about a robot is confirmed when another henchman calls in to report having heisted the mechanical man from the police, and that the inventor is being held at Kent's apartment.

After receiving a ransom call from Chopper, Horatio sets out to get rid of Jimmy so he can slip away to a meeting with the gang of crooks. When Jimmy fails to fall for the old 'go out and get ice cream sodas' routine, the inventor drops a gas pellet in Jimmy's face and makes his escape.

The plan is to force Horatio into making modifications to Hero which would allow him to break into the vault of the Metropolis Trust Company. When he refuses, he is locked up with the robot while the crooks formulate a more persuasive argument. Horatio uses the private opportunity to put through an emergency radio message to his assistant, **MARVIN** (Bob Easton), using a transmitter hidden in Hero's chest cavity.

Marvin telephone's Kent, but Lois intercepts the call. She immediately goes after Horatio and is ultimately captured. When the crooks threaten harm to her, Horatio agrees to the gangsters' demands. He effects necessary changes to Hero like fixing him up with a blow torch, and then operates the control device so the robot may successfully enter the vault. As the robot makes his escape with the money, Horatio forces the mechanical man to trip several fire alarm boxes.

Kent and Jimmy have been patiently waiting for some kind of break when they hear the fire alarms. Kent sends Jimmy to investigate so he may quickly become Superman.

Mousie has taken over control of the robot, and as he is about to send the robot after Lois, Superman arrives. The robot is instructed to attack the strange visitor from Krypton. It falls apart in the process. Superman then quickly captures the crooks, and brings Lois and Horatio to safety.

The wrap up scene in Kent's apartment has Henderson arriving to point the finger of responsibility at Horatio for the missing jewels from the original robbery. Kent points to the basket full of robot parts and Henderson quickly recovers the missing jewels. When the playful robot gives Henderson a hot set with a quick blast of his blow torch, everyone breaks out in laughter. The serious Inspector threatens to jail anyone who will admit to thinking his hot seat was funny.

The entire episode was played for laughs and

not at all characteristic of a first season production. If Robert Maxwell had produced more shows of this caliber, he may never have been asked to leave. In retrospect, it would have been a small sacrifice to prevent what Whitney Ellsworth ultimately did to this sharp, action-packed, adventure series.

Oh, and don't forget: XP127Y4.

EPISODE 18

DRUMS OF DEATH

directed by LEE SHOLEM
written by DICK HAMILTON

Jungle stories would become familiar to the Superman family of players before the series ran its course. This story begins in Perry White's office where he and Kent are watching the last piece of documentary film footage to arrive from Perry's jungle exploring sister, Kate. We also learn that Jimmy Olsen is with her and neither have been heard from in over a week.

A frightening view of a voodoo witch doctor before the tail of the film slaps around the take-up reel of the home movie projector sets the mood for this episode. Kent announces he will go to Haiti and investigate. In spite of Kent's claim to be able to travel faster without him, Perry insists on going along.

Stock footage of a Pan American airliner brings us to a hotel room in Haiti where Perry and Kent have checked in. Here, they are soon visited by a friendly Haitian police official, **MR. BERGERÉ** (Milton Wood). As he offers his assistance to locate the missing Americans, jungle drums are heard beating in the distance. Bergeré explains they are not voodoo drums, but the local form of native communication announcing to anyone who may be listening that two white visitors have arrived, referring to Perry and Kent.

Their next visitor is **WILLIAM JOHNSON** (Henry Corden). He initially offers his services as a guide, but when Kent and Perry show him the picture of the voodoo witch doctor enlarged from Kate's film footage, he retracts his offer and suggests they leave the searching to the authorities. He wants nothing to do with any voodoo cults.

After Johnson leaves, Kent reaches outside and grabs an evesdropper named **LELAND MASTERS** (*Leonard Mudie*). He claims to understand the jungle drums and offers his services as a guide. They agree to meet in the morning.

Kent discovers a bandanna left behind by Johnson, who was using it to wipe the sweat from his forehead. Kent finds it curious for some unknown reason and suggests to Perry that they both should get some rest. Of course, we know that to be just an excuse for Kent to slip away and change into Superman.

If you watch his takeoff through the window carefully, you'll see Superman is carrying a stick of dynamite. Hmmm. Even more curious is how much the window reminds us of the Daily Planet. See the review of episode 21 for more details.

Superman arrives in the nearby jungle. Seeing through a temple wall, he listens as a voodoo witch doctor tells **KATE WHITE** (*Mabel Albertson*) that she is under his power. He wants to know why she was taking pictures in a secret corridor of the citadel? She claims to know nothing and is apparently in some sort of hypnotic trance.

Later, Superman visits Kate in confinement. She is convinced that she is being held captive by what Superman assures her are only chains made of paper. She is afraid and refuses to let Superman free her, claiming that she must obey Legbo, the voodoo witch doctor.

Superman locates Jimmy in another part of the temple. He is faking a trance and tells Superman how Kate drank some tea that he didn't, which is probably what put her under the voodoo spell. Superman hides quickly as Legbo arrives to question Jimmy as to why he and Kate were snooping around the temple. Jimmy continues his fake trance and again tells Legbo he doesn't know anything. When Legbo exits, Superman tells Jimmy to keep up his act until he can figure out what is going on and who is responsible.

The next day, while Kent is away with Bergeré visiting **DR. JERROD** (*George Hamilton*) in another city they reached by airplane, Masters leads Perry into the jungle where they walk into a trap. Legbo locks Masters up inside a block cell and then leads Perry into another cell behind bars. Kate and Jimmy are brought in to join Perry for a final confrontation. Jimmy decides its time to drop his act and try to escape, but he fails. When Legbo still cannot get the confession he wants, he leaves the prisoners in the cell with the walls closing in on them.

Meanwhile, Jerrod gives Kent the test report of the analysis of Johnson's bandanna. It had significant traces of cocoa butter. Kent exits quickly and becomes Superman for a return to the jungle. He arrives just in time to rescue Kate, Perry, and Jimmy from being crushed to death. Knowing that cocoa butter could certainly be used to darken one's skin, he rubs the face of Legbo to reveal he is really Johnson in the disguise of a voodoo witch doctor. Perry claims Masters is also part of the mysterious plot which proves to be a scheme designed to keep people away while they have been searching for a buried treasure.

Later, they are all gathered at the hotel room drinking tea. Kate assures them it is not laced with any mind altering drugs. Kent walks in to join the party and hear how Superman saved the day. When Bergeré arrives, he is shocked to see that Kent has returned before him.

"Mr. Kent? How did you get back here so quickly?"

Kent touches his glasses and smiles after a pause, "Why, I... flew."

EPISODE 19

THE EVIL THREE

directed by TOMMY CARR
written by BEN PETER FREEMAN

This is another dark tale which begins with the establishment of a precarious setting in the lobby of the broken down Hotel Bayou. Here, old **COLONEL BRAND** (*Jonathan Hale*) is about to attack **MACEY TAYLOR** (*Rhys Williams*) with a sword. From the balcony at the top of the stairs, **ELSA** (*Cecil Elliott*) sits in her wheelchair and watches the two men throw each other around in an almost playful fight scene until they are distracted by the arrival of an automobile outside.

"This used to be a fine hotel," remarks Perry White, looking around the dusty lobby as he and Jimmy approach the front desk.

Jimmy nods a qualified agreement by saying, "Year One, maybe?"

Macey attempts to discourage the two weary travelers from registering, but Perry insists they are too tired to drive and he wishes to fish a nearby stream in the morning. When Perry goes outside to the car, Macey begins to play on Jimmy's fear by telling him how the place is haunted by the ghost of his Uncle George.

Meanwhile, Perry puts through a call to Kent back at the Daily Planet *(MEtropolis-6-0500)* from his mobile telephone. He tells Kent where he and Jimmy are staying the night and instructs him to find out what he can about a George Taylor who used to own the old hotel. They plan for Kent to return a call to the car in an hour. Perry's mobile number is *MX39162*.

As they begin to unpack for their stay in what Jimmy refers to as 'a crummy dump', Perry explains that he smells a story. The old owner of the hotel didn't trust banks and probably hid his money away somewhere.

Jimmy sees the face of a ghost outside the window, but Perry doesn't turn around in time. *This is one of several shots that did not appear in the Kellogg's editions of the show in its initial run.*

Perry sends Jimmy off to his own room to get some rest while he stays awake for Kent's return call.

From his room, Jimmy hears laughter outside the door. He moves out into the hall to investigate. Perry catches him and tells him he had better get some sleep, reminding him they have a six o'clock wakeup call for an early start in the morning.

Later, Jimmy is visited by someone in the dark. *A shot of the ghostly visitor was also cut for the original Kellogg's editions.*

Jimmy yells out. When Perry comes running, of course, no one is there but Jimmy. They soon discover a hidden doorway that reveals a ramp leading down under the hotel. Unwillingly, Jimmy accompanies the headstrong editor down the ramp where they discover a skeleton. It must be that of old George Taylor. As they are about to escape, Macey and the Colonel arrive to over power them with a shovel. Elsa sits at the top of the ramp in her wheelchair, screaming how she wants no more killing. Macey has other plans. He sends the Colonel to get rid of the visitors' car

outside. These nosey reporters must be silenced for good.

When Kent has no luck getting through to Perry's mobile phone, he quickly changes to Superman. The Colonel puts Perry's car into neutral gear and rolls it off a nearby cliff out of sight. Perry and Jimmy manage to escape the underground trap and return to their rooms to quickly pack for a getaway, but Elsa blocks their way with a gun from her wheelchair. She explains how Macey killed his Uncle George and that he and the Colonel have been scaring guests away from the hotel while they search for the buried savings of old George. Elsa claims to know where the money is hidden and offers to lead the two reporters to it if they will help her escape.

As Perry and Jimmy return to the basement to dig up the buried loot, Macey is waiting for them, ready to attack. Superman lands outside the hotel where he meets the Colonel. After inquiring about the two visiting reporters, the Colonel leads Superman away toward a nearby cottage where he claims Perry and Jimmy are staying.

When Superman challenges the wild goose chase, the Colonel informs him that the old man and the boy are dead. He quickly raises his sword and breaks it on the Superman's tough skin. The sharp viewer may notice the break in the background footage of blowing trees in the process shot of Superman in the woods.

Macey shoves old Elsa down the ramp in her wheelchair after putting away Perry and Jimmy. *And this shot was edited for the Kellogg's editions.*

Macey is about to escape when Superman arrives.

"Tell me where they are or I'll break every bone in your body!" says Superman.

Our hero obviously has no patience for nonsense as he pushes past Macey and down to the basement where he finds Perry and Jimmy locked up behind a giant boulder.

Not long after, Elsa is being dragged out of the hotel on a stretcher by two medical men and Macey and the Colonel are lead away in handcuffs by the local police. Superman offers to fly his two friends, now without a car, back to Metropolis, but Perry insists they've had too much excitement already. Jimmy smiles and asks for a raincheck on the flight.

"Sure thing, Jim," replies Superman. "Anytime at all."

Jimmy smiles with, "Golly," just as the show fades to black.

EPISODE 20

THE RIDDLE OF THE CHINESE JADE

directed by TOMMY CARR
written by BEN PETER FREEMAN

A quiet restaurant in Chinatown is the location of a meeting between a second rate crook named **GREER** *(James Craven)* and **HARRY WONG** *(Victor Sen Yung)*. From their conversation, we learn that Wong is assisting Greer in a scheme to steal the Kwan Yin jade, a priceless antique figurine that belongs to the family of Wong's employer, Lu Sung.

Wong explains to Greer how he may gain access to the apartment of Lu Sung by way of a secret tunnel that leads from Wong's house across the street. His motive is to raise cash for his future with Lilly, Lu Sung's niece, after they are married. But he is having second thoughts. Greer assures Wong that he is doing the right thing. Lu Sung is about to donate the family heirloom to a museum, and Greer maintains it will do much more good if it can be sold on the open market.

The next day, Kent and Lois are getting an interview with the elderly **LU SUNG** *(Paul E. Burns)* and his lovely niece, **LILLY** *(Gloria Saunders)*, regarding his decision to donate the jade antiquity to the Metropolis museum. They are interrupted by an explosion in Lu Sung's antique shop downstairs from a bomb thrown through the window by Wong and Greer across the street. Kent, Lois, and Lu Sung rush down to investigate, leaving a frightened Lilly alone. She is apparently

Lois Lane *(Phyllis Coates)*, Lu Sung *(Paul E. Burns),* his daughter, Lilly *(Gloria Saunders),* and Clark Kent *(George Reeves)* are all admiring the "Chinese Jade" statuette.

John Greer *(James Craven)* is about to be punished for making off with Lois Lane and the antique jade statuette.

shaken by the explosion and is resting on the couch.

Downstairs, Lois gets on the telephone to Inspector Henderson while Kent and Lu Sung walk through the shambles of the shop. Henderson will bring a few members of the bomb squad over to investigate.

Meanwhile, Greer and Wong enter the upstairs apartment through the hidden doorway in the wall to steal the jade. Lilly attempts to stop the theft and because she recognizes Wong, Greer insists that she come along as a hostage. Wong reluctantly agrees and the three go back through the secret passage down into the tunnel. Lilly is so upset that she faints and drops to the ground. Greer says they are now committed to the plan and orders Wong to cooperate.

As Kent and Lu Sung pick through the wreckage, Harry Wong enters and tells that he was asleep in his home across the street when he heard the terrible explosion. He is introduced to Kent by Lu Sung as the manager of this shop.

When Kent asks Wong if he has any ideas, he shakes his head innocently and replies.

"If I searched my mind for a century, I could not think of who would do this."

A scream from Lois brings Kent running up the stairs to find out that the jade is gone and so is Lilly. When Wong enters, Kent notices some flakes of sawdust on his shirt.

Henderson arrives and wants to question Wong as a suspect, but Kent persuades against it, arguing that Lilly may be in danger. He tells Henderson about the bamboo dust he saw on Wong's shirt and that the box containing the jade figure was also filled with bamboo dust.

Lilly is being held captive by Greer in Wong's apartment. Wong tries to convince her that he has done this crime to make a better life for them both. Sensing her disapproval, Wong insists if he isn't paid by Greer immediately, he is going to return the jade to its rightful owner. Greer engages in a fist fight with Wong. The fight, obviously staged by stuntmen who look nothing like our principal players, ends with Wong being the loser.

Meanwhile, Henderson is grilling Lu Sung in his apartment and suggests that Lilly has something to do with the missing statue. Henderson blames Kent for talking him out of arresting Wong when he had the chance. He decides to go to Wong's apartment and question him. Kent insists on going along.

Greer opens a trap door in the floor and escapes with the unconscious bodies of Wong and Lilly down into the tunnel. Henderson and Kent arrive to enter an empty room. Down below, Greer opens a sewer valve, and as the tunnel begins to fill with water, he makes his escape with the jade before Kent uses his x-ray vision to see what is happening.

Lois is assuring Lu Sung that she believes Lilly had nothing to do with the theft of the statue when Greer enters through the secret door in the wall, pointing a gun. Lu Sung sees that he has the jade and makes a quick move to get it. Greer knocks him out cold with the butt of the gun. He then tells Lois that she gets the same if she fails to cooperate.

Kent has given Henderson the slip in order to appear, walking in the street, as Superman. A crowd of curious chinamen gathers around as Superman zigzags, watching the ground with his x-ray vision until he locates Wong and Lilly. They are unconscious and about to be drowned in the rising water of the tunnel. Superman then stoops down and begins to use his fist as a jackhammer to open a hole in the pavement.

During the diversion, Greer is escorting Lois outside at gunpoint. He warns her not bleat or she's finished. He then forces Lois to move up the sidewalk.

Superman rescues Wong and Lilly as Henderson arrives with some uniformed police. Then he sees Greer and Lois and chases them down an alley with Henderson not far behind. Backed into a dead end, Greer has a gun pointed at Lois and wants to make a deal. Henderson flatly refuses, but Superman instructs him not to do anything right away and goes running off. Greer asks Lois who the man is in the circus suit, apparently because he never reads the Daily Planet, and then sarcastically remarks that the funny looking man doesn't seem so super now.

Superman flies up and then back down to land next to Greer for a surprise attack. Once again, he saves the day with several rapid punches.

With the jade statuette back in the proper hands, Henderson listens to Wong attempt to make apologies for his actions, claiming he did it only to make a better life for his beloved Lilly. Since Lu Sung apparently does not wish to press charges against his future nephew-in-law, Henderson decides to be judge and jury and let Wong off free of all charges. Lois and Lilly move in on Henderson from each side and plant a kiss on his cheeks. Kent enters just in time to witness this display. He suggests that Henderson is trying to become a superman. Then he smiles and winks at the camera for the final fade out.

EPISODE 21

THE HUMAN BOMB

directed by LEE SHOLEM
written by RICHARD FIELDING

The Metropolis City Club is where the socially elite lounge around a comfortable sitting room for brandy, political discussions, and a good cigar. **BUTLER** (*Trevor Bardette*) is contemplating the incredible power of Superman. When a fellow club member named **CONWAY** (*Lou Krugman*) begins to make fun of Butler's obsession with the Man of Steel, he is soon caught up in a challenge proposed by Butler. Conway agrees to pay him $100,000 if he can successfully hold Superman at bay for thirty minutes.

At the Daily Planet, Butler is dressed in a long trench coat. He gets past the **RECEPTIONIST** (*Aline Towne*) and gains access to the office of Lois Lane. There he introduces himself politely as 'Mr. Bomb' and when that fails to make an impression on Lois, he offers up his first name as 'Human.'

As Lois is about to make a run for the door, Butler grabs her arm and handcuffs himself to her. He opens his trench coat and reveals a vest with pockets full of dynamite and a detonator mechanism at his finger tips. After allowing Lois to call for help, Jimmy comes rushing into the office and demands that this crazy man release Miss Lane immediately. In order to prove his

Two henchmen *(Ted Ryan, Lou Lubin)* working for "Bet-A-Million" Butler *aka the Human Bomb* are now in custody.

intent, Butler offers a stick of dynamite for Jimmy's examination.

If only Superman were here! But that is exactly what Butler demands, the appearance of Superman, and he sends Jimmy off to inform Perry White of the situation.

Jimmy rushes into Perry's office and finally convinces the editor that the situation is serious enough for him to investigate. As they leave Perry's office, you can see a golfbag full of clubs that will play into the action later when Jimmy decides to take matters into his own hands.

Expecting the room to soon be crowded with curious reporters and policemen, Butler leads Lois out the window and onto the ledge overlooking the street below.

Perry and Jimmy return to the empty office. Jimmy is confused and Perry begins to doubt again until he yells out into the hall to **SAM** *(voice of Steve Carr)* who confirms that Lois never left the room. After moving to the window and confirming Lois is being held against her will by a crazy man, Perry puts through a call to **INSPECTOR HILL** *(Marshall Reed)* who is apparently filling in as the resident police official while Inspector Henderson is on vacation.

In a tense moment with Lois on the ledge, she accidently loses her shoe. It falls to the sidewalk many floors below. Kent happens to be standing there and instead of rushing into a nearby alley or telephone booth, he instead rushes upstairs to the office to meet with Perry and Jimmy.

When Kent hears that Butler demands to see Superman, he quickly works up a plan to leave the scene without drawing suspicion. Kent accuses Perry of cooking up this ridiculous publicity scheme that is dangerously risking the life of Lois and this stuntman. He insists on wanting nothing to do with this cheap trick designed to sell newspapers. He storms out of the office. In the hallway, we see Kent rush into the storeroom for a quick change of clothing.

Meanwhile, Butler decides to calm his nerves with a cigarette. When Lois offers a pleading protest, Butler realizes that a lit cigarette may not be a wise thing to do with a vest full of dynamite strapped around his waist. Of course, if this scene was played out today, Butler would encounter any number of newspaper reporters and clerical workers standing out on the ledge exercising what is left of their freedom to enjoy a smoke outside of what would have by now been declared a smoke-free work environment.

Finally, Superman arrives on the ledge to confront the crazy terrorist. Lois seems surprised to see him, but Superman reminds her that this entire event is hardly a secret as he points out the crowd that has gathered at the street below them. Butler then declares his intention of enjoying Superman's company for thirty minutes, assuring the costumed hero that the danger and the dynamite are real.

Superman takes the stick of dynamite offered to Jimmy for verification and fixes it to a camera's flashgun. Then he leaps out the window. *This window exit was filmed for this episode as Superman makes the leap with dynamite in hand. However, the shot was used in several other episodes of both the first and second season. Watch for it in episode 18 and again in episode 37. Can you find it in any others? Watch for window exits where Superman leaps out to the left over a chair.*

Superman flies high into the sky where he detonates the explosive. It is the real thing and now everyone knows this human bomb character is definitely serious. Butler explains the bet he has with Conway. In exchange for Lois' freedom, Superman must remain within his sight for thirty minutes while two of his accomplices execute a robbery of a nearby museum. They will steal only one art object to prove the bet and later return it unharmed. Butler makes it perfectly clear to Superman that he has no intentions of hurting anyone or stealing anything permanently. All he wants to do is keep Superman occupied for the half hour to win the prize money. Superman reluctantly agrees, but says he must wait inside because he cannot stand to see Lois Lane in such terrible danger.

Inspector Hill and **OFFICER RILEY** (*Dennis Moore*) have been watching out the window with Perry and Jimmy when Superman jumps into a nearby window which just happens to be Clark Kent's office. Riley begs to go out on the ledge with a couple of his men, but the Inspector orders him to wait. Meanwhile, two of Butler's **HENCHMEN** (*Lou Lubin, Ted Ryan*) have been watching the event unfold through binoculars from a nearby building. They decide it is time to exit and act out their part of the plan.

Superman is in Kent's office and quickly rearranges some of the furniture. He aims a small desk lamp at the wall within Butler's view. He sends Jimmy into Perry's office to get a tape recorder while he positions himself in a chair so his shadow is cast on the wall. When Butler yells to Superman to verify his presense, Jimmy records his response on tape.

"No comment until the time limit is up!"

As Perry moves in front of the window to momentarily block Butler's view, Superman quickly changes places with Inspector Hill who casts a shadow very much like Superman himself. The next time Butler asks a question, Jimmy replays the taped voice. The plan appears to be working, so Superman excuses himself for a short time while he rushes off to prevent the museum robbery.

After almost losing the taped voice of Superman, Jimmy fears the plan will fail and decides to take matters into his own hands. He quickly rifles through the telephone book and mutters, "It isn't there, the guy is a fake." Then he rushes into Perry's office and telephones someone named Miriam to say he may be late for their date. He grabs one of Perry's golf clubs and moves out onto the window ledge.

Superman arrives at the museum as the henchmen attempt to get away in their automobile. At first, they suspect a stuck parking brake or faulty transmission, but a glance in the rearview mirror reveals the source of their car troubles. Superman gathers the two crooks and promises to deliver them to the nearby police station where they are sure to receive free room and board.

When Jimmy approaches Lois and Butler on the narrow ledge, he exposes the scheme set up by Superman with the tape recorder and accuses Butler of having only fake explosives. When Butler begins his escape, Jimmy attempts to capture him with the swing of the golf club. Jimmy loses his footing and falls toward the street. Superman flies by just in time to catch him. During the confusion, Inspector Hill and his men move out on the ledge, capture Butler, and drag him inside.

When asked why he attempted such a foolish stunt, Jimmy says he had to save Miss Lane and brags that he knew the dynamite was phoney. Lois quickly points out that just because there was no listing for an Apex Company in the local telephone book does not necessarily prove the dynamite manufacturer was imaginary. And when Superman reminds Jimmy that the first stick did indeed explode, the cub reporter realizes his mistaken logic and faints. Superman smiles and quickly makes an exit. Within seconds, in walks the returning Clark Kent.

"I'm glad to see you all came to your senses and cut out that crazy publicity gag!" says Kent with a smile.

"And where were you?" asks Lois.

"Me? I went fishing," replies Kent as he looks over at Jimmy. "Caught a big one, too."

It's amazing of course that no one ever wondered how Kent managed to get out of town, do some fishing, and then return fully dressed in his business suit in less than an hour. Maybe that is one reason why these are called the *amazing* adventures of Superman.

EPISODE 22

CZAR OF
THE UNDERWORLD

directed by TOMMY CARR
written by EUGENE SOLOW

The deadly menace of organized crime is the target of Superman in this two fisted episode, originally titled *Murder on Stage 13*. Clark Kent is selected to act as a creative consultant on a Hollywood film production. It is to be based on a series of biting articles he has written documenting the affairs of a suspected underworld leader named *LUIGI DINELLI* (Tony Caruso). Of course, the gangster is considerably upset when he discovers this planned exposé is in the works.

Kent is about to leave his office with Henderson to catch a plane for the West Coast when the telephone rings. The two are completely unaware that they are being watched from a window across the street by two of Dinelli's henchmen. When Kent picks up the phone, he is greeted by Dinelli calling from California.

"Hello, Kent. They tell me you and Inspector Henderson are coming out here to work in the movies."

Kent smiles. "That's right, Dinelli. National Studios bought that series of articles I wrote about you for the Daily Planet. Czar of the Underworld, do you remember?"

"I didn't like what them articles said in the paper, Kent," says Dinelli, speaking slowly in order to give his henchmen an opportunity to get Kent in the sight of their rifle. "I'm gonna like them less in the movies."

"Well now that's too bad, Luigi." says Kent "What do you suggest?"

"Friends of mine tell me that picture shouldn't oughta be made. They say you and Henderson should call off your trip."

Meanwhile, Henderson has moved to the open window, unknowingly blocking the gunman from getting a clear shot. When Henderson finally moves away, the rifle trigger jams up. As the gunman works feverishly to fix the rifle, Kent continues to gab with Dinelli.

"And another thing, Luigi. You better tell your friends that Czar of the Underworld starts shooting tomorrow morning. Inspector Henderson and I intend to be on hand for the occasion."

Wanting to get in on the conversation, Henderson grabs the phone and puts in his two cents worth.

"And you can tell them for me, Dinelli, this picture is gonna pack more wallop than a tommy gun. When you see the stuff we're putting into it, you won't be able to find a hole deep enough to crawl into." Henderson hands the phone back to Kent as he once again backs up to the open window.

"Well, how do you like that?" remarks the gunman after fixing his rifle. "I finally get it working again and all I can see is that copper's back."

Kent continues, "I'm sorry, Luigi. But I'm afraid we'll have to cut this short. We have to shove off for the airport. See you in sunny California."

"I'm warning you, Kent. You and that copper won't leave California alive if you go ahead with that picture!"

"It's too late to stop them now," says Kent. "They start shooting tomorrow morning."

"Some friends of mine are libel to start shooting, too." replies Dinelli, hoping to hear a gunshot. "It might be sooner than you think!"

A gunshot rings out. Kent and Henderson hit the floor. Dinelli laughs loudly over the telephone as Henderson crawls toward the window.

"Keep back, Inspector!" warns Kent.

"But they tried to plug you!" says Henderson. "That call was a plan to get you to the phone! It was an attempted murder!"

"We haven't got time to worry about that now!" insists Kent as he moves for the door. "Come on, let's go!"

After an unsuccessful attempt to assassinate Kent, Dinelli decides to go to an alternate plan. He sends some muscle headed up by a character named **OLLIE** (Paul Fix) to sabotage the film production company.

In Hollywood, Ollie takes the place of the driver sent by the studio to pick up Kent and Henderson at the airport. He drives the two visitors to an abandoned garage with a phoney excuse to check one of the tires. Then as Henderson is saying how wonderful it is to be in Hollywood, the garage door closes, leaving the two unsuspecting visitors in the dark.

Outside, Ollie tells an accomplice that the boss wants to take care of these two nosey visitors himself. After locking up the garage door, Ollie makes his getaway.

Within a minute, Kent foils another attempt against him and Henderson by knocking out the hoodlum guard. Then he forces the garage door open.

"How'd you do it?" asks Henderson. "We were locked in here."

"One of the little tricks that Superman taught me," replies Kent with a smile.

"You know, Kent, sometimes I get the feeling you *are* Superman."

"I may have to be to get this picture made," replies Kent a little more seriously.

In a brief montage of stock film footage, we see that the gangsters are making every attempt to stop the film company from completing the documentary. But the production continues, even after one of the star movie actors is killed by a prop gun with real bullets. Here is where producer Robert Maxwell and writer Gene Solow add some irony to the story by setting the action at a movie company called National Studios in homage to the comic book producers, and they draft *Steve Carr* to portray the fictional movie director in the story, who is actually the brother of the episode's real director, Tommy Carr.

Hoping to force the gangsters into the open, Kent announces that he will be spending the night at the studio in the dead actor's trailer on stage 13. Dinelli soon gets word of this and orders his man on the inside to make his move.

However, before another attempt to kill Kent can be carried out, Superman pays a visit to Dinelli. After disarming the bodyguards, Superman takes Dinelli for a short flight to the movie studio. He puts the unconscious gangster in the trailer where Kent said he would be spending the night.

Soon after, Superman returns to stage 13 with Inspector Henderson. They find that someone has attached a hose from a running automobile's exhaust pipe to the trailer's air vent. Superman quickly stops the car as Henderson opens the trailer to let in some fresh air.

"That little carbon monixide deal was meant for me!" exclaims Superman.

"For you?" asks Henderson.

"I mean for Kent," says Superman. "I better take a look at Dinelli!"

Luigi Dinelli is still sleeping, safe and sound. Superman sees a visitor up on the stage rigging and leaps up to chase him after the man takes a shot at Henderson. When the man falls from the high rigging, he is recognized as the studio **GUARD** (John Maxwell). Before he can confess to being Frank Dinelli, Luigi's missing brother, Luigi appears at the trailer door and shoots him dead. Superman quickly apprehends Luigi and tells Henderson to handcuff him. When Luigi claims they have nothing on him, Superman reminds him that they now have him for murder.

With a necessary assist from Superman, Kent and Henderson put an end to Dinelli's crime career. The show is over before we realize the absence of Lois and Jimmy. All things considered, it is still a classic example of Superman as an effective enemy of gangland tyranny.

EPISODE 23

GHOST WOLF

directed by LEE SHOLEM
written by DICK HAMILTON

With the season nearing an end, the production shifted locations for a change of pace to the forest in the vicinity of *The Lone Pine Timber Company,* the primary source for newsprint paper used by the Daily Planet. The opening scenes of this episode reveals **SAM GARVIN** (Stanley Andrews), the company's chief operations officer watching **JACQUE OLIVIER** (Lou Krugman) through a pair of binoculars as he runs from a timber wolf. Olivier comes running to the shack to tell Garvin that he cannot continue to work for the lumber company because he believes the stories about a legendary werewolf that is suppose to be able to change its form to that of a woman. When Garvin puts through a call to Perry White to give him the news of how all the lumber workers have quit their jobs over a crazy werewolf rumor, Perry tells him to hold out until he sends his people up to investigate.

Stock footage of a commercial airliner and some aerial shots of forest covered hills brings Kent, Lois, and Jimmy to the final leg of their journey. They are passengers in the caboose of a logging train snaking its way through the mountains. Then a railroad **WORKER** (Harold Goodwin) announces how relieved he will feel after the train passes the high tressel bridge stretching over Devil's Gorge. He explains that there have already been several attempts by persons unknown to wreck the train recently. Kent decides to take a little walk. As he moves toward the door at the front of the caboose, Lois is almost thrown off her feet by the jolting motion of the train. She orders Kent to tell the engineer to slow down.

Kent is standing outside on the porch of the caboose. He notices the main support beam for the upcoming bridge has been nearly split by an axe. "Great Scott!" says Kent and he quickly takes to the air as Superman.

The Man of Steel arrives at the foot of the tressel. He is just in time to prevent the destruction of the bridge long enough for the train to make a safe crossing. As Lois and Jimmy are watching the bridge collapse behind them, Kent walks in acting as if nothing ever happened.

The three reporters arrive at the lumber camp and begin to question Garvin. He suggests the collapsing bridge was merely the result of rotted timber. He then goes on to explain how all the workers have quit after stories were circulating about a mysterious woman who roamed the countryside, changing at will into a wolf. Kent confesses to Lois that he believes Garvin knows more than he is telling.

That night, Lois wakes up screaming after seeing a wolf at her window. Kent and Jimmy come running along with Garvin, who is fully dressed even though it is the middle of the night. Kent wants to excuse himself for an opportunity to look around, but Lois refuses to let him. She insists on moving into the bunk house with him and Jimmy.

In a classic exchange of contentious dialog, Lois demonstrates her liberated, no-nonsense attitude by giving the men their orders long before the *N.A.G.* gang made it fashionable.

"I think it would be a good idea if we all turned in," suggests Mr. Kent.

"Oh, you do, do you?" replies Lois. "Why is it, Clark, everytime trouble starts, you want to sneak off someplace?"

"Trouble is over now, isn't it?" remarks Kent sheepishly.

"I'm not so sure!" says Lois. "Did you notice Garvin was fully dressed? He hadn't even been to bed!"

"Yes, I did," replies Kent calmly.

"Why?" Lois insists on an answer.

"I don't know," says Kent.

"Alright, Clark. Don't cooperate," Lois gives in with a sigh. "But for once, you are going to stick around and be useful."

"Alright, how would you suggest I stick around and be useful?" replies Kent sarcastically.

"Well, for one thing," replies Lois sharply, "you can help me move my things into that bunk house with you and Jim."

"Now wait a minute!" says Kent. "That's the *men's* bunk house!"

"With a hundred and twelve bunks, I'll have plenty of privacy," says Lois. "You and Jim can sleep at one end and I'll sleep at the other. But if you think I'm gonna sleep in this shack here alone tonight, you're nuts! Come on!"

The next morning, Lois walks to a nearby river to wash up while Kent and Jimmy have breakfast. It is interesting to note how Kent is always the business man, fully dressed in a three piece suit at the rustic breakfast table.

Lois discovers a gold earring on the ground just before she comes face to face with a growling wolf. Once again, her electrifying screams bring Kent and Jimmy running to investigate.

Now Kent insists on going out alone and tells Lois and Jimmy to stay put. But, of course, they decide to go out on their own armed with wooden clubs. They soon discover a forest fire in the making. Garvin is watching from the shack with his binoculars as Olivier is setting fire to some bushes.

Lois and Jimmy soon find themselves trapped by the rapidly spreading fire. Garvin is attacked by Olivier with a blow to the head. Superman saves Lois and Jimmy while Olivier is threatening Garvin. Poised nearby is **BABETTE** *(Jane Adams)* with her pet timber wolf. When Olivier orders her to release the animal against Garvin, she refuses. Garvin recognizes Babette as the daughter of the lumber company's owner who recently died.

Superman arrives just in time to prevent Olivier from killing Garvin. Olivier, it seems, has been trying to convince Babette that it was Garvin and the lumber company that was responsible for her father's death. Garvin assures her that her father died of natural causes and that he has all this time been keeping her inheritance safe and accounted for in a nearby bank. Olivier's plan was to marry Babette and make himself rich at the same time.

With the forest fire threatening the future paper supply of the Daily Planet, not to mention the lives of everyone nearby, Superman takes the lead end of a huge coil of telephone wire. He explains his plan for flying up into a high thunder storm in the hopes of creating a rain shower by catching a bolt of lightning. Here follows the famous forest take off scene. It actually ended with *George Reeves* crashing to the stage floor when one of the specially designed lift wires snapped.

Superman manages to successfully execute his plan and bring down a pouring rain. Back at the shack, everyone is getting to know that Babette's pet wolf is quite harmless. Kent enters, fully soaked in rain water. When comments are made about how wonderful it is that Superman has brought the life saving rain. Kent smiles and says in closing, "Too bad you can't get him to stop it."

EPISODE 24

CRIME WAVE

directed by TOMMY CARR
written by BEN PETER FREEMAN

The last of the first season's thirty minute stories begins with a montage of stock crime fighting footage from previous episodes as a narrator gives us a tense introduction to the plot. In fact, almost every one of the filmed shows from this season are represented in this first ten minute sequence.

"Bursting upon Metropolis almost without warning, a crime wave of tremendous proportions has all but paralyzed the city. . . beginning with a series of gang war shootings. . . from the innocent deaths of truck drivers. . . to the machine gun deaths of all sorts of gangsters. . . seems to indicate the revival of the long gone protection racket.

"The racketeers have launched an all out attack. . . Frightened businessmen have unleashed a flood of frantic calls for police protection. Lights have been burning day and night at the state's leading newspaper where editor Perry White, long known as a hard hitting enemy of corruption, joins in the battle to end the rein of terror!"

See the notes on page 57 regarding the two versions of this episode in circulation.

A meeting has been called in Perry's office of several members of the Citizens' Committee. Everyone expresses they are fed up with the current crime wave. Perry concludes his dramatic speech by introducing Superman as the number one citizen of Metropolis. Superman promises to dedicate himself fully to the war against crime. Clark Kent is conspicuously absent from what appears to be a key meeting. It is never made clear how he managed to avoid it. Inspector Henderson offers the full cooperation of the police department, and also present is **WALTER CANBY** (*John Eldredge*), the leader of the committee for clean government, who nods an approval to the assembly.

Next, we see Superman addressing a gathering crowd of angry citizens. He is standing at a podium next to a large poster that lists the top twelve known criminals that he will either capture or run out of town. The list contains names like *Greasy, The Fish, Shortcake,* and *Crusher.* Nick Marone and Big Ed Bullock are number three and two, with a big question mark for number one. Who is the mysterious Mr. Big?

We soon catch a glimpse of Mr. Big getting a rubdown by **TONY** (*Bobby Barber*) as **NICK** (*Phil Van Zandt*) and **ED BULLOCK** (*Al Eben*) enter the room. They tell the boss how Superman is filling the jails with their men. The boss tells them to go out and pour it on.

A radio **ANNOUNCER** (*Bill Kennedy*) delivers the following update to the listening audiences, "The entire nation has its eyes trained on Metropolis where the mighty Superman is battling the hoodlums, racketeers, and strongarm men who have held the city in a rein of terror. The city jail is filled to overflowing, and the mobsters still at large are cowering with fear as Superman continues his crusade against organized crime with unabated fury!"

Yes, this is the same Bill Kennedy who later hosted matinee movies on channel 50 in Detroit, Michigan. He portrays a racetrack announcer in the first adventure of the 1955 season, and he provides most of the voice-over narration for the opening title sequence of every episode.

Marone and Bullock are eventually captured and Henderson attempts to scare a confession out of them, but he is unsuccessful, even with Superman watching from the shadows of the interrogation room. When the two leaders of crime are released, they regroup with the still unseen Mr. Big to lay out a plan. **SALLY** (*Barbara Fuller*), the gangster's moll, will roam around the Daily Planet and try to get close to all of Superman's friends. Her orders are to come up with a way to lure Superman into some sort of trap.

Sally soon returns with some home movie footage of all the series regulars in the midst of doing various activities, including a rather revealing shot of Kent running into an alley where Superman quickly appears for a leap into the air. It catches our eye as it does Mr. Big, who has Sally replay the projector so we can see the same scene again. The glaring error of the story is that no one realizes the implications whatsoever.

Anyway, Sally makes a telephone call to Kent, who happens to be in Perry's office. She tells him that the mysterious Mr. Big everyone has been talking about is ready to give himself up, but only to Superman at a special hideout up on Dover's Cliff. Kent hangs up, tells Perry to hold tight for a rework of page one, and then he quickly makes an exit.

Waiting in a specially constructed concrete room are Marone, Bullock, and the **PROFESSOR** (*Joe Mell*). When Superman arrives, he is bated into a room that locks him off from the others. The Professor quickly throws some switches that showers Superman with a rain of electrical sparks which eventually brings him to the floor. The three enter the room to declare him dead. It's time to call the boss.

Perry is at his desk. He calls down to the press room and gives the order to start printing. Jimmy and Lois are sleeping in the chairs. Perry mutters to himself that Kent has finally let him down.

Back at Dover's Cliff, Walter Canby arrives to examine the dead Superman.

He smiles, "And he was gonna get me!"

Then Superman leaps to his feet and exclaims how surprised he is that they believed the fireworks would actually harm him. He then proceeds to clean up the room.

The final scene has Perry, Lois and Jimmy about to exit.

"I knew Clark would never come through with that story," says Lois as we hear a swooshing sound of Superman landing on the ledge outside

Perry's window. He enters the room with Canby in tow by the collar.

"Would you sign for this delivery, Mr. White?" asks Superman in a rather harsh tone. "Clark Kent's page one story in the flesh! Walter Canby, chairman for the citizens' committee for clean government and the number one man behind crime in Metropolis! Now you can print that statement Mr. Canby wanted you to print, there is no number one crime boss in Metropolis... anymore!"

EPISODE 25

THE UNKNOWN PEOPLE
—Part One

directed by LEE SHOLEM
written by RICHARD FIELDING

This show begins at the Havenhurst experimental drilling site of the National Oil Company. Standing at the base of the tower structure is **BILL CORRIGAN** *(Walter Reed)*, the project supervisor. He has a clipboard and is noting down pieces of digging equipment as his men are reluctantly tossing them into a hole for burial. When **EDDIE** *(Steve Carr)* asks why so many brand new tools are being discarded, Corrigan sharply tells him to mind his own business.

Clark Kent and Lois Lane arrive at the site in a car driven by **JOHN CRAIG** *(Ray Walker)*, the public relations officer for the oil company, on a routine inspection. As they get out of the car to look around, Craig eagerly asks what Lois thinks of the project?

"Looks just like any oil well," replies Lois, rather bored with the entire affair.

At 32,740 feet, it's the deepest oil well ever drilled!

When the guard, **POP SHANNON** *(J. Farrell MacDonald)* announces much to Craig's surprise that the well is being shut down, Craig quickly

Clark Kent tries to calm the townspeople of Silsby after word gets out of an invasion by creatures from the center of the earth. *Jeff Corey, Phyllis Coates, George Reeves, Walter Reed,* and *Irene Martin.*

Publicity photo of the Mole Men at the oil well with their deadly weapon. *Jerry Maren, Tony Boris, John Banbury,* and *Billy Curtis.*

rushes over to see Corrigan. Lois sarcastically remarks how happy Perry White will be to hear they made the trip all the way from Metropolis for nothing.

Kent and Lois approach Corrigan and Craig arguing over the company's order to shut down based on a report filed by Corrigan. Kent asks about the contents of the report, but Corrigan insists it is confidential, which makes Craig even more unhappy. He claims the company should have kept him informed, and he apologizes to the reporters for the wild goose chase. As Kent takes a curious look at the equipment in the hole, he comments that there may be a story after all.

That evening at the Silsby Hotel, Lois meets up with Kent in the lobby, since there isn't much to do in a town with a population of 1,430. Kent expresses an interest in going out to the well site to look around. Lois senses he has a hunch and insists on going along with him.

Meanwhile, at the oil well, the cap that has been bolted onto the top of the drill shaft is popped open from below. Two humanoid creatures *(Billy Curtis, John Banbury)* with fuzzy outfits and oversized bald heads emerge to have a look around.

Kent and Lois arrive soon after and as Kent looks over toward the guard shack, he exclaims, "Great Scott!"

Kent runs and Lois follows to discover Pop Shannon lying dead on the floor. Lois figures it must have been a heart attack and sees no reason to make anything more of it.

While Kent takes a look around outside, Lois is about to put through a telephone call to Craig when she sees the two creatures peeking in at her from outside the window. Her loud scream quickly sends the two creatures away and brings Kent running fast.

Soon, the **SHERIFF** *(Stanley Andrews)* arrives to investigate with Craig, Corrigan, and **DOC SANDERS** *(Harry Harvey)* who concludes that Pop

Ray Walker, Walter Reed, Phyllis Coates, and *George Reeves.* They are all wondering what "Luke Benson" will do now that he knows aliens are loose in Silsby.

Shannon must have died of a heart attack. They make a phone call to summon Jeff Regan to come out and collect the body. Kent volunteers to stay and wait while the others see that Miss Lane gets safely back to town. The Sheriff has doubts about her story of little furry men.

Corrigan stays with Kent at the shack and decides to let the reporter in on some more of the strange story. After the drilling crew reached a depth of 32,600 feet, they found the drill head had broken through into thin air. Kent suggests the possibility of the earth being hollow and

Corrigan agrees. Micro-organisms were discovered on the drilling equipment. Corrigan believes there must be life, perhaps a civilization, far below the surface.

Then they get a phone call reporting that Jeff Regan has just driven his car into a ditch after seeing two strange creatures. Kent and Corrigan decide its time to act. As they turn out the lights of the shack to leave, Kent notices the oranges on the floor are glowing in the dark. If they were handled by the creatures, it could mean that they are radioactive. They must warn the town.

Phyllis Coates, George Reeves, Hal K. Dawson, and Jeff Corey.

Meanwhile, the two creatures make their way into the town. They soon come upon an open window into a little girl's room *(Beverly Washburn)*. She makes an attempt to talk to them.

Kent and Corrigan arrive at the Silsby Hotel where a crowd is gathering, led by **LUKE BENSON** *(Jeff Corey)*. Kent inquires about the excitement. **ESTHER POMFREY** *(Irene Martin)* testifies that she has seen the little creatures, and **JEFF REGAN** *(Byron Foulger)* shows off his broken arm as the result of driving off the road to avoid hitting the strange visitors. Kent admits they may exist and attempts to warn them of the dangers with these creatures. Benson tells Kent to mind his own business and tries to push past him with a shotgun. Kent begs them to listen, but Lois suggests that they should not interfere.

Back at the little girl's house, she is playfully reacting to the mole men by rolling a toy ball across the floor. They seem tame enough until the mother *(Margia Dean)* enters the room and screams.

This, of course, incites the crowd, and Benson leads them out of the hotel to investigate. Kent watches for a moment and then rushes off by himself. Lois remarks on how Kent always gets himself into a jam and then runs away.

Kent runs into a nearby alley and emerges as Superman. He leaps into the air and flies over the running mob to get over to the little girl's house just before the mob arrives. From the front porch of the house, Superman announces the girl is alright, only a little frightened.

When Benson refuses to put away his shotgun, Superman takes it and bends it into a pretzel, saying, "It's men like you who make it difficult for people to understand one another." Benson refuses to listen and orders his men to get the dogs on the scent of the creatures.

Lois arrives with Craig and Corrigan. She's very happy to see Superman. Luke Benson comes out of the house and announces that he will not tolerate these invading creatures coming after little kids. Then he rushes off into the woods with the mob. They follow **MATT** *(John Phillips)* and the dogs to track down and destroy the uninvited creatures.

Superman instructs Corrigan to take the little girl and her mother into the hospital for decontamination, as they may in fact be radioactive.

"That is the one thing Benson and his men don't know," says Superman.

When it sounds as if the dogs have caught up with their prey, Superman leaps into the air in a spectacular wire lifted take off shot as Lois, Craig, and Corrigan watch with amazement.

Benson and his men are standing at the base of a canyon below a huge dam. The two creatures are trapped up above, as shown by the search lights of Benson's mob. The narrator *(Jack Narz)* breaks in as we see a close shot of the two frightened creatures.

"Hunted by men and dogs!... Trapped on the high parapet of the dam!... These strange little creatures from the dark center of the earth are now at the mercy of Luke Benson and his mob!... What will happen? Stand by for a preview of part two of 'The Unknown People" in the *Adventures of... Superman!*"

EPISODE 26

THE UNKNOWN PEOPLE
—Part Two

directed by LEE SHOLEM
written by RICHARD FIELDING

This adventure opens with a few key scenes from the previous episode, played under the following narration. "When Clark Kent and Lois Lane, star reporters for the Metropolis Daily Planet, were assigned to write a story on the deepest oil well ever drilled, they little realized what was going to happen," says the narrator *(Jack Narz)* like a true story teller. "In the darkness of the night, two strange furry creatures—half human, half animal—crawled out of the abandoned well shaft." The voice goes on to say how the mob led by Luke Benson chased the creatures to the dam outside of town and trapped them high above the valley as we join the present story.

Superman drops out of the sky on Benson and

a few of his men and warns them not to try and harm the potentially dangerous creatures. Remember, Superman believes they may still be radioactive. After withstanding bullets fired from Benson's gun, **CHUCK WEBBER** *(Hal K. Dawson)* takes a shot with his rifle at one of the unknown people. The little creature cries out in pain and falls over the edge of the dam. Superman makes another spectacular leap and in a combination of animated and processed shots, he flies by to catch the falling figure.

Superman takes the wounded creature to the town hospital. Benson, Webber, and Eddie follow Matt and his hound dogs after the other creature who escaped the dam in the confusion of the thrilling rescue. They follow and corner the second creature in an abandoned shack. They set fire to the old shack, and when it appears the creature is cooked, they break up and head back toward town. What they do not realize is the clever little creature has escaped through some loose floor boards and is on his way back to the well shaft where he drops out of sight.

Benson returns to the Sheriff's office to brag how they cornered and killed the little menace. When he learns that the other one was saved by Superman and is in the hospital making a recovery, he threatens to seek and destroy again. The Sheriff orders him to remain still. When deputy **JIM** *(Phil Warren)* moves to put the handcuffs on Benson, he pulls a gun and makes his exit.

Meanwhile, Superman has convinced the young **DOCTOR REED** *(John Baer)* and his **NURSE** *(Adrienne Marden)* on duty at the hospital to defy the order of the chief **ADMINISTRATOR** *(Frank Reicher)* not to admit the strange creature. Kent assists in an operation to remove the bullet from the wounded patient. As Kent and Dr. Reed come out into the hallway, Lois arrives demanding to know what is going on? The following lines of dialog not only advance the story, but also set the design of these two main characters that was strictly held throughout the first season episodes and modified only slightly for the rest of the series.

When Lois asks if Kent knows about the little creature being shot down by Luke Benson's mob, Kent replies that he and Dr. Reed just removed the bullet from the creature's chest.

The little creatures are hunted by men and dogs. . . Superman confronts *Hal K. Dawson, Jeff Corey,* and *Steve Carr* at the foot of the dam.

Adrienne Marden, Frank Reicher, George Reeves, and *John Baer.*

George Reeves and *Billy Curtis.*

"I brought... er, that is, Superman brought it to the hospital," says Kent as he smiles and touches his glasses.

"Then you know about Superman?" asks Lois.

"If I don't, who should," quips Kent.

Dr. Reed excuses himself to make his scheduled check of the ward and promises to keep an eye on the little creature if he doesn't get fired. As he walks away, Clark Kent comments

that Dr. Reed is indeed a young man with courage.

"Well, I wish I could say the same for you," says Lois.

Kent fires back at her, "You know, Lois, one of these fine days—"

"One of these fine days, what?" asks Lois.

After a pause, Kent says, "Never mind. I've got to find Corrigan."

As they walk off toward the front door of the hospital, Lois continues to badger poor Mr. Kent. "You always do that. Start to say something and then abruptly change your mind."

"I do?" asks Kent as he fiddles with his hat.

"What are you afraid of? What are you hiding?"

"Hiding?" repeats Kent.

"Well, you give the impression you're leading a double life," insists Lois.

"Really?" says Kent, smiling.

Then Craig and Corrigan come running up the street toward the hospital. They warn of Luke Benson coming with the gang after they have found out about Superman bringing in the wounded creature. The talk is about a potential lynching, and nothing will be able to stop them.

"I wonder," says Kent as he starts to move back toward the hospital.

"Clark, where are you going?" asks Lois.

"I'll be right back!" says Kent as he disappears into the building.

Lois is disgusted with the cowardly Kent, but there is little time to think about it as the mob approaches carrying guns and clubs. As Benson tries to push his way past Corrigan and Lois, Superman steps out from inside the hospital. He informs the mob that no one is allowed inside.

"Now I'm going to give you all one last chance to stop acting like nazi stormtroopers," lectures Superman very seriously. He goes on to say how the little creature has rights to live just like anyone else. He reminds them that it was the surface people that invaded the little creatures' world, and when they come up to visit, they were greeted with dogs and guns. When someone in the crowd fires a bullet that almost hits Lois Lane, Superman decides they can no longer be trusted with guns and he proceeds to take them away.

Later, the creature that had escaped comes back up from the drill shaft with two companions *(Jerry Maren, Tony Boris)*. Together, they tote a deadly ray gun that looks very much like an electrolux vacuum cleaner. The story soon comes to its logical conclusion when the three little creatures storm the hospital to retrieve their wounded companion. After Superman saves Luke Benson by stepping between him and the deadly light rays coming from the creature's weapon, he helps them carry their wounded friend back to the well shaft.

As Lois and the two oil men arrive, Superman learns from Corrigan that the supposed radioactive glow was merely harmless phosphor. Then a high pitched squeal is emitted from the well shaft just before it collapses in an explosion. As they watch the burning fire consume the well structure, Lois makes a closing comment.

"It's almost as if they were saying, you live your lives and we'll live ours."

Superman nods an agreement as we fade out to closing credits.

The unknown people were played by four of Hollywood's leading midget actors. *Billy Curtis* will always be remembered for his performance in "The Wizard of Oz," and he later appeared as a Martian in a color episode of Superman entitled "Mr. Zero" from the 1956 season. *Tony Boris* was known as one of the touring Phillip Morris mascots.

NOTE: Initially, the *Adventures of Superman* was not intended to be a children's show as one can easily conclude by comparing the high level of violent action contained in the first season episodes to the kinder, gentler stories from the rest of the series. Whether it was the decision of National Comics, the advertising agency, or the Kellogg's people, the final editions of the Robert Maxwell episodes were deemed unacceptable for television. They recut the episodes before prints were made for distribution. The three episodes with scene variations that are most often topics of discussion among film collecting Superman fans are *"The Stolen Costume," "The Evil Three,"* and *"Crime Wave."*

The Kellogg's version of *"The Stolen Costume"* has a shorter death scene at the end when Ace and Connie slip from the icy slopes of their exile. *"The Evil Three"* episode has a number of shots removed for the Kellogg's edition, with Elsa shoved down a flight of stairs being the most provocative. However, the variations in *"Crime Wave"* are of particular interest because it is the episode which has been most easily examined in recent years. If you have access to a videotape of the Nickelodeon broadcast from a few years ago, compare the first ten minutes or so of it to the first ten minutes of the version released by Warner Home Video. The Nickelodeon version begins with a montage of action accompanied by a narration which clearly sets up the premise of the episode. The Warners version has a similar montage, though not exact from cut to cut, but the narration is missing. Then following the first appearance of Superman before the citizen's committee in Perry White's office, the episode continues with further variations. At first, neither version seemed to be any more violent than the other until I noticed the Warners edition contained a scene where a freight worker is crushed between a truck and a loading dock. Evidently, Nickelodeon's package of episodes contained a survivor from the Kellogg's days.

Before they were sacrificed for extra commercial time in the later years of syndication, the first season episodes ended with a quick collection of preview scenes from the next show. They were reminiscent of the theatrical trailers from the saturday matinees of the old days. Patrons were teased into returning the following week for the next thrilling chapter of the current movie serial with short clips of the best action sequences. In the *Adventures of Superman*, about a minute of air time was ear marked for a montage of action scenes from the following show with a forceful narrator and the end credit theme music creating the excitement.

"Don't miss the next thrill-packed episode in the amazing Adventures of Superman!

"Join with the Man of Steel as he wages war against the forces of evil. . .

"Thrilling adventure and tense excitement. . . !

"Pounding action and spine-tingling mystery. . . !

"You'll find them all in the next startling episode in the Adventures of Superman. . . !

"So don't miss it! . . . There's action! . . . adventure! . . . and mystery! . . .

"in the Adventures of Superman!"

The Episodes of
1953

WITH THE INITIAL SUCCESS OF THE FIRST TWENTY-SIX EPISODES ALREADY A PROVEN FACT, production of another twenty-six was ordered by National Comics. However, in the nearly two year hiatus since the first episodes were finished, some changes were made.

Whitney Ellsworth was brought in as producer to replace Robert Maxwell and Bernard Luber, with orders to tone down the violence and beef up the humor. After all, Kellogg was sponsoring the show, and they did not want to mix scenes of a brutal crime-drama with cereal commercials.

Phyllis Coates was otherwise committed and no longer available at the time, so the production was in need of a new Lois Lane. Ellsworth turned to the perfect replacement, an actress with just the right experience. *Noel Neill* was brought in to reprise the same role she portrayed for Sam Katzman in the 1948 and 1950 serials for Columbia.

Another refreshing addition to the production staff was special effects expert Thol (Si) Simonson, and to his credit, most of the new flying sequences were a considerable improvement.

Tommy Carr handled the bulk of the directing assignments with 17 episodes to his credit, and *George Blair* picked up the other 9 episodes.

PRODUCTION CREDITS

producer . . . . Whitney Ellsworth
production manager . . . . Clem Beauchamp
director of photography . . . . Harold Stine ASC
production co-ordinator . . . . .David S. Garber
film editor . . . . Harry Gerstad ACE
assistant director . . . . Ivan Volkman
special effects . . . . Thol Simonson
photographic effects . . . . Jack R. Glass
story editor . . . . Mort Weisinger
sound engineer . . . . Jean L. Speak

Publicity photo from 1953

EPISODE 27

FIVE MINUTES TO DOOM

directed by TOMMY CARR
written by MONROE MANNING

The first episode of the second season begins at the State Prison. The **WARDEN** *(Sam Flint)* is standing outside the visitors' room with Kent and the new **LOIS LANE** *(Noel Neill)*. **JOE WINTERS** *(Dabbs Greer)* is inside, a condemned prisoner, having a touching conversation with his **WIFE** *(Lois Hall)* and his young son. Joe is saying his final farewell as the Warden enters to indicate his time is about over. As Mrs. Winters and the boy walk out crying, Kent and Lois move in opposite Joe for an interview.

Kent outlines a proposition. The Daily Planet will pay $10,000 to his family if Joe will tell the exclusive story of events that led up to the time of the crime. Knowing the money would certainly help his family, Joe agrees to talk.

As he begins his story, Kent takes Joe's hand and monitors his heart beat like a lie detector. Through a series of flashback scenes and Joe's narration, the plot unfolds.

Joe Winters was the county building inspector when he discovered that a contractor named Wayne was using sub-standard steel on the construction of an overpass. The supervisor was a man named **BAKER** *(Dale Van Sickel)* with whom Joe had an argument over pouring cement before an inspection could be completed.

On another occasion, Joe confronted Baker again. While they were fighting in the supervisor's shack at the construction site, a gunshot killed Baker and a gun belonging to Winters was dropped inside.

Joe was arrested and put on trial for murder. Because of the evidence and Joe's history with Baker, Joe was convicted and now awaits the death sentence.

Joe tells Kent that he believes he was close to proving that Wayne was using cheap steel in the project. Wayne must have had Baker killed and Joe framed to hide the evidence. Joe confesses that even Superman could not get him out of this mess. Kent tells Joe not to give up hope as he and Lois conclude the interview.

The conversation with Joe was overheard by an informant. He gets on the telephone and tells **WAYNE** *(Lewis Russell)* about the nosey reporters. Wayne then calls an explosives expert, **TURK** *(John Kellogg)*, and arranges an accident.

While driving along the country road from the prison, the explosives expert manages to flag down a ride from Kent and Lois. He carefully places his lunch box on the floor behind the seat. After they drop him off a short while later, Lois interrupts Kent's concentration to ask him if he remembers the hitchhiker having a lunch box. Kent looks in the back seat and sees the bomb.

Quickly, Kent tells Lois to speed up the car. He reaches back and grabs the bomb. He jumps out of the car and rolls down the roadside hill. As the explosion goes off, Lois slams on the brakes.

Kent's clothing has been torn away, revealing his Superman costume. He asks Lois to toss him the trench coat he has conveniently carried in the car. Lois remarks that she has never seen anyone act so brave before.

"You mean it's something you'd only expect Superman to do?" he asks, smiling.

"Well, yes," replies Lois, missing the pun entirely.

Kent cannot resist the temptation to say, "Lois, sometimes I think you underestimate me."

The two reporters convince Perry White to allow an investigation. Kent and Jimmy examine the scene of the crime and determine that it was possible for someone else to have entered the shack, kill Baker, and escape without being seen. Lois has gathered information on construction specifications and inspection routines to suggest the contractor could have profited substantially if lower grades of steel were used. What they need now is proof.

Lois pays a visit to Wayne's office for an interview to get his reaction on a possible investigation. Wayne acts as predicted. He refuses to let Lois see the inspection reports when his **SECRETARY** *(Jean Willes)* produces them. He strongly insists that Lois leave his office at once.

Jimmy then disguises himself as a bumbling vacuum cleaner salesman and gains entry to Wayne's office. He manages to get his hands on the phoney inspection papers, but fails to sell Wayne a vacuum cleaner.

Now they have new evidence that could be used to get Joe Winters a new trial, but the telephone lines are down and time is running out. Superman flies out to see the **GOVERNOR** *(William Green)* to get a signed reprieve. Superman crashes through the prison wall just in time to save Joe from getting electrocuted.

At the wrap up scene in Perry White's office, Lois has her characteristic questions about how Superman managed to take over when Kent could not possibly get to the prison in time. The show ends on a humorous note when Jimmy comments that if he had tried harder, he probably could have sold Wayne a vacuum cleaner.

EPISODE 28

THE BIG SQUEEZE

directed by TOMMY CARR
written by ROY HAMILTON

In the opening scene, a quick panning shot of the city skyline takes us to Metropolis Furriers Inc. where Clark Kent sits in the office of **MR. FOSTER** *(Harry Cheshire)*. A trophy naming the Daily Planet selection for man of the year will be presented to one of Mr. Foster's employees of ten years service, Dan Grayson. Mr. Foster assures Kent they could not have chosen a better man.

Meanwhile, in the fur storage department, **DAN GRAYSON** *(Hugh Beaumont)* gets an unnerving call from an old acquaintance, **LUKE MAYNARD** *(John Kellogg)*. After hanging up the telephone, Dan accidently locks himself in the storage vault. Kent and Foster rush to answer the alarm and learn of Dan's confinement. The urgency is heightened when Foster tells Kent that there is no way to open the timer operated vault before Dan will fall victim to the special gases inside designed to help preserve the furs. With that, Kent rushes out of the room.

Within seconds, Superman arrives through the window and lifts the vault door off its hinges. You will note after leaning the heavy door against the wall, George Reeves has his hand on the vault door to keep it from falling over. As he turns to leap out the window, you'll also notice that the vault door is about to fall over before the camera cuts away. When we return to Foster and Dan, we

can see in the background the door now leaning at a much greater angle, probably adjusted by the stage crew between shots.

Dan gets the rest of the day off. When he arrives home, he is greeted by his lovely wife, **PEGGY** *(Aline Towne)*. As he is about to explain how his life was saved, the door bell rings and Dan is confronted by Luke Maynard. He explains to Dan about his little blackmail business where old prisonmates pay him to keep silent about their questionable experiences. **TIM GRAYSON** *(Bradley Mora)*, Dan's young son, overhears this conversation. It is obvious that the Grayson family is unaware of Dan's dark past.

At a meeting in Perry's office, it is firmly established that Dan Grayson is deserving of the award because he has been an outstanding citizen. In a moment of humor, Perry tells Lois to take care of the award background story, etcetera. He tells Kent to take care of the interviews, pictures, etcetera. Then he tells eager young Olsen to take care of the etcetera. When Jimmy gets out into the hallway, he stops smiling and says to himself, "What am I so happy about?"

Back at the Grayson residence, Peggy senses something is wrong when Tim enters the room and shoots a cold glance at Dan before running upstairs. When Dan meets with Luke, he agrees to pay the protection money. Luke says not to worry. He will call it even if Dan helps him heist some furs from his company vault. Dan decides to think about it.

Later, Kent and Lois arrive to give Dan the good news. They want pictures and the story of his life. Dan is very upset when he hears the story has already hit the papers. He insists they find another winner and asks them to leave immediately.

The next day, young Tim visits Kent at his office and begs him not to expose his father as a criminal. Kent assures Tim he won't let anything happen to harm his father. Kent goes to visit Dan at his work and explains how he wants to help. Dan tells how when he was a kid, he got involved in a prank car theft which got him three years in jail. Now Luke Maynard is attempting to blackmail him. Kent says not to worry and maybe he can get Superman to help out.

The plan backfires. Luke and **AL** *(Ted Ryan)* pull off a heist anyway and leave Dan to take the rap. Front page headlines say Dan Grayson is responsible for the theft.

When Luke and Al make their getaway, however, Dan hides in the back of the car. Jimmy is also hot on their trail which leads to a cave in the nearby mountains. Luke isn't worried because the cave is lined with lead, not even Superman will be able to find them. Jimmy calls Kent and Superman arrives outside the caves. When Luke decides to crack some walnuts, Superman detects the sound with his super hearing and crashes into the hillside. Luke tries to shoot the man of steel, but the usual happens when Superman grabs the gun from his hand and crushes it like a toy.

The show ends with the presentation of the award on television to Dan Grayson. Kent gives a speech on how people who make mistakes should be given an opportunity to prove themselves worthy of society's forgiveness.

EPISODE 29

THE MAN WHO COULD READ MINDS

directed by TOMMY CARR
written by MONROE MANNING

The entire cast of the series assembles at the beginning of this episode. It is nighttime in this residential exterior setting while Henderson is discussing a stakeout with a **SERGEANT** (Russell Custer). The hood of his car is the command post. He quickly dispatches a squad car to patrol the area on the lookout for someone armed and dangerous. Two more cars arrive, one with Perry and Kent, and Lois and Jimmy in the other.

Note how the scene begins as a day for night exterior, but when the Daily Planet staff arrives, the scene switches to a studio set for closeup shots with a projected background. On the modest budget of the series, Ellsworth had to count on day for night shooting on exteriors.

Henderson and Perry are arguing over the tone of the news coverage regarding the recent phantom burglaries. Jimmy pulls Lois away and convinces her to go with him on his own patrol in hopes of getting a scoop. As they cruise the area, Jimmy is contemplating how the headlines

will read when he and Lois capture the infamous Phantom. When Lois gets a look at a hooded man running across a front lawn, Jimmy stops the car and chases after him. They struggle for a moment, but the villain gets away in a waiting car. Jimmy quickly picks up a small object dropped by the villain, returns to their car and chases after the escaping vehicle.

All through the following sequence, some of the best background music of the series accents the excitement of the chase. When the **PHANTOM** (Richard Karlan) starts shooting at Jimmy and Lois, Kent and Henderson hear the shots. Everyone moves to his car to get in on the chase.

With Perry driving, Kent is watching in the distance to see how Lois and Jimmy are being fired upon. Here, the sharp-eyed viewer will note that when Kent tells Perry to stop the car, stop it does! In a freeze frame that holds for at least five full seconds, we hear gunshots and exciting music. The giveaway is that the dust kicking up from behind the car seems to freeze in stop motion with Kent perched on the car door looking off camera. Finding themselves short of footage for this sequence, the film editors probably had to stretch this one shot by reprinting the last frame. The low budget could not afford any retakes.

Kent then makes a lame excuse to get out of the car while Perry continues the chase. We hear a drum roll and then the opening strings of the theme music as Kent quickly runs behind some rocks and majestically appears as Superman. He executes a beautiful springboard takeoff over the head of the cameraman.

Another gunshot. Lois screams. The car blows a tire and goes out of control. Superman lands behind the car and grabs the bumper just in time to keep it from plunging over a cliff.

Perry arrives to get in on the conversation regarding the clue found by Jimmy. It is a little toy top that Superman cleverly associates with a night club in Metropolis called the *Tip Top Café*. Perry tells Lois to go pick up Kent back at the office and snoop around. Jimmy gets stuck having to change the flat tire because Superman must excuse himself for a pressing appointment.

The scheme unfolds for the viewers at the Tip Top Café as a rather affluent couple arrives. They have their car parked by the valet. We see Monk (the Phantom without a mask) as he checks out the glove compartment of the parked car to get an address off the vehicle registration.

Kent and Lois arrive at the club to witness the feature attraction, **THE SWAMI** (*Lawrence Dobkin*). **LAURA** (*Veola Vonn*) circulates through the audience and picks up objects from the patrons. Through a secret transmitter in her costume, she whispers the object's identity to the Swami who is blindfolded and miraculously reveals the object to the amazed audience. Kent has it all figured out, but he makes no connection to the fact that Laura gets wax impressions of house keys that match up to addresses acquired by Monk from the parking lot.

While the affluent couple enjoys their evening at the club, Monk is driven by a henchman to their home as he makes up a duplicate house key. Monk boasts how they have the sweetest racket in Metropolis that even Superman cannot discover.

The burglary makes another headline. Lois and Jimmy make the connection between the victims and their attendance of the Tip Top Café. Jimmy disguises himself as a visiting foreign dignitary, *Don Alvarez Ortega.* Lois accompanies him to the Swami's performance using the key to a set up hotel suite as bait. For some comic relief, Jimmy is dragged into dancing the tango with Laura before the Swami comes out on stage.

Meanwhile, Clark learns from a copyboy, **DOUG** (*Tom Bernard*), that Lois and Jimmy have set out on the town in disguise to play a prank on somebody. Clark concludes the Tip Top Café would be the logical place to find them.

Later, Lois and Jimmy are waiting in the dark hotel suite for the arrival of the phantom burglar. When he enters, they get the drop on him. But when the Swami and Laura arrive, the tables are turned. Jimmy and Lois would have been forced to jump out the window if Kent hadn't been able to figure out what was going on. Using a familiar stock shot from the first season, we see Superman leap up from an alley and land on the balcony in time to capture the gang and save Lois and Jimmy from certain death.

As was becoming the usual routine, the villains waste bullets on Superman. He takes and crushes their guns in his hands. Then he lifts them into the air to smash their heads together. This holds them until the police arrive.

"The Phantom Bandit of Gotham City" is an illustrated adventure appearing in *Batman #81* which shares some plot elements with this episode.

And for a final bit of trivia, *Lawrence Dobkin,* who portrayed the phoney fortune teller, later directed the first *STAR TREK* episode to appear on television in the mid-sixties entitled "Charley X." You may also remember Dobkin appeared in television commercials advertising a dream-away weight reducing product in the late 1980s. However, he will always be remembered by this author for his portrayal of *Caleb,* an assistant to Moses, in *The Ten Commandments.*

EPISODE 30

JET ACE

directed by TOMMY CARR
written by DAVID CHANTLER

This episode begins out at the Metropolis branch of the U.S. Airforce. The whole gang is in an executive office with **GENERAL SUMMERS** (*Selmer Jackson*) sitting at his desk. They all listen to air traffic chatter over a loud speaker. We soon discover that a new jet fighter plane is being flight-tested by **CHRIS WHITE** (*Lane Bradford*), Perry's nephew. During a dive, Chris sounds like he is about to go unconscious. Kent knows he must act immediately and exclaims, "He's in trouble! I can't stand it! I've got to get out of here!" With that, he slips away to make a quick change to Superman.

When all seems lost, Superman lands on the fuselage of the plane and causes it to return to level flight. Chris manages to land the plane safely, and Kent returns sheepishly to take some abuse. Lois informs him that everything is all right now. Perry remarks how lucky it was that Chris did not need to depend on Clark Kent!

Chris enters the room and is happily greeted by his worried uncle. General Summers turns angrily at **MARTIN** (*Larry Blake*), a reporter following Chris for a statement. When Martin sees the Daily Planet staff in the room, he makes a bitter remark about their getting special privileges and storms away.

Summers tells Chris they were worried about him and that he has been working too hard.

Perry offers to let him go off and rest at his hunting cabin in the mountains. There he can get some peace and quiet while he writes up his highly classified aircraft report.

At the cabin, Chris has completed his secret report. He rolls it up and hides it in the barrel of his shotgun. Then he is visited by **NATE** *(Ric Roman)* and **FRENCHY** *(Dick Reeves)*. They knock him out and take him for a ride.

Perry White learns from the helicopter pilot who delivers the mail in the area around the cabin that Chris has disappeared. He sends Kent and Jimmy to investigate.

Kent and Jimmy arrive at the cabin and find it empty. They hide as Nate and Frenchy return to look around for the secret classified report. After finding nothing, they drive away. Kent tells Jimmy to stay put while he runs into the rocky hillside and changes to Superman.

Nate and Frenchy are driving along the country road when Superman lands behind them and stops the car. He scares Frenchy into telling how he and Nate were hired by an anonymous phone call to kidnap Chris White and deliver him to an alley. When Superman drags the two out of the car to deliver them to the police, foolish Nate takes a swing at Superman's iron jaw and breaks his wrist.

The man behind the kidnapping proves to be Martin. He takes Chris back to the cabin to try and force him to give up the classified report. **TIM MALLORY** *(Jim Hayward)* comes to the door and introduces himself as the mail delivering helicopter pilot. Martin stands behind the door holding a gun on Chris while he gets rid of Mallory. Before he leaves, Chris tells Mallory to be sure the letter he picked up the other day is delivered to Perry White. Mallory leaves a little confused and Martin figures the report is on its way to the Daily Planet editor.

Martin ties Chris to a chair and gives him one last chance to give up the classified secrets of the fighter plane before he leaves the country. Chris refuses to deal, so Martin leaves the cabin rigged to go up in flames after he is long gone.

Meanwhile, Mallory stops in to see Perry White and they soon learn that Chris is back at the cabin. Kent runs off, changes to Superman, and flies up to the cabin in time to save Chris from a fiery death.

Note the window takeoff shot with Superman carrying a stick of dynamite from "The Human Bomb" episode.

Kent and Chris return to Perry's office. Perry calls in to report how they have found the cabin burned to the ground. Kent tells him that Chris is with him and that he is okay. Kent also tells Perry to have the police announce that Chris died in the fire because he has a plan.

Later, at the General's office, another test flight of the new jet has been scheduled and the media has been invited. When the voice over the loudspeaker is recognized as that of Chris White, Martin gets nervous. Then Chris enters the room to confront the would be murderer.

Martin runs out of the room, Chris chases after him and beats him unconscious in another office. Kent and Lois are standing in the doorway when Chris remarks how he almost needed some more help from Superman.

"Well, that's more than you got from Clark," says Lois. Kent smiles, ignoring the usual insults, and tells Chris he did a pretty good Superman performance himself.

EPISODE 31

SHOT IN THE DARK

directed by GEORGE BLAIR
written by DAVID CHANTLER

Superman returns to the Daily Planet to begin this adventure. After changing into Clark Kent, he collides with Perry White, who reprimands him for missing a story about how Superman saved ten people from a burning building. Upset because he had to read the story in a rival newspaper, White storms off to his office.

After totally confusing Perry White with a 'Gracie Allen' style conversation, **HARRIET HARPER** *(Vera Marshe)* enters Kent's office and begins to plead for help, addressing him as *Superman*. Jimmy is especially interested when she pulls an 8x10 glossy out of her purse. It is a photo appearing to be of Superman changing into Kent.

The two reporters accompany Harriet to meet the photographer, her nephew **ALAN**, *(Billy Gray)*. Prior to his appearance in this episode, he played the young friend to Klaatu in *The Day the Earth*

Stood Still and then later, he became a regular family member on *Father Knows Best.*

Jimmy forces the issue of the photograph taken with an infrared bulb in the alley behind the Daily Planet at night. Kent simply explains it away as an accidental double exposure. The possibility of Superman changing into the civilian clothes of someone other than Clark Kent is never an issue for debate. Neither is the fact that a double exposure would never have produced such a perfectly registered image, although that might have been on Jimmy's mind.

Kent smells something burning. He sends the group out into the hallway to investigate while he quickly rushes into Alan's darkroom to snuff a trash can fire. The sharp-eyed viewer may observe the shadow of a head on the wall in the lower right corner of the picture, perhaps of the cameraman. Since this was the first episode directed by *George Blair,* and because he may not yet have been used to the rapid 'setum up an shoot' routine, it could possibly have been his shadow in the foreground.

This shadow was observed while viewing a 16mm print of this episode. Subsequent viewings on television, where the picture is more tightly cropped, did not show the offending shadow.

Alan explains that a man who has made several increasing cash offers for the photograph he'd taken of him with a bouquet of tulips, attempted to steal the picture after Alan refused to sell. Kent learns that a burglar made off with the double exposure of Superman. He asks Alan if he might borrow the photo of the Tulip Man to see if it might be identified by the police. Jimmy wonders in which of the two photos is Kent more interested?

At his office, Kent is confronted at gunpoint by the **TULIP MAN** *(John Eldredge),* demanding to have the photograph. As Kent is about to hand it over, Jimmy breaks into the office. He snatches the photo and runs off down the hall. The Tulip Man is in hot pursuit, immediately followed by Kent. Lois, having witnessed the chase, decides to follow.

Jimmy manages to escape the chase by getting aboard the *Valley Express* subway train. Kent overhears the Tulip Man in a phone booth making plans to wreck the train. As Kent is about to rush away, he is intercepted by Lois. She insists on staying with him until she finds out what is happening.

Soon, two of the henchmen, **HANK** *(Frank Richards)* and **BILL** *(Alan Lee),* beat a subway conductor over the head and send his train full speed toward a collision with the Valley Express.

Meanwhile, Lois and Kent are walking the street. Kent uses a blast of heat vision to set off a burglar alarm. Lois rushes off to get a scoop on the story and Kent is free to change into Superman. A running takeoff from an alley leads into a nice flying shot panning the city in the background. Once again, the sharp-eyed viewer will notice Superman's cape getting tangled in the support wire attached to his waist.

Superman crashes down into the subway tunnel. He rips up the third rail to short out the electrical power and subsequently halt the speeding subway trains.

Jimmy returns to the office with the photograph and goes with Kent to Inspector Henderson's office. As they thumb through a mug shot book, they come to a positive identification of the Tulip Man. He is *Burt Burnside,* a confidence man who specialized in running insurance fraud games, but the record shows that he died in a traffic accident a few years back and that an insurance policy paid off $50,000 to his two associates.

And one more time, the sharp-eyed viewer will notice to the left of John Eldredge's picture in the police photo book is a picture of *Hugh Beaumont,* who appears in *The Big Squeeze* episode as a reformed criminal.

Henderson fails to see why Kent and Jimmy are interested in a dead crook until they point out to him the photo taken by Alan. It shows Burnside standing in front of a billboard that announces the playdates of a show that only opened two weeks ago. Henderson gives Kent twelve hours to solve the case before mobilizing the police force.

"It shouldn't take a man like Mr. Kent that long!" says Jimmy with a smile.

Back at the office, Kent doctors a news story to convince the bad guys that the photo they want will be on a mail truck in the morning. This trick of faking news stories to flush out criminals gets Jimmy in trouble in a later episode entitled *Jimmy Olsen, Boy Editor.*

As planned, the mail truck is hijacked by Hank and Bill. They shoot the driver and leave him for dead on the road. When the truck is out of sight, the mail truck driver jumps to his feet and sheds his coveralls to reveal his true identity—Superman. A running outdoor takeoff shot puts him in the air.

Arriving at Burnside's hideout with the mail truck, Hank and Bill quickly discover the mail bags are full of shredded copies of the Daily Planet. Superman crashes through the wall to apprehend the criminals, but Burnside proposes a deal. If Superman will fly him to safety before the police arrive, he will give Superman the revealing photo of his costume change. But Superman has already located the photo locked away in a safe. He destroys it with his heat vision, and then tells Burnside to face the police alone as he flies away.

Henderson storms in with Jimmy and several officers, followed by the entrance of Kent. Burnside opens the safe to find only ashes. He pulls a gun out of his ankle holster and shoots at Kent point blank to prove he is Superman. Kent hardly flinches except to reach into his breast pocket to quickly produce a bent silver dollar that has deflected the bullet. Henderson laughs off the preposterous idea that Kent is Superman. He takes Burnside away to see a judge and jury. Jimmy tells Kent how great he is even without being Superman. Kent looks to the camera and winks just before the fade out.

EPISODE 32

THE DEFEAT OF SUPERMAN

directed by TOMMY CARR
written by JACKSON GILLIS

Who is this strange visitor from another planet that always comes between the hard working criminal and his intended goal? That is the question on the mind of **HAPPY KING** (Peter Mamakos). For the answer, he looks to a self-serving scientist named **MELDINI** (Maurice Cass). Meldini talks up a good story about how native elements that were harmless to Superman on his home planet could certainly be dangerous, and perhaps deadly to him on earth.

To test what Meldini calls the Delthinian theory, King recruits an accomplice named **RUFFLES** (Sid Tomack) to rig up a machine gun loaded with bullets made of various elements, one of which is kryptonite. With a hidden motion picture camera in place, Superman is lured to an out of the way location and subjected to a shower of machine gun fire.

Later, when the gang views the captured film footage, it is obvious that Superman was adversely affected by the one bullet made of a small quantity of kryptonite. Meldini's theory has proven correct. Happy King gives the okay to proceed with the next phase of the plan.

With what would become the standard operating procedure of every gangster who wants to lure Superman into some sort of trap, King orders the kidnapping of Lois Lane to use as bait. As it happens this time, Jimmy is swept along for the ride. Superman is alerted to their captivity within a specially rigged basement.

When Superman arrives, Lois and Jimmy try to warn him of the danger. These criminals should not be taken lightly because they have a small block of kryptonite. Superman smiles and assures his two friends that nothing on earth can harm him. He then takes a run at the locked door only to find himself thrown back into the room.

"Did you say kryptonite?" asks a very worried Superman.

Jimmy brings the small block of metal a little closer for a better look. Superman drops to the floor. Lois and Jimmy are now painfully aware that they may in fact be witnessing the death of their hero. They make several attempts to rid the room of the kryptonite. When he sees they are having no such luck, Superman mutters something about lead pipes. Lois fights back the tears to help Jimmy jam the horrible metal block down into a drain pipe that is fortunately made of lead. Hopefully, it will shield Superman from its deadly radiation.

Success! Superman quickly regains his strength and decides the best resting place for this kryptonite is deep under water. He hurls the lead pipe far into the sky and out into the ocean. As it streaks across the sky with a high pitched whistle, it draws the attention of the three escaping villains. The distraction is enough to cause their car to go out of control and plunge over a cliff. Although Meldini and company are silenced forever, his discovery shows up again in the color episode #56 called *Superman Week*.

EPISODE 33

SUPERMAN IN EXILE

directed by TOMMY CARR
written by JACKSON GILLIS

A new theme was rapidly emerging in the series. If Superman could somehow be taken out of the picture, the reigning criminals could easily work their schemes without too much interference. With kryptonite in short supply, villains were continually relying on some wild scientific theory, or the kidnapping of one of his friends, to divert Superman long enough to do their work. Comic book readers may recall a similar situation as it was illustrated in the story called "The Spectral Superman" that unfolded in the pages of *Action #188*.

This episode begins with an accident that puts Superman out of service while a gang of jewel thieves led by a master mind named **FERDINAND** *(Leon Askin)* gives the Metropolis police force a run for their money.

In a great show with state of the art special effects, we see a nuclear reactor going critically out of control and posing a serious threat to the people of Metropolis. Superman is called to the rescue by the facility **DIRECTOR** *(Joe Forte)* to calm the potential explosion. Unfortunately, Superman is charged with a dose of radiation that would be lethal to any human who remained too close to him for very long. This forces him into exile high above the city on Blue Peak mountain.

When the news breaks, Ferdinand puts his two associates, **REGAN** *(Phil Van Zandt)* and **SKINNY** *(John Harmon)* into action. With Superman powerless to help fight crime, the local scientists work feverishly on a solution to relieve his contamination.

Before long, Lois finds herself caught up in Ferdinand's scheme. She gets kidnapped and hauled away in an airplane. Luckily, Superman has one more alternative. It is proposed that a huge electrical charge may be able to force the

radiation from his body. He decides to test the theory by flying through an electrical storm.

After a few lightning bolts flood his body, the mysterious radiance that once characterized his contamination is now gone.

Superman forces the getaway airplane to land and Ferdinand is soon in custody by the **SHERIFF** *(Gregg Barton)*. Kent makes a timely appearance which causes Lois once again to remark about how he and Superman always seem to share experiences. She confronts Kent with a sigh and says, "You and Superman. I still wonder."

"It's no wonder you wonder," Kent replies with a smile. "You're a pretty wonderful girl."

EPISODE 34

A GHOST FOR SCOTLAND YARD

directed by TOMMY CARR
written by JACKSON GILLIS

Clark Kent and Jimmy Olsen are winding up a European tour on a quest for news when they finally land in England. Jimmy is in search for a magazine at the newsstand across the street from the hotel while Superman is off recovering their lost traveller's checks. Jimmy learns of a mysterious prediction that has been making the local news from the magazine **VENDOR** *(Clyde Cook)*. It seems that a dead magician who was killed five years ago in a seemingly innocent traffic accident is about to reappear.

This is very upsetting news to **SIR ARTHUR** *(Colin Campbell)*, an old friend of Perry White, and his wife, **MABEL** *(Norma Varden)*. Asked to investigate by their stateside editor, Jimmy and Kent go out to visit the stately mansion of Sir Arthur. They learn from Mabel that Sir Arthur is late coming home and she fears the worst. It seems Sir Arthur has not been well as of late because of the expected return of Brockhurst, the man who vowed to come back to life for revenge.

While Jimmy offers comforting words to Mabel and their maid, **BETTY** *(Evelyn Halpern)*, Kent decides to slip away for a look see as Superman. A nice outdoor takeoff puts him in the night sky.

Meanwhile, Sir Arthur is driving his Rolls Royce along the country road near the edge of a coastal cliff when he sees the bodiless image of **BROCKHURST** *(Leonard Mudie)* drifting among the clouds. This frightens him to faint. Superman arrives just in time to prevent his runaway automobile from plummeting over the cliff.

It is Kent who helps Sir Arthur into the house for some much needed rest. **FARRINGTON** *(Patrick Aherne)* arrives from Scotland Yard to investigate. In a disguise, Brockhurst shows up on the estate long enough to use an extension telephone to call in a frightening threat to Farrington.

Superman later takes another look around the site of Sir Arthur's unfortunate automobile ride. He discovers a strand of motion picture film carelessly left behind. It has on it the image of Brockhurst that was projected on the clouds to scare Sir Arthur.

Meanwhile, Jimmy has gone out to the carriage house to investigate an extension telephone. He comes face to face with Brockhurst. In a monologue proclaiming this to be his hour of triumph, he threatens to detonate a bomb that will execute his long promised revenge.

Superman returns in time to save the evening in a curious display of weakness. He apparently cannot see Jimmy in the dark and requires the sound of his voice to locate him. Anyway, Superman manages to get hold of the bomb. He throws it up through the roof before it can be detonated and destroy the estate.

A nice closing scene has Jimmy back at the newsstand restating to the vendor his unwillingness to believe in ghosts. As Jimmy and Kent rush off to catch an airplane back to the States, the vendor gives the nice chaps from America a copy of the latest issue of *Superman* magazine.

EPISODE 35

THE DOG WHO KNEW SUPERMAN

directed by TOMMY CARR
written by DAVID CHANTLER

An adventure entitled "The Dog Who Loved Superman" appeared on the pages of *Superman*

#88 and may have at least been the inspiration for the title of this episode.

Clark Kent is giving his sports car a workout in the country when he happens upon a tragedy in the making and the beginning of an adventure. A little dog named **CORKY** is barking away in the background as the owner, **JOYCE** *(Dona Drake)* is letting her anger out on her gangster husband, **HANK** *(Ben Welden),* for being so careless to let the poor little pooch fall into an open well.

Kent quickly changes to Superman. Within seconds, all attention is on him as he dives into the earth and brings Corky up from out of the well. Almost as quickly as he arrived, Superman is gone. As Joyce and Hank move to their car, Corky picks up a driving glove that Kent accidently dropped before rushing away.

LOUIE *(Billy Nelson),* a member of Hank's gang, is waiting at the apartment when Joyce and Hank return with Corky. They are still arguing about Hank's carelessness as Joyce goes into the kitchen. When Hank removes the leash, Corky goes running out the open door. Joyce insists Hank go out and retrieve him. He claims not to be at fault this time because she had left the door open, but he promises to find the runaway dog even if he has to put an ad in every newspaper in town.

Meanwhile, Corky finds his way to Clark Kent's office. He recognizes Corky and tries to shoo him away as Lois and Jimmy enter the office. The dog barks, grabs Kent's other driving glove off the desk, and runs away.

As Corky is running out of the Daily Planet, Hank happens to be arriving. He catches Corky, sees the driving glove, and he begins to get the idea. Corky gets away again.

He returns to the apartment to tell Joyce he is offering a five thousand dollar reward for the return of Corky. He tells Louie to spread the word.

What better way to spread the word about Corky than have a newspaper story written about him? Louie calls Kent with the details. Kent tells him to come over to the office.

Meanwhile, Corky arrives again at Kent's office. Kent orders Jimmy to hide the dog until he can figure out why the owner wants him so badly. Outside the office, Louie recognizes Corky with Jimmy. He phones Hank with the news.

Soon, Jimmy is kidnapped by Hank and blindfolded before being taken for a ride back to Hank's apartment. They use a lie detector on Jimmy to learn that Corky is locked away in a kennel. Hank finally explains how he believes Corky will lead them to Superman's secret identity. Hank sends Louie to go pick up the dog.

Louie, on the other hand, does not care to tangle with Superman, so he goes to tell Kent about what is going on. When Kent learns what Louie has done with the dog to insure the secret of Superman, his reaction in favor of saving the dog is a surprise to Louie. He wonders if Kent is planning to double cross Superman.

Kent changes to Superman and leaps out the window. He soon locates the wagon of the **DOG CATCHER** (John Daly) where Corky has been confined and he makes the rescue. Kent returns to his office with the dog where Lois is waiting to find out what is going on. He tells her to wait with the dog while he does a little investigating and quickly leaves before she can resist. Then Jimmy rushes in and tells her how he was kidnapped and quizzed about the dog. Lois and Jimmy decide to do their own investigation by returning the dog to its owner.

When Lois returns the dog to the apartment, Hank is very happy to see him. He thanks Lois and tells her the reward check will be in the mail. As he tries to close the door, Lois insists on a story. Hank tells her to get lost.

Later, Hank is following Corky down the street near the Daily Planet. Kent is approaching from the opposite direction and is tipped off by Corky's barking. He quickly backs into an alley. When Hank and Corky come around the corner, they are greeted by Superman. He grabs Hank, very surprised, and hangs him up by his coat on a burglar alarm box attached high on the wall of the building to await the arrival of the police.

In Kent's office, he is explaining to Corky *(and all of us kids in the audience)* that he cannot allow the dog to stay with him. In a very touching moment, he tells Corky to go back with Joyce and not to worry about Hank because the kidnapping of Jimmy will put him away for a long time. Corky barks an agreement and leaves the office.

Lois enters a moment later to see an expression of remorse on Kent's face.

"You look like you just lost your best friend."

"Maybe I have, Lois," Clark Kent sadly replies. "Maybe I have."

EPISODE 36

THE FACE AND THE VOICE

directed by GEORGE BLAIR
written by JACKSON GILLIS

The story begins when a clever crime boss named **FAIRCHILD** (Carleton Young) recruits a punch drunk boxer named **BOULDER** (George Reeves) for some minor facial surgery and a voice training program. Boulder takes a last look at his beat up face in the mirror, the result of many lost fights, and agrees to participate in exchange for ten percent of the profit from the scheme.

Fairchild begins the project by sending **SCRATCHY** (George Chandler) to break into Perry White's office and steal a phonograph record. His appearance is noted by Jimmy, but Scratchy passes himself off as a shoe repairman summoned by the editor.

Scratchy gets the record and returns to the hideout apartment in time to witness the unveiling of Fairchild's new creation as **T-BONE** (I. Stanford Jolley) removes the bandages from Boulder's new face. Boulder now looks just like Superman, but his Brooklyn accent needs a lot of work. Fairchild tells Boulder about a voice coach due to arrive.

Later, at the Daily Planet, Kent meets Perry and Jimmy in the hallway. They have discovered the theft. The phonograph record was made by Superman when he recently gave a speech. Jimmy recalls the visitor from the night before, but Kent pays no attention to the minor mystery.

HAMLET (Percy Helton) is the voice coach who spends many long hours working with Boulder. The old boxer finally demonstrates his ability to speak like Superman. Fairchild is convinced the plan will work. He is ready to put it to a small test.

Next, we see Boulder (as Superman) entering a grocery store. He politely asks the **STORE CLERK** (William Newell) for all the money in the cash register. The clerk is so surprised, he hands the money over quickly. When he finally asks for a receipt, Superman merely turns and makes an exit.

The next day, Perry reads the headline to Kent and Jimmy about Superman turning into a super crook. Perry allows Kent to go question the store clerk. Kent suspects that he made up the story to cover up the fact that he stole the money himself.

Jimmy meets up with Kent later in his office. It seems the interesting point was that the store clerk never saw Superman fly away. Jimmy also points out that an amount of money equal to the amount stolen from the store was just anonymously donated to a local charity. Jimmy says it sounds like something Superman would do. Kent laughs and says he happens to know that Superman was home in bed when the robbery occurred. Lois Lane might have quizzed Kent about that remark, but she is nowhere around, and Jimmy never questions it.

Then we see Superman enter a jewelry store after closing time. He cleans out a display case as the **WATCHMAN** (*Nolan Leary*) stands nearby. Superman runs down the alley The watchman chases him and shoots his gun. Around the corner, Scratchy is standing near a camera tripod. He gives Boulder a trench coat and helps him into a getaway car.

Boulder returns to Fairchild and complains the element of risk is getting too high. He tells Boulder not to worry, they are now ready for the big payoff, a gold shipment worth two million dollars. By now, the real Superman is probably beginning to question his own sanity.

And that he is. Kent hears about the watchman taking a shot at Superman and Jimmy shows a picture of Superman flying away, claimed to have been taken by an eye witness. Kent decides to pay a visit to a **PSYCHIATRIST** (*Hayden Rorke*) for some reassurance. He tells Kent there is nothing on earth wrong with him. Nothing on earth, maybe, wonders Kent.

Jimmy pays a visit to interview the eyewitness. He recognizes Scratchy as the visitor to Perry's office. Scratchy realizes Jimmy is a potential problem and knocks him out until Boulder can complete the gold robbery.

Meanwhile, Boulder dressed as Superman visits with Perry at his office to turn over the jewelry he swiped the night before with instructions to give it to charity. Perry informs Superman that the citizens are getting angry at his Robin Hood behavior. Boulder reminds

Perry what the consequences might be if he decided to get angry at Metropolis. Then he makes a quick exit.

The real Superman finally figures out something is wrong and tries to convince Henderson. As he chases the Inspector around the desk in his office with a wild theory of an impersonator, a call comes in to report a gold robbery in progress. When they hear it is being perpetrated by Superman, Henderson finally begins to believe him.

Superman captures the escaping gold truck, rescues Jimmy from being kidnapped, and rounds up all the crooks before the final scene. Boulder is in a hospital bed being questioned by Henderson.

"It takes more than a face and a voice," says Boulder. "There's only one real Superman."

A quick panning shot using some trick photography reveals Jimmy and Kent standing nearby.

"He can say that again," adds Jimmy. "Right, Mr. Kent?"

"Right, Mr. Olsen," he replies, smiling.

EPISODE 37

THE MAN IN THE LEAD MASK

directed by GEORGE BLAIR
written by LEROY H. ZEHREN & ROY HAMILTON

The title character is a master criminal named Marty Mitchell. He is on the loose and trying to extort money from other members of his own profession by staging a scheme that would be much easier for present day gangsters to believe than those of Metropolis in the 1950s.

With the help of two other crooks, a man named **CANFIELD** (*Frank Scannell*) and a so called plastic surgeon known as **DOC** (*John Merton*), Mitchell plans to convince a number of wealthy gangsters that the Doc has succeeded with a new operating technique to change both face and fingerprints. The gangsters, **PAWLEY** (*Louis Jean Heydt*), **SCOTTY** (*Paul Bryar*), and **MORRELL** (*John Crawford*), listen with great interest as Canfield, pretending to be Mitchell, testifies about how his changed face and fingerprints have allowed him to begin a new life free of any criminal history. For a substantial amount of down payment money, the Doc will work the same magic for any criminal willing to pay the price.

As an introduction to help dramatize his scheme of selling new identities, Canfield hides his face in a lead mask to break into a post office. He steals only a wanted poster of Mitchell. By revealing a few facts about himself known only to Mitchell and the gang of wealthy criminals, Canfield begins to convince the prospective customers that he is really Mitchell. Then he shows that his fingerprints are also different than those of Mitchell recorded on the wanted poster.

Meanwhile, Henderson and the Daily Planet reporters discover the strange theft at the post office. When they begin to wonder what is going on, the usual happens with our series regulars getting tangled up in the crooked scheme. Superman is far too clever for the con act. He wraps up all the loose ends in time to keep anyone from getting hurt and bring Mitchell to justice.

In order to substantiate his claim to be the *real* Marty Mitchell, Canfield shows himself at a diner across the street from the Daily Planet building where he orders some food from the **WAITRESS** *(Lyn Thomas)* while Kent and Lois are having lunch. Kent begins to notice certain mannerisms performed by Canfield and begins to suspect him to be Mitchell. By staging a phoney telephone conversation with Jimmy from a nearby pay telephone, Kent manages to get a sample of Canfield's fingerprints by having him pass over a water glass.

After Kent rushes back to the office with the water glass, Perry White once again proves to having a life prior to becoming editor of the Daily Planet. His previous experience with police procedures allows him to examine the captured fingerprints. Although the prints do not match those recorded to be Mitchell's, Kent still suspects Canfield of some kind of wrongdoing.

This entire event has been staged by Mitchell so the newspapers will write a story to document how the authorities believed Canfield was Marty Mitchell. This convinces the gangsters that the Doc can really do his stuff.

Attempting to raise some quick cash to buy himself a new identity, Morrell sets out disguised in a lead mask to rob a safe at the *Ellsworth Jewelry Co.* Kent hears about the robbery in progress, changes into Superman, and then leaps out the window.

Watch for the stick of dynamite still gripped in Superman's hand from the Human Bomb episode of the first season.

Following a nice nighttime flying shot over Metropolis *(Hollywood Boulevard)*, Superman intercepts Morrell's getaway car which causes an accident that puts Morrell in the hospital.

Kent and Henderson listen to Morrell babble about a new face and fingerprints. Kent then borrows the captured lead mask from Henderson. As Superman, he follows the tire tracks of Morrell's car and locates the hideout.

Watch how the shadow on the garage reveals that Superman arrives by jumping into frame from a platform.

Superman makes his appearance at the hideout wearing the lead mask and a trenchcoat. Thinking Superman is really Morrell, Canfield gives him an order to accompany him on another robbery. This time it will be the payroll safe of the Daily Planet. However, when Canfield leaves the room to get his disguise, it is the real Mitchell who appears wearing another lead mask.

Got the picture? We now have two men in lead masks about to rob the payroll safe. One is the real Mitchell thinking the other is Morrell. The other is really Superman thinking he is accompanied by Canfield. In retrospect, it's amazing how clever we must've been as kids to follow this particular plot.

Anyway, when Superman soon gets a look at the other man's fingerprints, he realizes the scheme and returns to the hideout where he finally exposes both **MITCHELL** *(Joey Ray)* and Canfield to the other gangsters. The show closes with a bit of comedy as Jimmy gets his head stuck inside one of the lead masks. Superman quickly claims to be of no help as he winks to the camera before the final fade out. This gag was repeated with Jimmy and a pair of handcuffs in a later episode entitled *Semi-Private Eye.*

An interesting behind the scenes story is associated with this episode as told by the special effects expert, Si Simonson. In a syndicated television special of several years ago hosted by

Tom Bosley, Simonson relayed how George Reeves had to actually wear the head gear fabricated to appear as a lead mask. When Reeves realized how tight it fit, a moment of panic had him struggling to get the mask off and he bruised his face. It's also interesting to note that the mask was returned to active duty in one of the last episodes, *The Peril of Superman*. As the director of the show, Reeves stayed clear of wearing the mask himself.

Some of the plot elements of this adventure may be compared to those in the illustrated story "The Man Who Could Change Fingerprints" as it appeared in the *Batman #82* comic book.

EPISODE 38

PANIC IN THE SKY

directed by TOMMY CARR
written by JACKSON GILLIS

This adventure opens with somber music to a tracking shot along a city street which reveals an assemblage of people crowding the sidewalk, all looking fearfully toward the sky. A frightened woman tightly grips the arm of her **HUSBAND** (*Thomas Moore*) as he attempts to comfort her by saying not to worry, "it's only a meteor."

Only a meteor? Lois and Jimmy are watching from an office window at the Daily Planet building when Perry White rushes in looking for Clark Kent to lend some stability to the situation. Here, we learn that the threatening item in the sky is a five mile in diameter asteroid coming dangerously close to Earth. Jimmy is optimistic, as usual, and figures because the meteor already passed by Venus and Mars, that it will probably just pass by the Earth. Perry issues instructions to prepare an update story for the morning edition, if there is one.

At an observatory, located high above the city on the Metropolis equivalent of Mount Wilson, we meet **PROFESSOR ROBERTS** (*Jonathan Hale*), who many will remember as the boss of Dagwood Bumstead in the *BLONDIE* series. The Professor is closely monitoring the progress of our invading space rock through the eyepiece of a large telescope while Superman is standing nearby, watching the meteor with his own incredible telescopic vision. Superman remarks that the meteor appears to have stopped moving, but his great eyesight must've sacrificed depth perception because the Professor breaks the news that the asteroid is indeed coming straight toward them.

In spite of the Professor's warning lecture about the dangers of tangling with an unknown cosmic force, probably forgetting in the heat of excitement that Superman is one himself, the Man of Steel decides it's time to act. He executes a dramatic springboard takeoff over a low angled fence.

A panoramic shot of Superman flying up and away from Metropolis leads him toward his target, a glowing object that appears to be a large tin foil ball with Fourth of July sparklers lighting its path. His voyage terminates in an animated explosion, and it seems that Superman has once again saved the day, or night, in this case.

Superman returns to Earth, apparently by sheer instinct because it is soon evident that he has been knocked senseless by the collision with the panic in the sky. Luckily, he touches down on the rocky landscape of the Iverson Ranch, a location in the San Fernando Valley that has provided scenery for countless western movies filmed since before talking pictures were invented. From the moment he hits the ground, we are offered several hints that something is not quite right. His landing is shaky, at best, and then he staggers out of sight behind some large boulders. When a **FARMER** (*Jane Frazee*) drives up in an old jalopy, Clark Kent, complete with double breasted suit and black frame glasses, comes into view from behind the rocks.

Lois enters the office of Perry White, who is busily juggling telephone calls to and from leaders of the city. We soon learn that Superman is nowhere to be found. Coincidentally, neither is Clark Kent.

Jimmy has been dispatched to Kent's apartment. The door opens and in walks a dazed Clark Kent. As Jimmy presses him for details on his recent whereabouts, Kent moves in looking around, and he begins to loosen his tie and open his shirt to partially reveal his Superman chest emblem. Ironically, Jimmy is behind him as Kent mumbles about how he is tired and in need of rest. Jimmy volunteers to run for coffee and sandwiches, suggesting that Kent should take a shower and relax.

Now alone in his own apartment, Kent finds his way into the closet and accidently hits the button that slides open the secret panel to reveal two more Superman shirts hanging on the rack. Somehow, since *The Stolen Costume* episode of the first season, his Man of Steel wardrobe has been increased to better meet the demands of a busy superhero. When Jimmy returns a short time later, he hears a shower running and then a loud sound of crashing glass. Running into the bedroom, he discovers a broken shower door and Kent laying unconscious on the tile floor.

Somehow, Jimmy manages to get Kent into a pair of pajamas and tucked into bed before Lois and Perry White come charging into the place. Perry blusters inquiries as to what is going on as Lois remarks about all the shattered glass on the bathroom floor. Kent wakes up from the noise, fails to recognize anyone in the room, and doesn't seem to know where or who he is. Lois suggests amnesia and Perry appeals to great Caesar's ghost as the fade out leads to the commercial break.

The stage has been set for one of the best remembered and most popular episodes ever produced for the *Adventures of Superman*. It is precisely for that reason critics have been uncommonly severe in their reviews of this one particular show. In spite of its shortcomings, it is still the most imaginative story and very well executed. No one will dispute the gaping holes in the plot, but this is 1950's science fiction at its best. I once heard a story of a moviegoer who walked out of a theatre during the intermission of *Gone With The Wind,* and it wasn't until twenty years later that he discovered he'd only seen the first half of the picture. Certainly, no one ever walked away from their television set without waiting to see the conclusion of *Panic in the Sky.*

After the sponsors have had their say, we return to the observatory where Professor Roberts expresses to his **ASSISTANT** (*Clark Howat*) that he is still very much concerned with the dangers of the meteor and its twice a day orbit around the Earth. Meanwhile, Lois and Jimmy have been giving Clark a tour of the Daily Planet building with hope that it will jog his memory.

Both Jimmy and Lois recall antecdotes about their past here at the office, but Kent seems to only be humoring them with responses he believes they wish to hear. He cannot remember who he is, and certainly recalls nothing of Superman.

Lois and Perry White meet with Professor Roberts who reports that the gravitational influence of the orbiting asteroid is disturbing the rotation of the Earth. Tidal waves, earthquakes, and wind storms are occurring around the world. If something isn't done to correct the situation, life as they know it will soon come to a halt.

After tossing and turning in his sleep, Kent wakes up and takes a thoughful look at the special wardrobe in his secret closet. When Jimmy arrives, Kent quizzes Jimmy about Superman. Is it the costume that gives him his special ability? It would be years before the idea would flourish in *Steven J. Cannell's* Greatest American Hero series, and after Jimmy explains that it is not the clothing that makes the Man of Steel, Kent gives him the bum's rush. In the hopes that Olsen is wrong, Kent suits up and begins to pace his apartment, still wearing his glasses. In a fit of frustration, he smashes his fist on a discount department store end table. It all becomes clear, everyone insists that he is Clark Kent, Superman's costume is kept hidden in Kent's closet, therefore, he must be Superman! Harp strings and horns tingle loudly as he tosses his glasses on the chair, gets a good running start to leap out the bedroom window, and he is soon airborn over the skyline of Metropolis. His next stop, the observatory to meet Professor Roberts.

At the observatory, Lois, Jimmy, and Perry are discussing with the professor a plan to explode the meteor with a specially constructed bomb, if only they had a way to get it out to the asteroid. Then Jimmy, probably hearing the harp strings and horns, points up to the sky at an approaching Superman. Within moments, he gets a crash course on how to activate the explosive device, and then Superman makes another dramatic springboard takeoff over the cyclone fence. After a quick flight through a cloudy atmosphere, carrying the bomb like an end runner carries a football, he makes a landing on the desolate surface of the meteor.

While reviewing this episode to collect notes for the new edition of this book, my daughter happened to interrupt my study with a curious observation. It seems that if you listen carefully after Superman makes his landing upon the surface of the meteor, you can actually hear birds chirping in the background as our hero contemplates his next move. Could there be life on this drifting body of space debris? Imagine the flack Superman might have encountered today from the animal-rights whackos upon his return from saving the world at the expense of some hitherto unknown endangered species. Worse yet, would Superman have been forced to suspend his activities while the EPA dragged him through an intensive series of court hearings?

Anyway, Superman inevitably takes the decision to place the device in a strategic location among the rocks. Without hesitation, he sets a couple of switches, and then says what we all hope will not be his final words, "Well, no matter who I am. . . here goes."

Another fireworks display in outer space dissolves into a flying shot of Superman over a panorama of Metropolis. The world has been saved for sixty-six more episodes.

The closing scene is Clark Kent typing up the final news release under the watchful eye of Lois. She cannot help wondering how Kent knows so much about the recent events, and he confesses that his memory has totally returned. Admitting that he even knows who Superman is, Lois presses for a revelation. "Oh, just knock me on the head some time and you'll find out," he replies with a play on words and a smile as the show fades out.

To analyze why this episode is singled out by fans and collectors as the most remembered and popular show of the series would probably fill a psychologist's text book. It is riddled with flaws and factual inconsistencies, the special effects are mediocre and sometimes silly, and the main characters would have to be blind not to make the connection between Kent's loss of memory at the same time that Superman seems to have hopelessly disappeared. Nevertheless, *Panic in the Sky* presents a dramatic dilemma with the potential for world-wide consequences that mankind has feared throughout modern history. It is Superman at his very best.

EPISODE 39

THE MACHINE THAT COULD PLOT CRIMES

directed by TOMMY CARR
written by JACKSON GILLIS

One hot evening in Metropolis, **LARRY McCOY** *(Billy Nelson)* is trying to get some sleep in his dingy apartment when he hears his name mentioned on the radio news. When the **ANNOUNCER** *(Sam Balter)* refers to McCoy as an unsuccessful gangster *(a skunkweed)*, he smashes the radio against the wall. Now in silence, McCoy begins to hear the noise of bumps and whistles coming from another apartment. After banging on the water pipes to try and get the attention of the offending neighbor, he decides to personally investigate.

McCoy enters the apartment of the eccentric **UNCLE OSCAR** *(Sterling Holloway)*. Here he finds Oscar tending to a room full of noisey computer hardware with lights flashing and reels spinning. McCoy's anger soon turns into curiosity. He begins to express an interest in the mechanical brain Oscar keeps referring to as 'Mr. Kelso' and is fascinated to learn of its incredible thinking abilities.

For the sake of a demonstration, McCoy inquires hypothetically as to how a robbery might be executed without one getting caught. The answer clicks out of the ticker tape machine much to McCoy's amazement. "Too bad we're not criminals," says Uncle Oscar innocently.

Using this information, McCoy recruits an accomplice calling himself **NOSEY** *(Ben Welden)*, and together they put the plan to the test. Based on the carefully constructed timetable, Nosey easily obtains a sack of cash from a **BANK TELLER** *(Sherry Moreland)*. The successfull heist makes headlines in the Daily Planet.

Henderson calls Lois and Kent into his office to point out how the robbery was pure luck. It succeeded only because of a series of coincidences. The bank guard and beat patrolman just happened to be occupied at the time, and the traffic signal just happened to be right for the getaway. While Kent and Henderson are theorizing about the odds of calculating all of these variables and formulating a plan, a call comes in to report yet another robbery of the Second National Bank.

Mr. Kelso is so clever, he figures a way for McCoy to blackmail Superman with threats of exposing his secret identity in exchange for cooperation. Superman cannot take the chance that his identity may be revealed, so he actually assists the crooks with a getaway.

Kent decides to investigate. Lois follows him and eventually they are captured. They learn the gang plans to pull off one last job before eliminating the meddling reporters, and McCoy sends **PINKY** *(Stan Jarmen)* to kill Uncle Oscar and destroy the incredible machine.

Kent finds himself locked in the back of a panel truck, tied up, and looking for an opportunity to get away. After McCoy's brags a confession, Kent breaks free and knocks him out cold. After changing into his action suit, Superman crashes out the side of the moving truck to rush over and save Uncle Oscar from a lit stick of dynamite. He learns that Mr. Kelso has already figured out how the gang was using his incredible thinking power. The thieves are unknowingly on a getaway course bound for capture. They find themselves going the wrong way on a one-way street where a **POLICEMAN** *(Russell Custer)* writes Nosey a ticket.

An interesting scene has Superman flying over the city looking for the getaway vehicle carrying Lois Lane. A close shot of a smiling Superman shows the moving skyline background coming to a complete stop as if he were positioned motionless in the sky.

The episode ends on a clever bit with Uncle Oscar asking Mr. Kelso who Superman really is? He reads the response aloud to the viewers, "Wouldn't you like to know?"

You may audibly recognize Sterling Holloway as the voice of *Winnie the Pooh*.

EPISODE 40

JUNGLE DEVIL

directed by TOMMY CARR
written by PETER DIXON

A rather routine episode begins when Kent and Lois are assigned to investigate the disappearance of a husband and wife team of explorers working in a South American jungle. They have a departure time set for eight o'clock at Metropolis airport and Jimmy surprises them by his acceptance of being left out of this adventure when he wishes them both good luck and quietly leaves the office.

However, the inventive cub reporter has other plans. Jimmy reaches the airport before Kent and Lois and hides away in the cargo compartment.

After the **PILOT** *(James Seay)* puts the plane in the air bound for South America, he greets Kent and Lois in the passenger area with breakfast. The smell of food and hot coffee brings Jimmy out of hiding from the rear of the plane. After Kent gives him a token lecture about disobeying orders and how disappointed Perry White will be, he and Lois laugh and offer Jimmy a turkey sandwich.

The uneventful airplane ride is intercut with scenes of wild jungle natives dancing to drum music before their captives, **DR. HARPER** *(Damian O'Flynn)* and his wife **GLORIA** *(Doris Singleton)* while their trusty guide **ALBERTO** *(Nacho Galindo)* explains the ritual. It is performed to hopefully scare away the *jungle devil*. His colorful description makes this monster sound like just an energetic gorilla.

Now flying over the jungle, Kent convinces the pilot to fly a search pattern for the lost explorers in spite of a faltering engine. Kent has Jimmy and Lois watching intently out the windows while he slips back into the cargo hold for a change to Superman. He jumps out the door unnoticed for a quick look around himself.

Soon, Superman locates the native village and returns to the airplane in time to switch back to Kent as Jimmy summons him forward to see the pilot. The engine is now failing and they must attempt an emergency landing. Kent easily guides the pilot to a clearing in the heavily overgrown jungle. The pilot never questions Kent's uncanny aptitude for headings and airplane jargon.

Safely on the ground, the three reporters pack up for a hike through the jungle while the pilot tends to the aircraft. They soon walk into the sound of jungle drums and Lois is fearful of cannibals. Kent assures them both that everything will be okay just as they find themselves surrounded by a group of made in

Gloria Harper *(Doris Singleton)* and Dr. Harper *(Damian O'Flynn)* listen as Kent *(George Reeves)* considers the possibility of turning coal into diamonds.

Hollywood natives. Jimmy quickly reaches for his knife.

"Let's show them we can die like Americans!" boasts Jimmy, fearlessly.

"Put that thing away," Kent replies calmly. "Let's *live* like Americans."

Kent waves his arm in peace and figures they will be led to the Harper expedition. His hunch proves correct. After introductions, Alberto translates the native jibberish to explain how one white visitor must die in payment for the diamond taken out of an idol's eye. Gloria

explains how she removed the diamond to examine it and accidently dropped it in the quicksand when a native surprised her.

Kent invents a scheme to select the victim. Using a pith helmet, he collects five white stones and one black stone to see who gets sacrificed. His x-ray vision allows him to indirectly volunteer. He is led away by the angry natives.

As they are about to burn Kent at the stake, the jungle devil gorilla *(Steve Calvert)* arrives to terrorize them. A puff of smoke from the secret powder of the **WITCH DOCTOR** *(Leon Lontoc)* gives

The Tribal Chief *(Al Kikume)* watches with a degree of skepticism as the Witch Doctor *(Leon Lontoc)* makes peace with Clark Kent *(George Reeves).*

Kent a chance to change into Superman. He easily scares off the gorilla and is returned to the village a hero. To win back the respect of the **CHIEF** *(Al Kikume)* and the natives *(Henry Escalante, Bernard Gozier)* so the Harpers will be allowed to stay and continue their studies, Kent squeezes a block of coal into a diamond and pretends to find it lost in the quicksand. The natives are delighted when he restores the diamond to it's rightful place.

As the reporters make their way back through the jungle toward the waiting airplane, Lois remarks how for once Kent managed to save them from a dangerous situation without any assistance from Superman.

"Superman?" says Kent with a smile. "I wonder whatever became of him?"

Viewers will probably remember *Doris Singleton* made numerous appearances on the "I Love Lucy" show as Caroline Applebee, especially the episode, "Lucy Meets Superman" where *George Reeves* appears at Little Ricky's birthday party as Superman.

Damian O'Flynn appears as J. W. Gridley in "Jimmy, the Kid," the 1955 color episode of this series, number 71.

The Chief *(Al Kikume)* takes a stab at the mysterious jungle devil.

EPISODE 41

MY FRIEND, SUPERMAN

directed by TOMMY CARR
written by DAVID CHANTLER

This story revolves around the proprietor of a coffee shop who is being threatened by a gang of villains working a protection racket. The restaurant owner, **TONY** *(Tito Vuolo)*, who puts forth the best Italian stereotype performance since Chico Marx, refuses to buckle under the gangsters' scheme. It seems he is in possession of a unique souvenir, a rifle mounted on the wall that has a barrel allegedly twisted out of shape by his very good friend, Superman. In fact, Tony makes it very clear at every opportunity to anyone who will listen that his friend Superman will not stand by and allow him to be threatened by any cheap criminals.

Early in the show there is an interesting sequence where Superman returns to the Daily Planet from across the ocean. He lands in the supply room, sits down at a conveniently waiting typewriter, and quickly pounds out a written report before changing into his Clark Kent disguise. As he rushes into the hallway, he meets with an angry Perry White.

"Kent!" yells Perry. "Well? Where is it?"

"Right here, Sir," replies Kent as he hands over the freshly typed report. Perry then hurriedly looks it over.

"When on earth did you have time to do all this?" asks Perry.

"Well, Chief. Sometimes I can be pretty fast on that typewriter of mine," replies Kent with a smile as he coyly touches his glasses.

Fortunately for Tony, the familiar series regulars from the Daily Planet quite often patronize the coffee shop and Kent soon learns about the illegal insurance game. However, Tony becomes seriously concerned for the safety of Lois Lane when he is told by the **GANGSTERS** *(Paul Burke, Terry Frost, Joseph Vitale)* to either forget about signing any complaint against them, or be responsible for the demise of the lady reporter.

When Tony wonders if Superman will really take a hand in his problem, Kent reshapes the rifle barrel on the wall when no one is looking. He explains it must be Superman's way of telling Tony that he is on duty somewhere nearby.

At first, Kent isn't too concerned about Lois being out of touch as she had arranged to be away for a while. But when Perry reports to Kent that he hasn't received a scheduled contact from her, Kent begins to worry.

Meanwhile, Tony has made an amateur attempt to get some evidence by setting up a hidden microphone at the gangsters' regular serving table. The microphone is connected to Tony's wire recorder, but as he is about to get the inside information on the missing Lois, two energetic **TEENAGERS** *(Ruta Kilmonis, Edward Reider)* come dancing into the place and insist on playing loud music on the juke box.

A cute little subplot has Jimmy Olsen sort of infatuated with Tony's waitress, **ELAINE** *(Yvette Dugay)*. As they watch the two carefree teenagers, Jimmy remarks, "Look at those kids. It sure must be nice to be young." Elaine shoots him a cold stare.

Kent has changed to Superman and is pacing his apartment in hopes of hearing from Lois before the threatened deadline. He instead gets a call from Jimmy at the coffee shop. He and Tony are in the backroom and he explains to Superman (thinking he is Kent) about how Tony has recorded the crooks' conversation but that it has been garbled by the juke box. Superman has Jimmy play back the recording anyway. He is able to detect the voices by filtering out the offending background music long enough to hear the crooks remark about how they are happy Superman is off on a wild goose chase. Within seconds, Superman is out the window and on his way to the coffee shop.

Meanwhile, Lois makes a surprise appearance. The gangsters figure Superman is out of the way, but he shows up to prevent the criminals from escaping. Superman stands by as Tony and the rest of the customers pelt the thugs with a barrage of vanilla cream pies.

When the silliness is over, Tony is about to admit that he may have stretched the truth a little about his friendship with Superman, but our hero prevents him from revealing their secret. Then **GEORGE** *(Ralph Sanford)*, one of Tony's regular customers, announces his amazement in the closing line, "Well, I'll be darned. He really does know Superman."

On the wall is the rifle with the once again twisted barrel to prove it.

As a trivia note: Ruta Kilmonis later changed her screen name to *Ruta Lee*.

EPISODE 42

THE CLOWN WHO CRIED

directed by GEORGE BLAIR
written by DAVID CHANTLER

This story begins appropriately at the circus. **ROLLO** *(William Wayne)* returns to his tent dressed in his clown costume where he is confronted by his old friend and partner who we know only as **CRACKERS** *(Peter Brocco)*. After Crackers puts in a plea for a cash donation to his empty pockets, Kent and Lois arrive. Their mission is to ask Rollo to help them raise half a million dollars for the Children's Camp Fund. The Daily Planet is sponsoring a telethon and they are requesting Rollo's appearance as a guest performer.

Crackers is keenly interested in this great amount of cash. After Kent and Lois leave the tent, Rollo invites Crackers to join him in the telethon. Crackers agrees, but when Rollo turns his back, Crackers knocks him out cold.

Soon after, Jimmy arrives at the tent looking for Clark Kent. Crackers has assumed the disguise of Rollo. When Jimmy sees a pair of legs belonging to the real Rollo sticking out from behind a trunk on the floor, Crackers tries to make Jimmy believe they are props for his routine. To be sure Jimmy will not interfere, however, Crackers escorts him to the tent of **HERCULES** *(Mickey Simpson)*, the strong man. He gives the simple minded Hercules a hundred dollars to keep Jimmy tied up until after the

"Superman Flies Again"

George Reeves as "Superman" looks on while Rollo, the beloved circus clown, comforts a former partner who had assumed Rollo's character and attempted to rob a charity benefit, later plunging from a rooftop after a daring chase in this climactic scene from the 20th Century-Fox release, "Superman Flies Again" at the . . . . Theatre.   Mat 2C, Still No. B-14

An advertising mat cut from the pressbook used by theatre owners to promote one of the five feature releases from 20th Century-Fox.

telethon is over. Hercules believes Crackers is really his friend, Rollo, and he agrees because he needs the money to buy himself a new costume.

In spite of the serious situation, humor is not forgotten. Jimmy is first introduced to Hercules displaying fear of a mouse. A crushing handshake brings a casual remark from Jimmy about how he didn't need his hand anyway. And when Hercules wraps some iron chains around Jimmy to demonstrate a new trick, Jimmy remarks how he thinks the chains are around the wrong chest. Jimmy's clever jokes make his predicament seem less threatening than it should. No doubt, a preference of producer Ellsworth so as not to alarm the children in the audience.

Later, Kent and Lois are in the area near Hercules' tent in search for the lost Jimmy. Kent sees him bound and gagged and tries to excuse himself. When Lois refuses to let him slip away, he fakes an accident where he drops and steps on his glasses. Lois makes one of the usual 'Clark, you're a klutz' remarks. She offers to go and get him another pair from the office.

Within seconds, Superman appears inside the tent. After a few neat tricks with barbells and heavy weights, Hercules finds himself wrapped in iron. Superman sets Jimmy free.

Superman leaves Jimmy to confront the disabled strongman. A cute gag by *Jack Larson* has Jimmy give in to his prankster temptations. He pulls a hair from Hercules' beard and grins as he walks out of the tent.

Kent soon reappears in time to greet Jimmy at the tent. Jimmy tells about how he saw the legs in Rollo's tent before his unfortunate introduction to Hercules. Crackers overhears this conversation and quickly assumes the position on the floor behind the trunk. When Kent and Jimmy enter, he acts as if he were just waking up from a sleep. He tells them that Crackers knocked him out and got away with his payroll money. He tells them not to worry about it now, the show must go on.

The telethon is in full progress with Kent acting as the Master of Ceremonies. He introduces the **MAGICIAN** (*Harry Mendoza*) and then moves to talk with Perry and Lois at the telephone desk.

Meanwhile, the real Rollo is desperately trying to free himself from being trapped in the trunk.

Back to the telethon. Hundreds of requests are coming in for an appearance by Superman. Kent uses his dinner break as an excuse to turn the microphone over to Lois. As Kent walks behind a screen, we see his shadow eating a sandwich. Actually, it is the **SECURITY GUARD** (*George Douglas*) that Kent has offered to relieve for a while.

When Superman appears, Lois suddenly glances over to the screen and sees what she believes is Kent, still eating his sandwich. Of course, she has forgotten this trick used by Superman in *The Human Bomb* episode.

As the telethon nears its finish, Crackers does his act as Rollo. **TIM** (*Charles Williams*), the accountant, announces to Kent and Lois that cash is coming in from all over town. After Rollo finishes his act, he pulls a gun on Lois and Kent, announcing his plan to steal the proceeds. When he escapes, Kent is about to dash after him, but he is stopped by Lois saying they should leave the heroics to the police.

Rollo has freed himself and is rushing to the television studio in costume when he sees Crackers escaping with the bag of money. He chases the crooked clown up a fire escape to the roof of a tall building. Superman appears in time to see one clown push the other before they both come falling toward the street. Superman easily catches only one of them.

When they go to see the clown who hit the ground, Crackers asks Superman how he knew which one to save? That was easy says Superman. He knew the good clown Rollo would never push anyone over the edge of the building, even a bad clown who had disappointed him. A tender moment shows Rollo shedding tears for his old friend.

The show ends at the telethon. Rollo is doing his clown routines. When Lois remarks how Superman saved the show, Perry reminds her that some of the credit belongs to Clark Kent and Rollo as well.

EPISODE 43

THE BOY WHO HATED SUPERMAN

directed by GEORGE BLAIR
written by DAVID CHANTLER

In the Metropolis juvenile court office of **JUDGE ALLEN** (*Charles Meredith*), the immediate future of a young man named **FRANKIE** (*Tyler MacDuff*) is being decided as Kent enters the room. Frankie's uncle, Duke Dillon, is a criminal and has been captured with the help of Superman. While he awaits trial, the Judge orders Frankie to accept Kent's guardianship in spite of his obvious

Roy Barcroft was a veteran actor from the serials. Westerns, adventures, and sci-fi fantasies offered him a variety of character roles as he appears above in *Ghost of Zorro (1949), Manhunt of Mystery Island (1945),* and *The Purple Monster Strikes (1945).*

hostility to the idea. Frankie also blames Kent for his uncle's capture because of his hard-hitting news stories. Kent explains to Frankie the morality lesson played out in this episode, that loyalty is a fine thing when it is not misplaced.

Later, when Frankie pays a visit to **DUKE DILLON** *(Roy Barcroft)* in jail, he tells Frankie to accept Kent's offer of shelter. Maybe with him on the inside, he could find out what kind of evidence Kent has gathered against the Duke. Then his gang could arrange for payoffs and alibis to make the case too weak to stand up in the courtroom and give Duke his freedom to escape to South America.

That evening, another leading gangster, **FIXER** *(Leonard Penn)*, is trying to teach **BABE** *(Dick Reeves)*, his bumbling assistant, how to play chess when Frankie comes to visit. He explains his plan to get the evidence Kent has against his uncle. But in case he does not succeed, he wants to buy Fixer's guarantee that his uncle can be busted out of jail at the last minute. Frankie learns he needs more money to pay Fixer's price.

The next day, the opportunity to raise some ready cash presents itself when Frankie is in Kent's office. Lois walks in to get a cash voucher signed by Kent so she can pay for some television sets being donated to the Children's Hospital. When no one is looking, Frankie steals a voucher and slips it into his pocket.

That evening, Frankie is having dinner with Kent and Jimmy. When Kent excuses himself to go back to work at the office, Frankie takes the opportunity to tempt Jimmy into becoming a gangster in training. An expensive sports jacket and some cash as a gift from Frankie gives Jimmy something to think about.

Late that night, in Kent's apartment, Jimmy is asleep while Frankie searches the apartment for a key to Kent's confidential file cabinet. He locates the evidence on his uncle and telephones Fixer to come and pick it up. Frankie fakes being asleep when Kent returns quietly and moves into the next room. But the key to the file cabinet lying on the floor gives him away. With x-ray vision, Kent watches Frankie toss the evidence file folder out the window.

Kent makes a switch to Superman and leaps out the window. A nice special effects shot shows Superman flying over Metropolis.

Babe arrives to deliver the evidence to Fixer. Superman comes crashing through the window. "A little late for you to be up reading, isn't it?" asks Superman.

When Fixer tosses the file into the fireplace, Superman quickly blows the fire out and recovers the evidence. Fixer reminds Superman that he can do nothing to them because they found the file folder laying on the sidewalk. He asks Superman to open the door before making his exit.

The next day, Perry and Kent discuss Jimmy's recent behavior and Kent decides to question him about it. Jimmy confesses he was a little tempted by Frankie's stories of wealth and power as a gangster, but he soon realized Frankie was up to something. Jimmy decided to play along in order to find out what was going on.

Meanwhile, Frankie has been listening to Jimmy's confession from out in the hallway. When they meet up later, Frankie tells Jimmy to get lost. But Babe arrives to take Frankie for a ride, and Jimmy insists on going along.

They soon stop in an alley where Babe demands to have Frankie give him the money he is owed by Duke. Frankie refuses, claiming that he needs the money to give Fixer for Duke's release. Babe decides to set Frankie straight on his Uncle Duke by telling him how he was used by his uncle. The final proof is when Frankie sees

that Duke has only purchased one airline ticket for the escape to South America.

In a team effort, Jimmy and Frankie escape from Duke and return to Kent's apartment. Lois and Perry are waiting as Kent brings in a flaming cake to celebrate Frankie's birthday. He is deeply moved by this show of friendship and telephones Fixer to call off the jail break. Kent listens in with his super hearing to learn of the escape plan. When the lights go out to make a wish over the birthday cake candles, he slips away to become Superman.

Another special effects shot has Superman flying over the night lights of Metropolis. He lands in an alley just in time to prevent Duke from escaping up through a manhole by positioning a car conveniently parked nearby.

Kent returns to the party in time to ask Frankie how it feels to be a year older? He confesses to feeling wonderful and that he no longer hates Superman.

"He'll be happy to know that," says Kent as he shakes Frankie's hand. "Very happy indeed."

EPISODE 44

SEMI-PRIVATE EYE

directed by GEORGE BLAIR
written by DAVID CHANTLER

A spectacular sequence opens this episode as Superman streaks across the skyline of Metropolis just in time to prevent a shower of bricks from killing a man on the sidewalk. The man is **HOMER GARRITY** (*Elisha Cook, Jr*) and the bricks are from a chimney shoved off the top of a building by a hired assassin. The sequence continues with Superman tossing the bricks back up to reconstruct the chimney at super speed by means of a reverse photography effect.

Shortly thereafter, Perry is telling the story to Lois and Jimmy when Kent enters to claim he was an eyewitness. Perry is shocked to hear that he actually had a reporter at the scene of a breaking story for a change.

"Maybe he was nearer than you think, Chief," says Lois suspiciously.

Jimmy accompanies Lois to Homer Garrity's office to get an interview. Lois tells Garrity she wants him to follow Clark Kent for reasons she does not wish to disclose. Garrity says he will be free in the evening because he is just now completing his investigation of a blackmail case. Jimmy is disappointed to learn how dull a private investigator's life can be as Garrity explains that he will not even take part in the arrest of the blackmailer. Garrity also tells Jimmy he has never found it necessary to carry a gun in all his experiences.

To satisfy some of Jimmy's interest in how he works, Garrity leads him into the next room and demonstrates how he can watch his clients in the outer office through a one way window. When Garrity goes back out to talk with Lois, Jimmy watches the arrival of **CAPPY LEONARD** *(Richard Benedict)* and **NOODLES** *(Douglas Henderson)*. After seeing Garrity and Lois led away at gunpoint, Jimmy gets a telephone call from a pool hall proprietor named **MURRAY** *(Alfred Linder)* as a warning meant to tell Garrity that he is in danger.

Jimmy decides to assume the identity of a private eye to do his own investigation. He suits up in Garrity's trench coat and hat. During his parody narration in true Philip Marlow style, he decides not to take the gun because he might accidently shoot himself.

Jack Larson shines in this episode favored by many fans because of his sincerely charming rendition of the classic Bogart detectives from the great 40s films. When Larson playfully slips out of character a few times, you cannot help but conclude that he was having the time of his life.

Next, Jimmy enters the pool hall acting like a stiff shouldered tough guy. He soon gets the attention of Morrie and **FINGERS** *(Paul Fix)*. They exchange dialog with Jimmy who claims to be a shamus looking for Homer Garrity.

Jimmy follows Fingers to his apartment and catches him telephoning Cappy Leonard about Garrity. Jimmy attempts to force a confession out of Fingers with his tough guy impersonation, but he instead manages to get himself handcuffed to the steel frame of the bed. After pulling the telephone cord from the wall, Fingers leaves the room laughing. Jimmy is left alone to blame himself for being such a jerk.

Kent enters Perry's office to find out about a police report of a kidnapping. The victims are Lois Lane and Homer Garrity. When Kent goes to Garrity's office to investigate, he discovers a secret tape recorder that had been triggered by Garrity. Kent hears first hand about the kidnapping and also is quite amused at Jimmy's comic detective narration.

Meanwhile, Cappy is trying to force Garrity to turn over the blackmail evidence with threats. Lois encourages him to hang tough and not give in to Cappy Leonard. Fingers arrives and reports some nosey kid playing detective is on to something. Cappy tells Noodles to lock up Lois and Garrity in the celler.

Jimmy has managed to get free from the bed frame and arrives at the hideout pretending to have a gun in his trenchcoat.

"Alright you guys, back against the wall," Jimmy drawls. "I got an itchy trigger on this finger. . ."

Jimmy steps into position and soon falls into a trap when a door in the floor beneath him opens up and he finds himself caught with Lois and Garrity.

Superman arrives at Morrie's pool hall and confronts the informer. After Superman crushes a few billiard balls, Morrie decides to spill the location of Cappy's hideout.

When Garrity once again refuses to reveal the blackmail evidence, Cappy and Noodles fill the room with poison gas. Superman arrives in the nick of time to inhale the gas and save the captives. As the thugs try to escape, Garrity and Jimmy use judo to flip them both on the floor as Superman carries Lois out of the room to safety.

When Jimmy is about to tell Superman how all this got started, Lois speaks up and tells Jimmy not to say anything. She does not care to expose her suspicions of Clark Kent being Superman just yet for fear of embarrassment. The show ends on a comical note as Jimmy once again manages to accidently handcuff himself to the arm of a chair.

This show definitely ranks as one of the best of the series. It has a believable story with just the right blend of humor and danger. Certainly, the better stories unfolded when our heroes accidently stumble into the plot rather than when they are purposely pulled into the villains' schemes. You will also note that although the role of Fingers was played by *Paul Fix* from episode 22 and the "Rifleman" series, he is billed in the closing credits as Peter Fix. Perhaps another of his screen names or possibly a mistake by the credit writers.

EPISODE 45

PERRY WHITE'S SCOOP

directed by GEORGE BLAIR
written by ROY HAMILTON

Borrowing from an illustrated story called "The Deep-Sea Diver Mystery" as it appeared in *Batman #83*, this adventure begins when a man dressed in a deep sea diving suit is shot in front of the Daily Planet building. As the injured **DIVER** *(Tom Monroe)* lies on the emergency table, the series regulars are gathered around to hear the man utter his dying word, "Quincy."

Later, when Jimmy rushes into Perry's office, we learn that the clever editor has a plan to crack the case. Perry explains to young Olsen how the story of the murdered diver has been written in the newspaper in an attempt to flush the killer or killers out in the open.

"Here's the early edition, Chief. Hot off the press," says Jimmy as he hands the newspaper to Perry. "It's got your story in it. But, Mr. White, sir, I don't get it?"

"You don't get what!" barks the gruff editor. "It's written in clear, concise, newspaper style. Any idiot could understand it!"

Jimmy points out the text, "This part right here." Jimmy proceeds to quote the story, "The man in the diving suit before his death made startling and important disclosures to Perry White, editor of the Daily Planet."

"Well?" says Perry.

"Well, did he?" asks Jimmy

"He said Quincy," replies Perry.

Jimmy frowns. "That's a startling and important disclosure?"

"In itself? No," explains Perry. "But the killer or killers don't know what the poor devil said. All they know is what they read in the paper. And I write the paper!"

"Then it's a deliberate fake!" exclaims Jimmy.

"Certainly. The killers are probably worried

sick right now about how much I know. That's what will make them come to us."

Here Jimmy learns an interesting lesson in newspaper procedure which he later puts to use himself in a future episode called *Jimmy Olsen, Boy Editor* and gets himself into lots of trouble. But that's another story.

To add more cheese to the trap, Perry and Jimmy rent a diving suit. They are observed by several people including **MAX** *(Jan Arvan)* who later reports to **MARIA** *(Bibs Borman)*. Max insists they knock off the nosey editor before he goes to the police. Maria keeps a cool head, however, and decides the editor should be followed carefully to see if what he knows will lead them to the secret before their competitors find out.

Meanwhile, **BINGHAM** *(Robert Wilke)* reports to his boss, **LYNCH** *(Steve Pendleton)* about the editor and his new diving suit. He tells Lynch how Max is also hot on the trail. Lynch concludes that Perry is the key to the puzzle.

Back at the office, Jimmy is trying to help Perry get into the diving suit when Kent enters the room. He uses his super strength to bend the hard helmet out of shape so it won't fit over Perry's head. He then volunteers to take the suit and have it refitted.

Next, we see a man in a diving suit walking out the front entrance of the Daily Planet. A gunman takes a few shots at the diver from a passing automobile. The diver removes his helmet to reveal he is Superman and quickly apprehends the assailant.

After they discover the gunman knows nothing, the reporters decide to investigate based on the secret word uttered by the murdered diver. Believing Quincy to be a telephone exchange, they locate a gym in that area as being the only possible place to have a quantity of water large enough to support a diver. There is a water tank above the building that houses the Quincy Athletic Club which proves to have a swimming pool.

Kent and Perry dress up in sweat suits pretending to seek a workout at the gym where they are greeted by Bingham, the supervisor. They are soon caught snooping around and forced at gunpoint to get into two weight reducing steam cabinets.

Faced with certain death, Perry finally admits

to knowing nothing. Lynch and Bingham turn up the steam and rush off to follow Max and Maria. Perry passes out from the steam and Kent quickly breaks free to save him.

On the rooftop, they have recruited Jimmy to climb into the almost empty water tank where he finds only a goldfish with a coded message attached to it. Kent quickly decodes it as a railroad car number 763792 (nice work). Perry sends Kent back to the office to file the story with orders to meet him and Olsen at the railyard.

Perry and Jimmy locate the railroad car and find a few cases of rolled paper. The four crooks arrive to point out the paper is specially equipped with silk threads for printing counterfeit money. The mystery is solved, but it seems too late for Perry and Jimmy. After removing the paper, Lynch and Bingham lock up Maria and Max with the reporters and leave them to burn up in a railroad car fire.

Kent and Lois arrive in time for Kent to switch to Superman. He saves the captives and rounds up the escaping crooks. Before the final fade out, Perry asks Superman not to tell Kent how he needed his help to get the story.

"Don't worry, Mr. White," says Superman with a smile. "He'll never learn about it from me."

EPISODE 46

BEWARE THE WRECKER

directed by GEORGE BLAIR
written by ROYAL COLE

There are some nice action sequences in this episode, which is actually a slightly reworked version of *Crime Wave* from the first season. A series of destructive incidents involving the major transportation systems is being blamed on a villain known to the media as the Wrecker. As in *Crime Wave,* we finally discover the leader of the terrorist operation is in fact a highly respected leader of the community. His motivation is revealed to be greed that he is satisfying by collecting on inflated insurance policies.

The episode begins with a narration over the opening title shot of the Metropolis skyline. "It all began about a year ago. . . Metropolis murmured with the usual hum of activity as the wheels of industry turned. . . breathing life into the city. . ."

As stock footage shows some airport activity, the narration continues.

"Shortly before noon at the city airport, the *Silver Star* was taking off on its regular run to span the continent. The plane had already passed the city's outskirts and was gaining altitude— when it happened!"

A streak of light strikes the airliner in mid-air and an explosion fills the sky. Editor Perry White then receives a telephone call demanding $100,000 from the city, or the Crane Steamship Lines will be next on the list of destruction perpetrated by *the Wrecker.*

Perry immediately warns the steamship company and a full scale search of the harbor is set in motion in hopes of finding any hidden explosive devices. But as the S. S. Colossus steams out of the harbor, it explodes without warning.

Another similar telephone call precedes the destruction of the transcontinental express train. Inspector Henderson arranges for a private meeting in Perry White's office.

Present at the meeting are representatives of the three transportation industries. **MR. CRANE** (William Forrest) represents the steamship companies, **MR. KILGORE** (Pierre Watkin) speaks for the airlines, and **MR. MORGAN** (Tom Powers) sits in for the railroad. Henderson has called the meeting to review the situation. When asked if they should give in to the demands of the Wrecker, Henderson responds, "You don't starve a blackmailer by feeding him."

"And you don't run a railroad by permitting its destruction," replies the Railroad Director.

"Or a steamship line," adds Crane.

When quizzed about the telephone calls, Perry reveals an important clue. He has been trying to identify a strange sound always heard in the background, a repeated thumping noise followed by the clanging sound of a bell. Kent suggests the anonymous caller is using a portable telephone hookup because the police have had no success in tracing the threats.

Almost on cue, Crane receives a call from the Wrecker. As Henderson listens in with Crane,

Kent and Lois listen in on the extension. The next target will be a luxury liner due to set sail from pier 19 this afternoon. Henderson arranges for full police coverage and Perry issues a newspaper notice to alert Superman.

At the pier, watch for the sign announcing the departure of the SS Beauchamp, most likely named for this season's production manager.

When they all gather at the dock, Kent slips away to become Superman. He hears and then gets sight of an approaching model airplane, apparently operated by radio control, and he quickly leaps into the sky to retrieve it.

Henderson and the newspaper people review the new finding made by Superman. Another call comes in from the Wrecker. He now threatens to destroy a dozen targets at one time if his demands are not met immediately.

Even Superman cannot be in more than one place at a time. This, of course, is long before Superman met Professor LaCerne in the *Divide and Conquer* episode.

Henderson finally agrees it's time to pay the money. The scheduled drop point is a tree stump in the city park. Of course, Henderson arranges full police coverage again, and the payoff package is nothing but blank strips of paper. The Wrecker succeeds in recovering the payoff while no one is watching by coming up from the ground sewer through the hollow tree stump.

Lois and Jimmy are disappointed because they missed a chance to capture the Wrecker. Kent, however, has another idea. He takes the two reporters to a carnival in an outward attempt to cheer them up.

What actually unfolds is a clever scene designed by Kent to let Jimmy and Lois come up with the key lead to the Wrecker's hideout.

"Ring the bell and win the Superman medal of merit!" cries the *CARNIVAL BARKER* (Renny McEvoy) in attempt to lure patrons to his game.

The game is smash the hammer down on the lever, propell the ball up a shaft and ring a bell.

After watching one man succeed in ringing the

Sanders *(Murray Alper)* wants to know why Kent is snooping around the docks.

bell, Lois and Jimmy convince Kent to take a shot and give it his best try. He smiles, picks up the hammer, and with one hefty swing, he knocks the bell clean off the top of the shaft.

"Golly, Mr. Kent," says Jimmy. "You wrecked the whole thing."

"I'm very sorry," Kent apologizes. "I'll be more than willing to pay for any damages."

"I don't want any pay," says the Barker in amazement. "I just want to know how you did it?"

"I guess sometimes I just don't know my own strength," says Kent sheepishly as he leads Jimmy and Lois away from the gathering crowd.

Amazingly enough, they never even consider the true meaning of what they just witnessed. Instead, Lois makes a rather comical remark about Kent having enough fun. He quickly redirects their attention to the sounds they have just heard. Lois finally relates the thudding and bell ringing to the sounds heard in the background of the Wrecker's telephone conversations.

After splitting up into territories for a search of the carnival, Lois and Jimmy discover a little house on the edge of the grounds. Here, they catch up with an explosives expert named *EMIL HATCH* (*Denver Pyle*) as he is unwrapping the payoff package retrieved from the city park. They manage to tie him up, but when they return a short time later with Kent, they find Hatch has been murdered.

In the final scene, Henderson shows up at Perry's office by an invitation from Superman. With him are the three transportation leaders. Superman arrives within seconds with a promise to unmask the Wrecker. When Jimmy flies a model airplane into the office via radio control, Crane makes a run for the door exposing himself as the mastermind behind the extortion scheme.

When Perry complains that Kent has been away far too long, Superman replies in his defense.

"Oh, I think he's around somewhere, Sir."

The writer of this episode, *Royal Cole,* brought with him some previous experience in the action-adventure genre. He was a co-writer on the first Superman serial for Columbia in 1948. He also worked with *William Lively* and *Sol Shor* on a serial for Republic Studios called *King of the*

Rocket Men, which starred Tris Coffin as the title character.

EPISODE 47

THE GOLDEN VULTURE
directed by TOMMY CARR
written by JACKSON GILLIS

This episode demonstrates how the perfect blend of creative elements can produce a very entertaining experience on such a low production budget. A solid story, excellent direction, and great performances by all involved make *The Golden Vulture* a classic example of the series.

The adventure begins aboard a salvage ship with a very stern *CAPTAIN MACBAIN* (*Peter Whitney*) verbally abusing one of his mates, a man named *SCURVY* (*Vic Perrin*). It is easy to see there is no love lost between these two seamen, and the mystery continues when Scurvy quickly scratches out a note, puts it in a bottle and drops it overboard.

Soon, we see Jimmy Olsen by the seaside fishing off the breakwater. After his attention is drawn to the bottle floating in the morning tide, he wades out to retrieve it and then returns to the Daily Planet.

When Jimmy brings the bottle to show all at Perry's office, they quickly discover the writing on the note has washed away. The paper does, however, bear the almost invisible identification of a certain ship which has just docked in the Metropolis harbor, the Golden Vulture.

Lois and Jimmy decide to investigate by paying a visit to the ship. They meet Captain MacBain and are initially treated as welcome guests, that is, right after the first officer, *BENNET* (*Robert Bice*), stages a fake accident where he ends up stepping on and destroying Jimmy's camera.

In MacBain's cabin, he treats the visiting reporters to a display of recovered treasure, presumably fresh in from the Caribbean. When Scurvy enters to offer refreshments, he is caught trying to pass Jimmy a warning note. Now the Captain has no other choice but to keep the two reporters prisoner until he can figure out a way to properly dispose of them. Jimmy takes his best

Captain McBain *(Peter Whitney)* confronts Superman aboard the "Golden Vulture" salvage ship.

shot at intimidating the pirate by warning him that his mother will soon begin to worry if he isn't allowed to go home.

Meanwhile, Kent becomes concerned when the two reporters fail to return. He goes to the docks to take a look around. Here he meets up with a man named **SANDERS** *(Murray Alper)* supervising a shipment being prepared for the salvage vessel. When Kent accidently bumps into a **DOCK WORKER** *(Wes Hudman)* carrying a crate, he quickly takes a peak with his x-ray vision. He discovers the crates actually contain jewelry in spite of Sanders' claim it is food and supplies bound for the Golden Vulture.

Great second season background music as Kent snoops around the warehouse creates an authentic mood of impending danger. Kent changes into Superman and executes a great running liftoff from the cargo pier to pay a quiet visit to the ship. Upon his arrival on deck, he ducks out of sight and changes back to Clark Kent. He soon meets up with Scurvy who has been locked up in the brig. He explains how MacBain uses the scavenger ship as a front for an

operation where stolen jewelry is refashioned into phoney pirate treasure and sold to museums and collectors as the real thing.

After taking a quick look around, Kent again meets up with Sanders who has just arrived by motor boat. Approaching him from behind, Kent uses his pointed finger to make Sanders believe he has a gun in order to get some information.

After Bennet attempts to render Kent unconscious, the reporter manages to get chased around the deck by several menacing shiphands *(Saul Gorss, Carl Saxe, Dan Turner, William Vincent)*. Kent puts up a very good fight, but as he is about to slip away to change into his action suit, Jimmy and Lois block his escape.

With all the nosey reporters closing in on him, Captain MacBain decides to exercise his right as a pirate and force the intruders to walk the plank. Kent is the first one up and the other two are unwilling witnesses to what will soon be their fate as Kent is pushed into the dark ocean at the point of a sword. Within seconds, Superman appears from the sky and takes what seems like an eternity to poor Lois to clean up the phoney treasure peddlers. MacBain refuses to admit defeat until he sees his sword bend easily against Superman's chest. Then Superman takes an eternity to secure the crooks for the authorities. Lois finally convinces Superman to dive in and save Clark Kent who is hopefully still holding his breath.

"But I'm finished here," Superman warns. "I won't be back."

"I don't care," Lois pleads. "Just save Clark."

Superman dives into the harbor while Lois and Jimmy anxiously wait to see if Mr. Kent has held his breath long enough.

When the soaked reporter finally reaches the surface, Lois hurriedly kneels to extend a helping hand.

"Clark, are you alright?" Lois begs. "Superman waited so long and. . ."

"Yeeees?" Clark asks.

"And you appeared right after he disappeared," Lois continues until Clark pulls her down into the water.

"What did you say you were thinking, Lois?" Clark asks innocently.

"Nevermind," she replies as she thrashes water next to the world's biggest clutz. "It couldn't be. It just couldn't be."

Music up and fade out.

"*Yo-ho-ho and a bottle o' rum.*" An all-around good show.

EPISODE 48

JIMMY OLSEN, BOY EDITOR

directed by TOMMY CARR
written by DAVID CHANTLER

In an opening narration by *Tris Coffin*, over a montage of scenes showing Perry White having a sleepless night, we learn the city of Metropolis is celebrating its annual Youth Day. When Perry arrives for work in the morning to find a **CUSTODIAN** (*Jack Pepper*) removing the editor's name plate from his office door, Superman reminds him that this is the day when key positions in the government and the media are temporarily handed to selected juniors. Perry

White reluctantly agrees to turn over his duties to Jimmy Olsen, Boy Editor.

Jimmy's first order of business is to stretch his newly acquired power of the press by releasing a false story. He claims to be in possession of evidence that will conclusively prove an underworld character named **LEGS LEEMY** (*Herburt Vigran*) was responsible for a two million dollar armed robbery which took place exactly seven years ago tomorrow. The story is designed to bring the hoodlum and his gang out of hiding into the hands of the police.

At the gangster hideout, a **HENCHMAN** (*Keith Richards*) brings Jimmy's story to the attention of Legs himself. Angered by the idea of being brought down with less than a day to go before the statute of limitations runs out, Legs and the gang decide to storm the newspaper office.

Kent returns to his office to find Perry White attempting to balance a pencil on his nose to help fight the boredom of his temporary duties as office boy. Kent goes to Perry's office where Jimmy is manning the editor's desk. Here, Kent cleverly activates the intercom so he and Perry can listen in from Kent's office.

Within moments of Kent's return to his own office, Legs and his two thugs enter Perry's office and hold Jimmy and Lois as hostages for the duration. Perry and Kent listen in on the event over the intercom. Lois manages to sweet talk **TOOTS** (*Dick Rich*) into handing her his machine gun. She quickly empties the gun into the ceiling, but as she and Jimmy attempt to exit the office, Legs pulls out a handgun and orders the two newspeople to take a seat.

Most of the balance of the episode is a waiting game. Kent finally senses the event has gone on far too long. He changes into Superman, flies to Mercy Hospital, and has a quick meeting with the **HOSPITAL DIRECTOR** (*Anthony Hughes*). Superman borrows a can of a new experimental knockout gas and quickly returns to the Daily Planet. From the basement, Superman directs some of the gas up the air shaft to put everyone in Perry's office asleep.

Kent returns to his office where Perry is listening to the intercom. The only noise coming from the other end is snoring. Now is the time for Kent and Perry to storm the office.

Kent helps Lois, and Perry assists the young

editor over to the window for some fresh air while Legs and his gang lie asleep on the floor. Perry hangs Jimmy's head out the window and says to Kent, "I'm surely tempted to do something I'd probably never regret."

Jimmy wakes up to say, "What happened?"

"That's what we'd like to know!" insists Perry. "Whatever made you all go to sleep?"

"It was merely the power of suggestion," says Jimmy with a smile. "I knew if they saw me yawning and falling asleep, their subconscious libido would force a chain reaction into the cerebellum inducing involuntary slumber."

Within moments, the **JUNIOR MAYOR** *(Ronald Hargrave)* and the **JUNIOR POLICE CHIEF** *(Bob Crosson)* arrive to make the very important arrest of Legs Leemy and his gang. All Perry wants to do now is go home, go to sleep, and hopefully wake up to find this whole episode was a dream.

Comic book collectors may enjoy comparing this episode with the illustrated story called "Jimmy Olsen, Editor" as it appeared in the comic magazine *Superman #86*.

EPISODE 49

LADY IN BLACK

directed by TOMMY CARR
written by JACKSON GILLIS

Great background music sets the mysterious mood in this episode. Clark Kent is working late at the office when his typing is interrupted by a telephone call from Jimmy Olsen.

Jimmy is sitting on the couch of old Mrs. Jones' apartment that he is occupying while his mother is off visiting relatives in Michigan. With all this small talk, Jimmy finally confesses that he's been hearing strange noises and quickly rattles off *360 Appletree Lane* as the address hoping Kent will do him the courtesy of a visit. Kent is amused, and after Jimmy tells him of the hot dogs, ice cream, and pickles he's been eating and the mystery novel he's been reading, Kent assures him that he is only suffering from indigestion of the imagination. Kent follows with advice to get a good night's rest and hangs up.

Jimmy begins to pace back and forth when he notices the abstract painting of one large eyeball

hanging from the living room wall. Then he hears more noises from below the floor. Across the hallway, the door is open to the apartment of **MR. FRANK** *(Frank Ferguson)*, the building manager. Jimmy asks about the noises and Mr. Frank suggests he is only hearing old steam pipes. When Mr. Frank agrees to go investigate the basement, Jimmy quickly follows after him and slams into something in the dark.

Later, Kent tries to telephone Jimmy. When he gets no answer, he rushes to the store room, switches to Superman and leaps out of his favorite window. An impressive flying shot over the city at night brings Superman to a landing through the open window of Mrs. Jones' apartment. He finds Mr. Frank tending to Jimmy's bump on the head that he apparently received from a low ceiling beam in the basement. Jimmy swears he heard noises. Mr. Frank assures him that they must have come from the cat chasing mice.

Superman accepts the explanation that Jimmy is suffering from an overdose of hot dogs and reckless cats, and then he jumps out the window. Mr. Frank also makes an exit, and Jimmy is left alone with a painting on the wall that now has *two* eyeballs.

The next morning, Jimmy seems to be in a more stable mood and admits to himself that he must have been imagining things the night before. He picks up the mystery book, *"The Lady in Black,"* smiles and shakes his head, and then tosses the novel into the trash can on his way out as a gesture to reality.

But out on the sidewalk, things again take a turn for the weird. Jimmy is confronted by **SCARFACE** *(John Doucette)*, who inquires about the address of his apartment building and then insists that Jimmy remain quiet about ever meeting him. On the corner, Jimmy meets **GLASSES** *(Rudolph Anders)*, who in turn has a cryptic discussion with a mysterious Lady wearing a black veil over her face.

The Lady in Black inquires about an address and then becomes very nervous when Jimmy tells her about the man with the scar. She quickly forces him back into the apartment building to hide, begs him to hold her package safe until she can return, and then rushes out the back door. When the package falls apart in Jimmy's hands and spills bundles of cash on the hallway floor, he goes running after her but is greeted by a dagger sticking in the door frame.

Jimmy rushes into his apartment and quickly telephones Kent to tell him the story when the phone goes dead. Jimmy goes back into the hallway, sees the money is gone and Mr. Frank apparently lying dead on the floor. Jimmy rushes out to the sidewalk to summon a **POLICE OFFICER** *(Mike Ragan)*.

Superman flies once again to the apartment building, finds Mr. Frank very much alive. Superman apologizes to the police officer and then explains to Jimmy that he is letting his imagination get the best of him. When **MRS. FRANK** *(Virginia Christine)* enters with a bag of groceries and produces a rubber knife she found stuck in the screen door by some crazy kids, Jimmy confesses that he cannot understand why all this is happening to him in broad daylight. Superman would love to stay and lecture Jimmy on the evils of practical joking, but he must get back to the office, that is, to help Mr. Kent with some work.

After Superman and Jimmy exit, Mr. and Mrs. Frank expose the story. They and their two henchmen have knocked a hole in the basement wall to an adjoining art gallery warehouse and are slowly replacing original paintings with fakes. This charade has been set up to destroy Jimmy's credibility, especially to Superman, to insure they will be able to continue undisturbed.

Later that evening, Jimmy is troubled with more noises. Then Kent receives another phone call from 'nervous Olsen' but this time his super hearing picks up on voices coming from the basement. Within seconds, Kent is gone.

Superman appears at the art gallery, tears the door off the vault and finds the two thugs *(John Doucette and Rudolph Anders)* trying to escape. Superman crashes through the wall and knocks them out.

Back in the apartment, Jimmy's nightmare has returned as the Lady in Black. Meanwhile, Superman comes up from the basement into a shower of bullets from Mr. Frank's gun. As he backs away from the advancing Man of Steel, Mr. Frank trips and knocks himself out cold. When Superman enters Jimmy's apartment, he explains that this has all been a trick to keep him from

being a threat to the scheme. With a rush of wind from Superman's lungs, the veil is blown away to reveal the Lady in Black to be Mrs. Frank.

As he escorts the lady out to meet the police, Superman pulls the mystery novel out of the waste basket and gives it to Jimmy. When he rushes back to the phone to ask if Mr. Kent could hear what was going on, Superman replies with a smile, "sure he did, Jimmy," and then turns to wink at the camera as the final fade out ends the show.

This episode might have been inspired by a similar situation experienced by Batman's youthful ward in a story called "Dick Grayson's Nightmare" as it appeared in the comic book pages of *Batman #80*.

EPISODE 50

STAR OF FATE

directed by TOMMY CARR
written by ROY HAMILTON

This episode opens with a close-up shot of an ancient Egyptian jewelry box which is wrapped in lead foil and sitting on a table. As the camera pulls back to a full shot, we see Lois and Kent standing by as **AHMED** *(Ted Hecht)* explains the last wishes of his master and owner of the artifact. The box is to be auctioned off to the highest bid from one of two old acquaintances. **DR. BARNACK** *(Lawrence Ryle)* is an egyptologist, and **MR. WHITLOCK** *(Paul Burns)* is the owner of a local curio shop.

Ahmed claims to know nothing of the contents of the box. Barnak is convinced it contains something of great value. Whitlock is concerned about the dangerous curse attached to the box.

Lois and Kent sit nearby as the bidding proceeds. Kent explains that even Superman would not know what is in the box because of its lead foil wrapping.

The mystery begins.

When Kent leaves the room to go run a check on the two serious bidders, Lois catches a glimpse from the wall mirror as Barnak points a gun at Whitlock's back. The bidding comes to a conclusion, and Barnak exits with the treasure.

Whitlock chases Barnak into the hallway and begs him not to open the box. He warns that it is evil and carries with it an ancient curse. Barnak pushes Whitlock aside and makes a hasty departure with his secretary, **ALMA** *(Jeanne Dean)*.

Barnak and Alma return to his home and quickly remove the lead foil to reveal the ancient jewelry box. Alma is curious to see what is inside, but Barnak decides to do some more research just in case there is some validity to Whitlock's claim regarding an ancient curse.

As soon as Barnak is gone, in spite of his warning, Alma opens the box. After she smiles upon seeing the large sapphire, she begins to clutch her throat. Within seconds, she is unconscious on the floor.

A short time later, Jimmy and Lois arrive to get a story from Barnak, but instead discover that Alma is barely alive. When Barnak returns, everyone realizes the box is gone. Barnak phones Whitlock to learn that he has taken the box.

At the curio shop, Whitlock is reviewing some ancient hieroglyphics with his assistant, **MARCH** *(Tony De Mario)*. Once again, the curse is soon tested by March as he sneaks a peek at the inside of the jewelry box and quickly falls to the floor unconscious.

Barnak sneaks up on Whitlock and forces him to close the curio shop before Kent and Lois have a chance to enter. As Barnak hides behind a curtain with a gun pointed at Whitlock, Lois and Kent are knocking on the door and watching from the window. While out of Barnak's sight, Whitlock puts on a small rescue performance with a Superman puppet he happens to have on a nearby shelf. Kent and Lois smile and walk away thinking Whitlock is just an eccentric artist who wishes to be left alone.

After the reporters are on their way, Barnak gags Whitlock and ties him up before moving toward the safe with a small bottle of nitroglycerin. When he discovers the safe to be unlocked, he sets the explosive bottle on the little shelf of the nearby cuckoo clock. Barnak then helps himself to the treasured box and several thousand dollars worth of jewelry before making his exit.

Meanwhile, Kent has fortunately realized the meaning of Whitlock's little puppet show. He makes a change into Superman and arrives at the

curio shop just in time to save Whitlock from the falling bottle of nitroglycerin as the cuckoo clock strikes the hour. Whitlock then happily informs Superman that Barnak has only escaped with a fake version of the ancient box.

With March and Alma under observation at Mercy Hospital, **DR. WILSON** *(Arthur Space)* explains that nothing is known about the strange effects of opening the ancient box. All he can report is the victims are in some unknown state of suspended animation, and they may only live for a few more hours if an antidote is not found.

Lois has been sitting quietly nearby with Kent. She finally voices her impatient opinion.

"It's ridiculous to believe such a superstition!"

Lois quickly moves to the box on the desk and opens it before anyone has a chance to stop her. As she faints, Kent catches her before she hits the ground and helps her over to a couch. While all attention is on Lois, Kent opens the box and discovers a needle hidden in the lock spring which injects a strong poison into the victim's finger. When the sapphire setting in a carved leaf is removed from the box, Whitlock interprets the hieroglyphics to reveal the legendary pyramid plant as the only antidote to the poison. Kent excuses himself so he may return to the office and attempt to contact Superman.

"I wonder," says Dr. Wilson. "Kent opened this box, too. Yet he didn't succumb to the poison. Why?"

"It is strange," replies Perry. "I'll have to ask him about that."

Meanwhile, Kent switches to Superman outside Dr. Wilson's office. If you watch carefully, you will notice his chest insignia is backward as Superman leaps out the hallway window.

Superman flies to Egypt, lifts the corner of the Great Pyramid, retrieves a few trimmings of the legendary pyramid plant, and returns to Mercy Hospital. The leaves are processed into an antidote to save Lois from an eternal coma.

Jimmy has taken it upon himself to go after Barnak. Superman intercedes in time to save the young reporter from Barnak's gunfire.

The final scene shows Lois recovering in a hospital room. As Perry and Jimmy stand nearby, she expresses her curiosity about how Kent managed to escape the effect of what Dr. Wilson claimed to be a very dangerous poison. When

Kent enters the room, they all discover he is wearing an adhesive bandage on his thumb. Jimmy proposes that to be the likely reason why Kent was not injected by the poison needle.

"I don't know," says Lois. "I'm pretty confused."

"So am I," replies Kent with a sigh. "So am I."

This episode shares its title with an illustrated story that appears on the comic book pages of *Superboy #34.*

EPISODE 51

THE WHISTLING BIRD

directed by TOMMY CARR
written by DAVID CHANTLER

Clark Kent is asleep at his desk as we begin the story. He wakes up somewhat embarrassed as Jimmy arrives to introduce **NANCY QUINN** *(Allene Roberts),* the niece of Professor Oscar Quinn. We already know Uncle Oscar as the eccentric inventor of Mr. Kelso, who appeared in *The Machine That Could Plot Crimes* episode. Nancy reports that her Uncle has been working on a hydro-molecular experiment and is now ready to test the results. Kent and Jimmy have been invited to witness the demonstration which has been a complete secret from anyone other than *Schyler.*

Schyler is the whistling bird, Uncle Oscar's pet parakeet. When Kent and Jimmy arrive to meet **UNCLE OSCAR** *(Sterling Holloway)* at his basement laboratory, they learn how the Professor has instructed Schyler to recite a key phrase of the secret formula. The plan has proven to be good insurance because an unknown burglar arrived the previous evening and walked away with a written copy of the Professor's secret discovery. Fortunately, his work cannot be duplicated without the crucial information known only to Schyler.

The Professor finally reveals his ultimate scientific achievement, a glue for postage stamps that will be made available in six delicious flavors: beef stew, liver & onions, ham, lamb, veal, and vegetable.

"Professor, the secretaries of America will erect you a statue," proclaims Kent with a smile.

Kent is given the honor of licking the first prototype stamp. When he slams his fist down to seal the stamp to the envelope, the room explodes in a cloud of smoke. It seems the Professor has accidentally invented the most powerful explosive concentrate known to man.

Jimmy decides to commemorate this monumental occasion by taking a picture of Uncle Oscar with Kent and Nancy. It is also decided, however, that this event must be kept top secret until the proper authorities can be notified.

Later, when the photograph is developed, Kent takes note of a man and woman peeking in through the window in the background. The Security Commission of the Federal government is then notified of Uncle Oscar's important invention. The possibility of foreign spies attempting to gain possession is considered.

With his laboratory destroyed by the explosion, Uncle Oscar retreats to the city park with Schyler. Hopefully, with the help of the caged bird, he will be able to reconstruct his experiment by reviewing his notes.

When **DOROTHY MANNERS** *(Toni Carroll)* walks by the park bench a few times and drops a scented handkerchief, Uncle Oscar finally pays her some attention when Schyler lets out a whistle. He apologizes for the bird's rude behavior and invites her to sit down.

Kent arrives and introduces himself. Recognizing Dorothy as one of the people in the photograph, Kent excuses himself along with Uncle Oscar for a private conversation. He explains how Dorothy may have witnessed the private demonstration of the explosive stamp adhesive. Kent suggests Dorothy will attempt to question Oscar about his work, and that he should carefully act as if he does not suspect her espionage intentions.

When Oscar returns to the park bench, Dorothy is gone. He and Kent are both relieved to find Schyler is still safe inside his cage. Kent encourages Uncle Oscar to return to his laboratory while he returns to his office to await instructions from the Security Commission.

Back at the laboratory, Oscar realizes the bird in the cage is not Schyler. He telephones Kent to report how the birds must have been switched in the park.

Uncle Oscar's laboratory. *Jack Larson, Allene Roberts, George Reeves,* and *Sterling Holloway.* Schyler is in the cage.

Suddenly, Dorothy enters the laboratory. With her is an enemy agent called **SPECK** *(Joseph Vitale)* and a foreign **SCIENTIST** *(Otto Waldis),* and they force Uncle Oscar to hang up on Kent. Jimmy boldly warns the three uninvited visitors that Kent will undoubtedly contact Superman and they won't stand a chance. Speck is holding a gun on the group and is quite sure Uncle Oscar will cooperate by helping them outwit Superman.

Kent quickly responds to the situation by running to the storage room to make his change into Superman. When he arrives at Uncle Oscar's laboratory, he finds only Lois Lane.

"Where are the others?" asks Superman.

"What others?" replies Lois. "There's nobody else here."

Superman cannot understand how everyone managed to get away. Perhaps it was a trick and

they were never here in the first place? Lois is totally confused, but she figures Kent will gladly bring her up to date. Superman agrees and suggests she return to the office.

After Superman and Lois are gone, a wall panel opens up and everyone reappears in the laboratory. The enemy scientist compliments Uncle Oscar on the cleverly designed hiding place for doing secret experimental work behind lead shielding. Uncle Oscar is then ordered to manufacture a new batch of liquid explosive or something bad will happen to Nancy and Jimmy.

When the new explosive liquid is completed, Speck forces Oscar, Nancy, and Jimmy into the lead lined room and locks the door. The trio then escapes with most of the formula and Schyler, too.

Back at the office, a government security **AGENT**

Sterling Holloway and *George Reeves.*

(*Marshall Reed*) informs Kent and Lois that his agency is doing everything possible to identify the enemy spies. All they can do now is wait.

While locked in the laboratory, Uncle Oscar paces back and forth, trying to solve the error in is stamp adhesive formula. Jimmy notices a sprinkler head in the ceiling. Fortunately, Nancy is carrying some matches, and Jimmy reasons the sprinkler system could be used to set off a fire alarm and bring help. Uncle Oscar and Nancy lift Jimmy high enough to light a match under the sprinkler head. The water quickly begins to fill the room. Nancy and Jimmy cheer at the sound of an alarm outside.

"Well, that's very fine," says Uncle Oscar. "But no one knows this room is here."

They sadly realize the fire department will arrive, find no one, and dismiss the alarm to an accidental short circuit. The room will ultimately fill with water and the three will undoubtedly drowned.

"Oh, why was I born so clever?" says Jimmy.

A telephone call alerts Kent to a fire at Professor Quinn's house. As Lois and the Security Agent start to leave, they notice that Kent is remaining at his desk.

"There's nothing I can do now," says Kent. "And if something's already happened, there's no sense in my going in the first place."

"Old reliable Clark," sneers Lois. "I'm glad there's **one** man around here!"

Alone at last, Kent quickly changes into Superman and flies to Uncle Oscar's house. His super hearing detects the sound of running water, and he soon finds a way through the floor to the hidden room to make a rescue.

Uncle Oscar suddenly realizes his mistake in the formula. Superman rushes into the laboratory and quickly drinks down the flask of bubbling liquid before it explodes. Schyler makes a timely reappearance at the window. When the bird repeats a new word, *Eldorado*, Jimmy recognizes it as the name of a ghost town up north. Superman figures that must be the enemy hideout.

Superman catches up with the enemy agents and finds some more of the bubbling liquid. Rather than drinking it again, he recommends the three spies should leave immediately before the unstable explosive is detonated.

After the enemy agents are turned over to the authorities, Lois and Uncle Oscar return to the office to tell Kent how Superman has saved the day. When Schyler begins to call out Superman's name, Lois shakes her head.

"Until now, I thought Schyler was a pretty smart bird. But when he starts to call Clark *Superman...*"

When Schyler begins to whistle, Kent replies with a smile, "He just whistled at you, Lois. What do you think of his mind now?"

Lois smiles as the episode fades to black.

EPISODE 52

AROUND THE WORLD WITH SUPERMAN

directed by TOMMY CARR
written by JACKSON GILLIS

The title of the last regular episode photographed in black and white describes the grand prize in a Daily Planet contest sponsored for children. The script resembles an adventure called "The Girl Who Didn't Believe in Superman" that appeared in the comic book pages of *Superman #96*.

The story opens as Superman flies across Metropolis to attend a meeting in Perry White's office. After reading the winning entry, a letter submitted by Elaine Carson, he happily approves of the selection and then leaps back out the window to resume his duties as Clark Kent.

Lois and Kent arrive at the apartment building of the contest winner to verify the contestant and get an interview. They are surprised to discover

that *ELAINE CARSON* (*Kay Morley*) is a full grown adult and not qualified to have entered the contest. This is no disappointment to Elaine because she knows nothing about and wants nothing to do with them. Kent apologizes for the disturbance and waits for Elaine to disappear around the corner of the hallway.

When Kent knocks on the door of the apartment, they are greeted by a young girl, *ANN CARSON* (*Judy Ann Nugent*). They have come to announce the winner of the Daily Planet contest and Ann is very excited to hear her mother will get a trip around the world. The two reporters soon realize that Ann is blind. She entered the contest for her mother. Ann also expresses her disbelief in the existence of Superman. She insists the newspaper honor her winning entry and give her mother the world tour.

Ann goes on to explain how she was in a car accident a while ago. Her father had been driving and her life was never the same after her parents split up. Then Elaine returns and is very upset to find the two reporters have entered her apartment. When Jimmy arrives and quickly begins to take some pictures, Elaine insists they all leave immediately or she will call the police. She also threatens to sue the newspaper if they dare print any word about her in regard to the contest.

"The perfect contest! Great Caesar's Ghost!" Perry screams. "Of all the silly mixed up messes! Where's Kent?"

Lois explains in defense that Kent believes they should stick with Ann Carson as the winner. He is presently off on a visit to hopefully straighten everything out.

Perry continues his raving, "A little girl who's mother wants to sue us, who doesn't believe in Superman, who can't even see where he would take her. A poor little mixed up girl who's got everything wrong." After a brief pause for contemplation, Perry looks to Lois and Jimmy and shouts, "Well, get going! Do something about this mess!"

Kent is with *DR. ANDERSON* (*Raymond Greenleaf*) where he discovers that Ann's blindness is the result of injuries to her optic nerves. Dr. Anderson also explains that Elaine has a bad attitude because she separated from her husband. Life for her has been pretty rough. Kent

George Reeves and *Judy Anne Nugent* flying around the world.

suggests a particle of something from the accident is the cause of Ann's damaged eyesight and asks if the possibility has been checked out.

"The finest x-ray machine in the world, Mr. Kent," replies Dr. Anderson. "Unless you know of a better one than that, I'm afraid it's quite hopeless."

Kent smiles and replies, "Perhaps I do, Doctor."

Kent returns to Elaine's apartment. With Lois standing guard downstairs at the door to watch for Elaine's return, Kent visits with Ann claiming to be Superman. When Ann remarks how he

sounds a little like Mr. Kent, he assures her he is really Superman and proceeds to prove it.

Meanwhile, Lois greets Elaine who is apparently running from **MURRAY** (*Patrick Aherne*), a man she recognizes as her husband's lawyer. Elaine finally breaks down and confesses to Lois how she blamed Jim Carson for Ann's affliction and drove him away. Now she believes it is too late to try and work things out. Lois convinces her the Daily Planet will do everything to help.

When Lois and Elaine enter the apartment, instead of finding Kent, they are greeted by

Superman. Ann quickly tells how Superman has used his x-ray vision to detect a small piece of glass inside her head. Superman explains that if Dr. Anderson is allowed to operate with his guidance, Ann may have a good chance to see again.

Of course, the operation is a success, and Superman makes good on his promise to deliver the grand prize. While he flies Ann around the world, his progress is monitored by a radio **OPERATOR** *(Max Wagner)* with periodic reports announcing Superman's location. Meanwhile, the Daily Planet arranges an even better surprise. Upon her return, Ann finds her mother reunited with her **FATHER** *(James Brown)* with a promise of a much brighter future. As the three members of the happy family exchange hugs and kisses, Lois smiles and says to Superman who is leaning against the door frame, "How about that?"

After a quick double take, Superman turns and makes a swift escape as Lois shakes her head, laughing. And that ends the last episode of the greatest adventure series to travel the airwaves of 50s television. . .

Oh, wait. . . Yes. . . That's right. . . The *color* episodes.

For George Reeves' next appearance on the set of another studio and an occasional exterior location for a new series of *adventures,* he would be outfitted in a full-color costume.

But first, a word from our government. . .

STAMP DAY FOR SUPERMAN

directed by TOMMY CARR
written by DAVID CHANTLER

You will probably never see this episode on television as it is not a regular part of the syndication package. However, before the sets were repainted for the color cameras of 1954, the cast and crew got together for a production to be donated to the United States Treasury Department.

The story begins as Clark Kent is walking Lois Lane home one evening. Lois seems to be stopping at every store window, and Kent begins to wonder if they will ever get to where they are going. As they stand in front of the Metropolis jewelry store, a burglar alarm screams out to break the silence. Lois decides to run back to an all night drug store to telephone the police and get a story. Kent rushes into a nearby alley and enters the jewelry store as Superman.

Inside, Superman discovers one of the two robbers who has decided not to run. He is a first time offender and he tells Superman if only he had managed his money properly, he never would have considered a robbery to solve his financial problems. As the police arrive, Superman tells the man he is doing the right thing by turning himself in to the authorities.

Outside, Kent returns a few moments later to hear Lois tell how she already filed the story. In fact, she thinks the other robber bumped into her on his getaway run. Kent says he hopes she doesn't bump into him again.

In Kent's office the next day, Jimmy is showing off his new portable typewriter when Lois arrives to show off her byline on the jewelry store robbery. Lois asks Jimmy how he was able to pay for a new typewriter. He explains how the savings stamps he bought in school were converted to savings bonds when he graduated. He just cashed one in to buy his new typewriter. Kent suggests they do a feature story on how the school kids can help themselves and Uncle Sam by buying savings stamps.

Kent and Jimmy arrive at one of the public schools where the **PRINCIPAL** *(Tris Coffin)* introduces them to two boys setting up the savings stamp booth. One of the boys tells Kent it would be great if Superman would show up and help their stamp sales.

Meanwhile, Lois gets a call from **BLINKY** *(Billy Nelson)* who introduces himself as the guy she ran into at the jewelry store. He tells her he will give himself up, but only if she meets with him before going to the police. Lois then calls Henderson with a promise to bring him a surprise.

Back at the school, the Principal explains the stamp program and how the kids handle the operation themselves. Kent puts forth a good word for the program. When he telephones Perry White, he finds out about Lois. Perry says that she just stuck her head in the door and said something about putting a heist man on ice. Kent figures out what she meant and makes a fast exit.

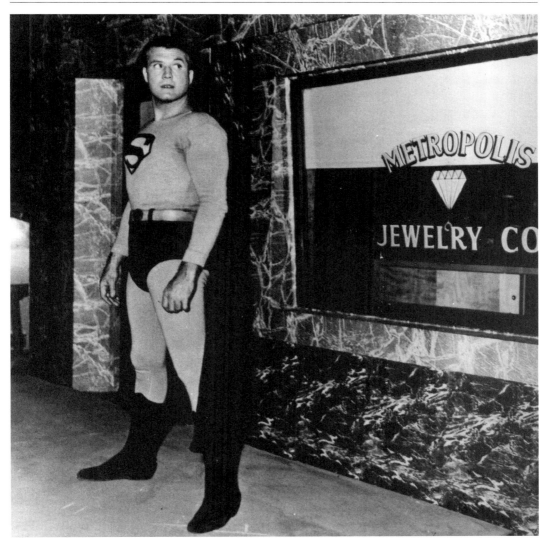

George Reeves on the set that appears in "Stamp Day for Superman."

Lois is tied to a chair with Blinky standing by for a call from the big boss who is going to pay him for the jewelry robbery. Blinky explains that he will be leaving the country with the payoff money and talks Lois into teaching him how to type so he will be able to write letters back home to his friends. Lois uses the opportunity to type up a send help letter in code. She folds it up into a paper airplane and manages to throw it out the window.

Kent is pacing his office when Perry brings in a paper airplane marked for urgent delivery to the Daily Planet. Kent sees the hidden message in the typewritten paper which reveals where Lois is being held captive. He exits, changes into Superman, and leaps out the window.

As Superman flies across Metropolis, Blinky gets the telephone call from the boss and figures now is the time to rub out Miss Lane. Superman crashes through the wall in time to save her and capture Blinky. He wraps a pole lamp around Blinky to hold him until the police can arrive. He tells Lois he has an important date and then leaps out the window.

Then Superman addresses a crowd of school children gathering around the savings stamp booth. He gives an inspirational speech on how they can help themselves and the government by regularly buying savings stamps just like their fathers do by buying savings bonds at work. They can be proud to be good citizens with savings stamps.

Kent returns to his office to present Jimmy and Lois with their own savings stamp book. He also has one for himself and one for his friend—Superman.

One final note: not too many years ago this particular show was readily available in super 8mm sound. Apparently, it is considered to be in the public domain. While doing some holiday shopping last year, I noticed *Stamp Day for Superman* was being offered on video cassette by a company calling themselves "Kids Classics" out of New York City. It was packaged with a prominent colorized picture of George Reeves which caught the attention of my two year old child from across the store.

Unfortunately, all three copies of this tape contained four or five color cartoons from the Fleischer series rather than the title named on the packaging, so I cannot report on the quality or content of their version of *Stamp Day for Superman*. You may have better luck if you wish to take a chance.

The Theatricals of
1954

BEFORE THE PRODUCTION TEAM GEARED UP FOR THE NEXT SEASON OF EPISODES TO BE filmed in color, National Comics apparently decided to cash in again on the theatrical market in 1954, over two decades before Christopher Reeve pulled on a costume. Five feature film titles were assembled for release through 20th Century-Fox. But rather than filming brand new adventures, they merely spliced together three of the second season television episodes into a single package.

There must have been some discussion as to the possibilty of staging some short "bridging" scenes to depict a smooth transition from one episode to another as indicated in photocopied scripts that have circulated the collectors' market for decades, but no one yet has produced any documentation to prove these special added scenes were ever photographed. They would have had to film these scenes at the end of the 1953 shooting season while the cast was still around and the sets were still intact. The *Exhibitor's Campaign Book* issued by 20th Century-Fox gives no evidence to suggest added scenes were included in the feature releases, and the fact that specific episode titles are named in the advertising material makes a strong case for the probability that each of the three episodes within the release remained intact.

Posters and lobby cards were created to give the impression of something new in the theatre. These paper advertisement items, by the way, are becoming quite scarce and are considered prized possessions to collectors. A one-sheet poster for *Superman Flies Again* was recently offered at a Southern California Collectors' Show for $350, and the lobby cards carry an asking price of anywhere between $50 and $150. Likewise, at the Camden House of Los Angeles auction in November, 1989, a poster (21x47) for *Superman and the Mole Men* sold for $770. These days (1998), that poster may well be worth $2000 to $2500. Now I wish I had made a few purchases back in the 80s when I was compiling information for the first edition of this book.

SUPERMAN
Theatrical Release Packages
through 20th Century Fox

Superman's Peril
The Golden Vulture
Semi-Private Eye
Defeat of Superman

Superman Flies Again
Jet Ace
The Dog Who Knew Superman
The Clown Who Cried

Superman in Exile
Superman in Exile
The Face and the Voice
The Whistling Bird

Superman and the Jungle Devil
The Machine That Could Plot Crimes
Jungle Devil
Shot in the Dark

Superman and Scotland Yard
A Ghost for Scotland Yard
Lady in Black
Panic in the Sky

THE PRESS BOOK

The following pages contain excerpts from the *Exhibitor's Campaign Book* utilized by local theatres to promote the release of the five Superman features. In the "Press Book" are several pages of release material in the format of news articles intended for public consumption with the intent of creating interest in the minds of the movie-going patrons.

PIX-BITS

The production crew which shot the SUPERMAN films started work with three Academy Award Oscars to their credit. Film Editor Harry Gerstad holds two Oscars—his first for his editing of *Champions*, Kirk Douglas-starrer, and his second for his editing of *High Noon*, which starred Gary Cooper. Clem Beauchamp, veteran production manager, also holds an Academy Award for his work in *Lives of a Bengal Lancer,* which brought Cooper to fame as a motion picture actor.

* * *

Although there is a long list of notable "dual-performances" by stars in a single picture, it remained for George Reeves starring as SUPERMAN to contribute three characterizations to a single film. In *Superman In Exile,* the initial *[actually, the second]* episode is based on a clever gangster's attempt to discredit Superman by utilizing plastic surgery and voice training on a thug who subsequently masquerades as Superman. In addition to enacting his regular characterizations of "Clark Kent" and "Superman," Reeves also portrays the thug who is "remodelled." Make-up artists were required to make Reeves as the thug look only vaguely like "Kent" or "Superman" initially. And production technicians had a tough assignment when the script called for Reeves as "Superman" to wrestle with Reeves as the thug.

* * *

John Hamilton, who portrays "Perry White, Editor of The Daily Planet," is a veteran of 25 years on the Broadway stage. In almost 20 years in Hollywood he has consistently been cast in "judge" roles. He has played every type of judge from a justice of the peace to Chief Justice of the United States Supreme Court in the recent production of *The Magnificent Yankee.* Of his sudden switch to the more adventuresome, less dignified role of an editor, Hamilton remarked: "Who says you can't teach an old dog new tricks?"

* * *

When a small fire broke out in the studios where SUPERMAN was being filmed, and excitable script girl turned in an alarm. But when the engines arrived the firemen were told they were too late—the fire was already out. Understandably curious, the Fire Chief asked who put it out.

"Superman took care of it," quipped a studio employee. Then seeing the Chief's face cloud over, the wit quickly pointed to George Reeves in his "Superman" costume stamping out the last embers.

* * *

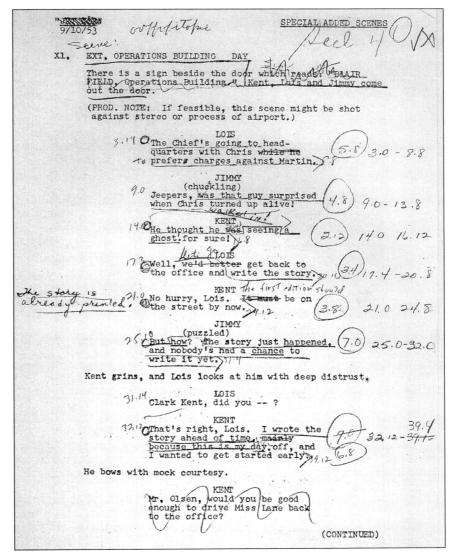

The first of two pages from a script titled "Superman Flies Again" by *David Chantler* containing direction and dialogue that would comprise a scene lasting about a minute to bridge the first episode, "Jet Ace," with the second episode, "The Dog Who Knew Superman."

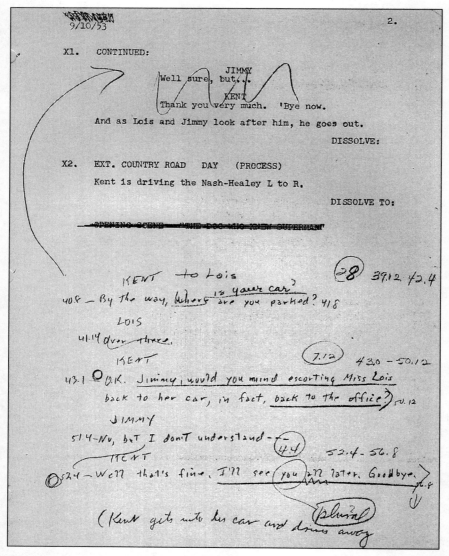

The second of two pages from a script titled "Superman Flies Again" by *David Chantler* containing direction and dialogue that would comprise a scene lasting about a minute to bridge the first episode, "Jet Ace," with the second episode, "The Dog Who Knew Superman."

When asked, during production, whether SUPERMAN was being filmed in 3-D, Producer Whitney Ellsworth quipped:

"Why SUPERMAN has been in and out of the fourth dimension for the last fifteen years. 3-D would be a step backward. . ."

✳ ✳ ✳

During the production of the SUPERMAN series, "Bud" Collier, who had portrayed Superman on the radio for many years, dropped in to visit on the set. When the film's star George Reeves was introduced to Collier, both men shook hands firmly for a few seconds seemingly scorning each other's strength. Whereupon an onlooker remarked, "Who do those guys think they are—Superman?"

✳ ✳ ✳

TYPE-CASTING IN SUPERMAN FILM

When after extensive auditions and tests, the trio of top stars was selected for ". . . ," coming . . . to the . . . Theatre, Producer Whitney Ellsworth discovered he and his staff had come up with a unique case of "type casting."

George Reeves, selected for the top role of "Superman," had been an outstanding athlete at Pasadena Junior College where he had displayed "Superman's" qualities of agility, strength and endurance as a light-heavy-weight wrestling title holder, boxer and football player.

Noel Neill, who portrays "Lois Lane" the Planet's crack female reporter, had started her professional career as a newspaper woman anxious to follow in the footsteps of her father, news editor of the Minneapolis Star-Tribune.

Jack Larson, who scores as cub reporter "Jimmy Olsen," was headed for a newspaper career until motion picture talent scouts sidetracked him. As editor of his high school paper, he was continuing his study of journalism at Pasadena Junior College when a Warner's scout signed him for *Fighter Squadron*.

The trio's uniquely appropriate pre-movie careers and interests enhance the production values of the SUPERMAN series, lending an exciting and unusual authenticity to the adventures of Superman and his "earth-bound" colleges.

Other prominent featured players include John Hamilton as "Perry White" and Robert Shayne as "Inspector Henderson."

✳ ✳ ✳

SCIENTIFIC SUPERMAN

Science-fiction fans are in for a treat with the forthcoming release of five feature-length films based on the picaresque adventures of Superman—himself one of the most popular and widely known contemporary science fantasy creations.

In several of the episodes in the forthcoming series of Superman feature-length films coming . . . to the . . . Theatre, Superman is involved in brilliantly unique science-fiction situations—entertaining in their fantasy and chilling in their plausibility.

In *Superman And Scotland Yard* there is an episode called "Panic in the Sky," in which a large meteorite plunges through the heavens toward the Earth, threatening to destroy a large portion of it with the impact of its collision. In a daring maneuver, Superman soars out to collide with the meteorite and destroy it. He is successful only in halting it and it hovers as a menace while Superman, jarred by the impact, returns to Earth suffering from amnesia. Later, he destroys it.

In the title episode of *Superman In Exile* an atomic stockpile in a laboratory runs wild and Superman, immune to the radiation, enters the deadly chamber and breaks the chain reaction, but becoming radioactive, he must exile himself until he discovers a way to dispel the radiation.

An eccentric scientist invents a "Machine That Could Plot Crimes" in *Superman And The Jungle Devil*—an amazing calculator that was meant to do good but falls into the hands of irresponsible criminals. And in *Superman's Peril*, the evil genius of a scientist discovers the one thing that can destroy Superman—the element kryptonite from his native planet Krypton—and the champion of justice encounters his most hazardous adventure.

Yet Superman himself remains the most amazing science-fiction phenomenon of all. The stranger from another planet, immune to all the deadly devices which would hamper any Earth man, is able to soar through the air with the speed of a bullet and muster the strength of a roaring train in his never-ending campaign to enable good to triumph over evil. His completely normal outward appearance, meanwhile, enables him to masquerade between adventures as Clark Kent, ace reporter.

✳ ✳ ✳

SUPERMAN TRIUMPHANT IN HIS EXCITING ADVENTURES

(REVIEW)

Soaring through the sky, sweeping through space, smashing injustice and evil wherever they appeared, Superman burst forth on the screen of the . . . Theatre yesterday, bringing to life the fabulous fictional hero from another planet who has caught the imagination of readers around the world for 16 years.

In a series of five feature films being released by 20th Century-Fox, the dual character of "Clark Kent, reporter" and "Superman, champion of justice" triumphs in 15 picaresque encounters with sinister gangsters and menacing threats from outer space.

George Reeves stars as "Superman" and Noel Neill and Jack Larson co-star as the Planet's crack female reporter and as a cub reporter who idolizes Kent. Kent admits to being a friend of the mysterious "Superman," and the trio keep an eye open for situations which require his assistance. More than once Kent is forced to jeopardize his secret identity when he has to come to the rescue of his adventuresome friends.

In the five features, Superman encounters a dog who detects his double identity, an ingenious machine which can compute perfect crimes, an evil scientist who discovers his only vulnerability, a sinister imposter, collides with a meteorite jeopardizing the Earth, and is forced into temporary exile by radioactivity after halting an atomic explosion among his other escapades.

ATHLETIC GEORGE REEVES SCREEN'S 'MAN OF STEEL'

It would almost seem as if handsome, talented, young George Reeves had planned his whole life

Handsome, rugged George Reeves won the coveted dual role of "Clark Kent—Superman" in " . . . ," bringing to life the adventures of the world-famed comic strip character soon at the . . . . Theatre.

to equip himself for the role of "Superman" when the filmed version of the world-famed hero from another planet finally went before the cameras. Selected from more than 200 actors who were interviewed and auditioned for the starring role of the dual character, "Clark Kent—Superman," Reeves breathes life into the world-familiar comic strip character which comes to life in " . . . ." now at the . . . . Theatre. And it is just as well that he has. The immediate and overwhelming popularity of the Superman films in the United States placed Reeves in a unique spot. Youngsters in his neighborhood and even strangers on the street were quick to recognize him as "Superman"—and were just as quick to ask for his aid to rescue cats trapped in trees, wayward kites, or even put a bully in his place. Flattered by people's confidence that he can rescue them from their calamities, Reeves nonetheless is often forced to decline the opportunity to perform virtually impossible tasks.

Reeves was born in Ashland, Kentucky, but moved with his family to Pasadena, California, as a child. At Pasadena Junior College he won the light heavy-weight wrestling title and found time to achieve recognition in boxing and football, too. Between the three sports he developed the agility, strength and endurance that were to distinguish him as the top contender for the role of "Superman." Today, he is six feet two-and-a-half inches tall and weighs 195 pounds.

While in junior college he became interested in famed Pasadena Community Playhouse, where he subsequently enrolled as an actor. He studied at the Playhouse for six years, landing his first film assignment in *Gone With The Wind*. A short time later Warner Brothers signed him to a long term contract.

Between screen appearances in more than a dozen films, Reeves acquired considerable radio and television experience in Hollywood and New York. His film credits include: *Meet the Fleet*, *Always a Bride*, *Blood and Sand*, *Lydia*, *So Proudly We Hail*, Marlene Dietrich's *Legend of Chuck-a-Luck* and *Bugles in the Afternoon*.

Lovely Noel Neill, in real life an ex-newspaper woman, portrays "Lois Lane" crack reporter on the Daily Planet in the forthcoming "Superman" feature released by 20th Century-Fox, ". . . .," to be shown at the . . . . Theatre, bringing to life the world-famed comic strip hero.

NOEL NEILL QUITS NEWSPAPER FOR FILMS—AS REPORTER

When the SUPERMAN script calls for "Lois Lane" to sit down at her typewriter and knock out a story, the versatile young actress who portrays the world's most famous newspaperwoman in the Superman series of films, feels right at home. Miss Noel Neill, who stars as the crack female reporter in ". . . ," coming . . . . to the . . . . Theatre, in fact, started out to be a professional newspaperwoman.

Miss Neill began her training with her father, who was news editor of the Minneapolis Star-Tribune, and she was soon writing articles for a living. Her newspaper career ended abruptly one summer, however, when Bing Crosby spotted her and hired her to sing at a nightclub he owned in California. Naturally, it was a quick step from there to motion pictures, her recent credits including *The Greatest Show On Earth*, *Invasion U.S.A.*, *Here Come the Waves* and *Gentlemen Prefer Blondes*.

Last August Miss Neill married Bill Behrens, an aircraft executive who shares her enthusiasm for swimming and volleyball. On the nights when she is tied up at the studios shooting a new SUPERMAN episode, Mr. Behrens assists in the preparation of dinner.

But between pictures Mrs. Behrens spends her time getting acquainted with her new home. The pert, trim—5 foot, 2 inches in stocking feet—young actress still enjoys spending any spare time at the beach. That, in fact, was where she and Bill met.

Since she is the screen facsimile of Lois Lane, youngsters always ask Noel whom she really prefers—Clark Kent of Superman. Her feminine wiles usually get her out of that tight spot. Recently, for instance, at a party at which she was guest of honor, the children offered her cookies shaped in the form of Clark Kent and Superman. Then they stood eagerly by to see which she would choose. Noel rose to the occasion by taking one of each.

FATE RULES IN LARSON'S PROFESSIONAL CAREER

Fate played a good-natured but ironic trick on young Jack Larson. But for a quirk of fate, Larson, who stars as cub reporter "Jimmy Olsen" in ". . . .," now playing at the . . . . Theatre, would have made reporting his real-life career.

Larson displayed his journalistic talents as editor of his high school paper and proceeded to continue his study of journalism at Pasadena Junior College. That is until one evening when an odd combination of coincidence dramatically thrust a stage, screen and television acting career upon him.

A Warner Brothers talent scout, looking for a young actor for a role in *Fighter Squadron*, hopefully attended a Pasadena Playhouse presentation. But it was a futile trip and he pessimistically wandered over to the Junior College where Larson was directing a musical he had written. It was dress rehearsal night, and although Larson had no part in the show, he happened to be on stage demonstrating the way he wanted a certain scene played. Biano was impressed and the following day Larson was tested and won the part.

Subsequently he has appeared in *A Wonderful Life, Starlift, Battle Zone, Star of Texas,* and *Three Sailors and a Girl* among other pictures. The handsome, 23-year-old actor is a member of a group of young Hollywood players who at present are studying under the great Michael Chekov, former associate of Stanislavski and the Moscow Art Theatre.

Talented, young Jack Larson was studying journalism in college when a movie talent scout spotted him and launched him on a film career. Ironically, Larson portrays a cub reporter in 20th Century-Fox's release of ". . . .," now at the . . . . Theatre.

A college letterman in tennis and swimming as well as a member of the tumbling team, he continues to excel in these sports as well as bowling. An expert bowler, he won the California Junior Championship when he was 14. He is five feet, eight inches tall and weighs 145 pounds.

The Episodes of
1954

COLOR WAS THE MAJOR CHANGE TO THE 1954 AND SUBSEQUENT PRODUCTION SEASONS OF the *Adventures of Superman*, although the television viewers would not know about it until years later. Before the cameras rolled in the Summer of 1954, the standing sets got a fresh coat of paint, and the wardrobes were reconsidered for their appearance on color film. Of course, the first thing to go was George's chocolate and gray action suit. Now Superman could be outfitted in his traditional red and blue uniform as it had been illustrated in the comic books, while still providing enough contrast between the shirt and cape to suggest the different colors in the black and white prints made initially. Remember, we were still more than a decade away from color broadcast capabilities for syndicated shows becoming commonplace with local stations across the fruited plains.

Another change was a drop in the number of new shows to thirteen produced per season for each of the next four years. *George Blair* directed eight of the season's episodes, and *Harry Gerstad* was relieved of his editing duties of the previous season to direct the other five.

PRODUCTION CREDITS

producer . . . . Whitney Ellsworth
production manager . . . . Clem Beauchamp
director of photography . . . . Harold Stine ASC
film editor . . . . Sam Waxman
assistant director . . . . John Pommer
photographic effects . . . . Jack R. Glass
special effects . . . . Thol Simonson
story editor . . . . Mort Weisinger
sound engineer . . . . Jean L. Speak

We will return
to the Adventures of Superman
in just a moment . . .

We are not alone. *The Adventures Continue,* published by Jim Nolt Enterprises, is the only magazine between here and Krypton that is devoted exclusively to *George Reeves* and the 1950s television series which earned him an eternal place in our hearts.

Since 1988, *The Adventures Continue (TAC)* has featured insightful articles about and in-depth interviews with those who knew and worked closely with George Reeves, including Noel Neill, Jack Larson, Phyllis Coates, Robert Shayne, Bette Shayne, Jane Ellsworth, Pat Ellsworth Wilson, Tommy Carr, Dabbs Greer, Jackson Gillis, Chuck Connors, Keith Thibodeaux, and many others.

Jim Nolt Enterprises also publishes a calendar with more than 250 events in the life of George Reeves and illustrations by Randy Garrett. More information about *The Adventures Continue,* the calendar, or TAC, Jr. *(a free electronic newsletter)* may be obtained by sending e-mail to JIMNOLT@AOL.COM or by writing to Jim Nolt Enterprises, 1935 Fruitville Pike #105, Lancaster, PA 17601 (WWW.JIMNOLTENTERPRISES.COM), phone/fax 717-560-6380.

EPISODE 53

THROUGH THE TIME BARRIER

directed by HARRY GERSTAD
written by DAVID CHANTLER

The first of the color episodes carries an exciting title, based on an illustrated story called "The Challenge of Stoneman" as it appeared in the comic book pages of *Action #201*. But unfortunately, there is more excitement in the new color opening sequence than what is played out within the scenes of this episode. Kent and Lois are waiting with Perry White in his office for the arrival of a gangster named *Turk Jackson*. They have ordered Jimmy to stand guard outside the door. As he is balancing a pencil on his nose to pass the time, a strange man whom we later learn is **PROFESSOR TWIDDLE** (*Sterling Holloway*) arrives. He insists on a meeting with Mr. Kent. Under his arm is a box that he claims to be the answer to everything.

"Can it get me a raise?" asks Jimmy.

"It will fix things so you won't need one," replies Twiddle with an impish smile.

Mr. Kent is in conference and cannot be disturbed. Jimmy asks the professor to come back later.

"Young man," warns Twiddle, "some of us may *never* come back."

As Twiddle moves away, **TURK JACKSON** (*Jim Hyland*) approaches and meets resistance from young Olsen. Jackson pulls out a gun and forces his way into the office. Once inside, Jackson explains that crime is no longer his chosen profession. He wishes to give himself up to the law as long as Kent promises to see that he gets a fair deal.

After signing a confession, Jackson and the Daily Planet staff head for the police station. In the elevator they meet up with Twiddle who uses the opportunity to introduce himself and his new scientific discovery. Kent is as amused as the rest of the group, but he insists they do not have the time.

"Time?" interrupts Twiddle. "That is just the point! I've conquered it with this machine."

Lois suggests he run along quietly and bury the weird device in his backyard. Jackson figures he won't get many laughs in jail, so he urges the

professor to amuse them with a demonstration. Within moments, the electronic machine in the box triggers an explosion that puts the elevator group back to 50,000 years BC.

"Jeepers," remarks Jimmy. "I should've left a note for my mother."

Only Kent realizes the seriousness of the situation. He insists Twiddle return them to the future. Unfortunately, the professor confesses to having never perfected the reverse process. Perry utters his famous phrase and Jimmy quickly points out that Caesar hasn't even been born yet.

They soon meet a **CAVELADY** (*Florence Lake*) and a **CAVEMAN** (*Ed Hinton*) from whom Jackson obtains a period wardrobe for everyone but Kent. Jackson makes it quite clear that he is taking over. He orders Jimmy to start carving a newspaper out of stone to impress future archaeologists. When Kent refuses to give up the professor's machine, Jackson slams him in the head with his gun. Kent falls down only after he realizes that Lois is watching.

"This guy doesn't know when he's knocked out," says Jackson as he moves off to hide the box of electronics.

The show is ridiculous. When the group attempts to put the rush on Jackson, he fires a warning shot that causes a landslide. It seems they are all hopelessly trapped. Kent loosens his tie and unbuttons his jacket.

"I guess it doesn't matter who knows now," says Kent. Then Lois calls attention to a strange odor. Twiddle sadly announces that it is coal gas and the end will come quickly.

After everyone falls unconscious, Kent jumps up and changes into Superman. He crashes a new entrance into the cave. The fresh air begins to wake everybody up, and Superman returns to his disguise as Clark Kent.

The caveman, having witnessed the mighty Superman's rescue, draws an 'S' in the dirt. Lois boldly informs Turk Jackson that he will never be boss now. She drags Kent off to search for Superman, who has somehow journeyed back in time with them.

The nonsense continues. All hope for any return is now up to Twiddle. He needs his machine and a small sample of a special metal that gives off neutral isotopic rays. It is called *coborium-x* and it is found only on meteors.

"I hope you can direct as well as you can edit," *George Reeves* may have said to *Harry Gerstad*.

Superman quickly fills the order for the missing metal, but Jackson will not reveal the hiding place of the missing machine.

When Perry finally remarks about how they haven't seen Kent around lately, Superman assures him that Kent can be found anytime, but finding the missing machine could take him years. Oddly, no one questions the absurdity.

"Well, let's face it," says Lois cheerfully. "We're cave people and that's the way it's gonna be."

"We can get society off on a better foot," adds Jimmy.

The story finally comes to an end after Jackson trades a cigarette lighter to the caveman for what he believes are uncut diamonds. With his new found wealth, Jackson reconsiders a return to modern times. He recovers the machine and gives it back to the professor.

After they all return to the elevator in the Daily Planet building, Jackson offers to buy everyone a new wardrobe. Then he considers buying the city. His aspirations are destroyed when the professor confirms that all he has returned with is worthless quartz.

What a way to start the new season.

EPISODE 54

THE TALKING CLUE

directed by HARRY GERSTAD
written by DAVID CHANTLER

The story begins at a police lineup where Clark Kent is standing among the suspects. **CLAUDE JAMES** (*Julian Upton*) is questioned about his participation in the recent robbery of the First Continental Bank. When Kent steps forward to be identified, Henderson asks him his name.

"Which one?" replies Kent coyly.

"How many do you have?" asks Henderson.

"Several," replies Kent as a little inside joke. Of course, Kent is merely doing his inspector friend a favor by filling out the suspect roster for witnesses to pick out James.

In Henderson's office, Kent is introduced to the inspector's son, *RAY (Richard Shackleton)*. One of his hobbies is collecting sound effects on a tape recorder. He demonstrates by playing a tape of bullets bouncing off of Superman. Kent must remember the trouble he nearly got into when *Billy Gray* caught him in the act of changing clothes in an earlier episode. He is relieved to hear that Ray made the recording from a police car while on an assignment with his father.

As Ray sets up his recorder to catch the sounds of the police teletype, Henderson explains his latest puzzle to Kent. He is desperately trying to get the goods on Claude James in order to catch his boss, a gangster named Muscles McGurk. An *OFFICER (Brick Sullivan)* enters with James on the way to the jail. Henderson opens the safe to get

the police file, and James notices that the tape recorder has picked up the clicks of the combination lock.

Later, after being captured and released on bail, James and *MCGURK (Billy Nelson)* are in their hideout playing card games. McGurk explains how they are going to make a chump out of Henderson with the help of his son.

Lois and Jimmy are at Ray's apartment to get a story on his unusual hobby. McGurk arrives to buy a recording for a hundred dollars. Lois is curious.

Then Kent is in Henderson's office when a call comes in about a robbery in progress at the secret weapons laboratory. Kent quickly changes into Superman and flies out to investigate.

When he crashes through a cement wall, you will notice Superman is covered with white powdered dust. In the next camera shot, Superman is miraculously clean.

James fires a heat gun at Superman, but it has no effect. James runs to escape and accidentally knocks himself out. McGurk barely manages to get away.

Back at Henderson's office, the inspector tells Kent how he had made a study of the city's

Promotional advertisement as it may have appeared in television listings of your local newspaper.

While viewing the color episodes, note the differences in the "S" insignia of the black and white costume *(left)* from the color costume *(right)*.

burglar alarms and reported on the weaknesses of the system. He has the report locked up in his safe, but he does admit to having dictated his findings to a recording tape made with his son's machine. Kent suggests sadly that Ray must be the information leak because Lois witnessed the sale of a spool of tape to McGurk. Ray is in trouble.

When McGurk arrives to kidnap Ray and his tape machine to a secluded hideaway in *Echo Canyon,* Ray manages to leave a few pieces of tape as a clue. When Henderson shows up with Kent, the inspector figures Ray has run away and really begins to believe his son is guilty of selling police secrets. Kent discovers the two pieces of recording tape.

We will return to the *Adventures of Superman* in just a moment! But first, a few words regarding a particular line of dialog in this episode. In his book entitled *Superman—Serial to Cereal,* author Gary Grossman calls attention to how the production of the color shows demonstrated a lackadaisical attitude toward flubbed lines. He sites as an example how Clark Kent says he has threaded two pieces of audio tape onto the beginning of a new *rule* when he should have said *reel.* In all fairness to Reeves, in one scene he says ". . .I'll splice these onto a new *spool.* . ." and then later he says the mistaken line. Obviously, Reeves had *reel* and *spool* in mind at the same time.

Anyway, the two sound effects of cannon fire and a voice spoken in an echo leads the search to Echo Canyon, a known hideout location of Muscles McGurk. Ray plays a recording of Superman in flight. McGurk thinks it is the real thing and tries to escape in his car. Superman drops a huge boulder onto the road and McGurk is captured.

Kent proves that McGurk did not hear of the alarm system report from the audio tape. It was the safe combination recording that McGurk used to get a look at the report in Henderson's safe. Ray gets an apology from his father for doubting his integrity. He asks Kent to thank Superman.

"I think he's already had his thanks, Ray," says Kent as he looks to the camera with a smile.

EPISODE 55

THE LUCKY CAT

directed by HARRY GERSTAD
written by JACKSON GILLIS

As the title might suggest, this is a story about the silliness of superstition. It begins as a crazy old man named ***BOTTS*** *(Harry Tyler)* attempts to warn Kent and Jimmy away from a house he has rented out to a group of men. The men belong to an anti-superstition club.

Production photo signed by *Robert Shayne* at a film collectors' convention in Los Angeles.

Mr. Botts reminds the two that it is Friday the Thirteenth and that all who enter the house will be sorry. When he is ordered off the property by the club steward, *MR. FREDRICKS (Ted Stanhope)*, Botts warns that they may never live to regret defying the superstitions.

After seeing a black cat cross their path, Jimmy would rather forget the whole affair, but Kent insists they go after the story Perry White sent them to get. Once inside, the two are greeted by *BILL GREEN (Charles Watts)* and asked to enter the meeting room by walking under a ladder. Green explains the idea behind the club. Kent agrees it is a good idea to put an end to all superstitious fears and practices.

Next, they meet another club member, *CHARLIE KING (Carl Harbord)*. He calls attention to the pins on the floor. They are intentionally not picked up by club members to tempt bad luck. King introduces himself as the owner of *King Chemical Company* that is having financial trouble.

The meeting is about to be called to order. Green smashes a mirror and explains how he will hop thirteen times across the room on the cracks in the floor. Kent notices a weakened floor joist as Green begins to hop toward the speaker's table. He quickly slips away and down into the basement as Superman just in time to keep the floor from collapsing under Green's weight.

Later, Kent is in Henderson's office explaining the threats to the club members, probably coming from the irate landlord, Botts. While Henderson is on the telephone to warn Mr. King, Kent hears an explosion over the phone and changes into Superman for a flight to investigate.

Superman arrives at King Chemical just in time to save Mr. King from a fire. Watch for the King Chemical sign when it shows up in a later episode entitled *The Big Freeze*.

Kent catches up to Jimmy and Lois as they are snooping around the basement of the clubhouse. They soon get locked inside by the villain that only Kent sees with his x-ray vision. Lois wonders if Superman knows of their whereabouts.

"Yes, he does," replies Kent. "But I'm afraid he can't come out in the open and help us now."

Kent and Lois discover that Jimmy has a lucky horseshoe he carries to protect himself from bad fortune. Kent remarks how Superman could probably make a magnet out of the horseshoe and use it to open the dead bolt on the door that holds them captive.

"Superman would knock a hole through the wall!" Lois remarks to silly Clark Kent as she leads Jimmy to the other side of the room, searching for a way out.

"Trouble is, too many people might see him *knocking* that hole," says Kent to himself. Kent moves to the door to execute his plan with the magnetic horseshoe.

After they escape, Kent sees the visitor upstairs with his x-ray vision. The visitor applies poison to the claws of the black cat used by the club as their mascot.

Later, Henderson is with Kent, Lois, and Jimmy as the club meeting is called to order. Kent

uses fear of the cat to expose the villain—Mr. King. He planned to frame old Mr. Botts for the fire in his factory and threatening the other club members so he could file for a big insurance claim to cure his failing financial situation.

"How did you know I was the one?" asks King.

"Maybe I'm lucky," replies Kent. "Or maybe I'm Superman."

"Big joke!" yells King. "You better knock on wood when you say things like that!"

As Henderson leads King away, Kent knocks on the wood over the fireplace and winks at the camera.

An outstanding episode with a cleverly constructed mystery, a commodity that would all too soon become rare in the following seasons of colorful adventures.

EPISODE 56

SUPERMAN WEEK

directed by HARRY GERSTAD
written by PEGGY CHANTLER

This episode has roots in an earlier story called *The Defeat of Superman* where a small block of kryptonite was pitched into the Metropolis harbor after it almost killed our hero. As all the resources of the city are mobilized in preparation for a celebration to honor their number one citizen, a thug named **SI HORTON** (*Herburt Vigran*) decides to plan a special event of his own. With the assistance of his partner, **TIPS** (*Paul Burke*), the two lay a trap for Jimmy. After getting him to drink a truth serum milkshake, the unsuspecting cub reporter reveals the whereabouts of the lost kryptonite.

As part of the festivities, a portrait of Superman is being painted by an **ARTIST** (*Tamar Cooper*) and a plaster bust of Superman has been crafted by a sculptor **VANDEGLAS** (*Jack George*). Horton schemes to create a little irony by having the kryptonite planted inside the plaster statue.

To make a dull story short, Superman outwits Horton and brings him to justice. But his last and greatest challenge is how to avoid the inevitable interview scheduled between Kent and himself on live television. Lois can hardly believe her eyes as she watches what appears to be Kent's head in the foreground, hat and all, addressing Superman who is facing the camera. The secret is soon revealed to be a prerecorded dialog tape of Kent's voice. We actually see the plaster bust is wearing Clark Kent's hat.

How Superman managed to arrange a private television studio to perform this clever stunt is never fully explained. The show finally closes with stock footage of a nameless ticker tape parade intercut with close-up shots of Superman waving to a faceless crowd. This is only a preview of the many low budget stories yet to come.

EPISODE 57

GREAT CAESAR'S GHOST

directed by HARRY GERSTAD
written by JACKSON GILLIS

From an illustrated adventure in the comic book pages of *Superman #91*, the story begins by appealing to every viewer's fear of being somewhere alone at night. Perry White is working late at the office. He is visibly upset when he telephones Clark Kent at home, only to be reminded that it is late and he himself has not been home the past few nights.

When Perry confesses that he forgot why he called, Kent asks if he might be worried about his upcoming testimony for the Morley Case hearings in which he is a star witness. Of course he's not worried. "Great Caesar's Ghost!" he replies just before hearing a noise outside his office which noticeably disturbs him. Kent assures him that it is only someone using the elevator. "How do you know that?" White asks as a **DELIVERY MAN** (*Jim Hayward*) enters with some coffee from the drug store. This seems normal until Perry begins to wonder if he ever ordered coffee. Then he hears a ticking sound coming from the desk. He yells to Kent on the phone— there must be a bomb in his office!

Next, we see Superman racing across the city skyline. He enters Perry's office from the window ledge to discover a very upset editor. He is in a panic over a paper sack containing only a cup of coffee prepared exactly as he likes it.

Superman suggests that Perry is working too hard and advises he get some rest. When Perry

accuses Kent of hanging up on him, Superman puts in a word of defense saying that Kent must have a good explanation. White agrees and almost admits to hearing voices.

The next day, Lois and Kent are outside White's office listening to him severely yelling at Jimmy. Lois remarks about Perry's repeated appeals to Great Caesar's Ghost. As Lois and Kent enter the office without an invitation, Jimmy is explaining to Mr. White that the ballplayer he was assigned to interview has been dead for thirty years. Perry attributes the mistake to the voices he has been hearing. Kent and Lois suggest again that he take some rest at his home in the country. Perry reminds Lois to get to work on the sample newspapers he provided to her. He tells Kent he called the night before to find out why he hadn't moved the wall heater closer to his desk as he'd requested.

As White turns his back to Lois in order to demonstrate to Kent how he wants the heater moved, Lois holds up the paper dolls cut out of Perry's newspaper. She whispers to Clark that the editor is losing his mind. Perry informs Kent that he wants the wall heater moved while he is away visiting Inspector Henderson.

Kent sends Jimmy and Lois away to stay busy while he attends to the heater for Mr. White. When Perry arrives at the elevator, he realizes he forgot his hat. When he returns to his office, he sees Kent lifting the heavy heater unit and bending the connecting pipes as if they were rubber. Perry figures he must be hallucinating and collapses into a chair as Lois and Jimmy enter. Kent also rushes to his side. Perry finally agrees to go home for a needed rest.

Aboard an airplane, **JARVIS** (*Olaf Hytten*), Perry White's trusted butler, is ordered by Perry to go up front with the pilot and leave him alone to relax. After he mutters another "Great Caesar's Ghost," a voice begins to call out to Perry. Reasoning that the voice is coming from outside, Perry begins to work at opening the airplane exit door.

Kent happens to be watching the airplane pass overhead from his office window by some stretch of coincidence and immediately sees the need to become Superman. He makes a quick change and flies up to meet the airplane. He arrives just in time to keep Perry from falling out.

Superman settles Perry back safely into an airplane seat as Jarvis returns. Perry confesses that he has been hearing voices. A quick scan of the airplane with x-ray vision reveals no solid source for projecting a voice. Now Perry is more convinced than ever that he is really losing his mind.

After the commercial break, Perry is unsuccessfully attempting to relax in his country home, muttering about how pills and warm milk will not make him sleep. Perry utters his usual "Great Caesar's Ghost" again. A voice replies and appears as a man with a chalk white face, dressed in a suit of Roman armor. He claims to be Caesar's Ghost for whom Perry has called one million times.

Some clever dialog between this ghostly figure of *JULIUS CAESAR (Trevor Bardette)* and Perry leads them out to the patio. When Jarvis arrives, he claims to not be hearing the voice of Caesar.

"Great suffering catfish!" exclaims Perry.

"I wouldn't go summoning up any catfish, Perry. Squirmy little creatures," replies the ghost.

"Don't tell me what to do and stop trying to be funny!" Perry screams in a fit of frustration.

Meanwhile, Kent has taken on the duties of editor back at the office. He tells Lois and Jimmy that Jarvis has reported Mr. White is having conversations with imaginary voices. Henderson enters and immediately complains to Kent that his star witness in the Morley Case now has a reputation for seeing ghosts. The inspector also reports that Perry has now taken to yelling "great jingle bells" and has begun to study Latin. Kent realizes an urgent need to visit the confused editor and sends Olsen out to investigate.

When Jimmy arrives unannounced at Perry's home, he overhears the voices of Perry talking to the ghost. Superman also arrives in time to learn with Jimmy that Jarvis is part of the plot. Members of the Morley gang are making it appear as if White is too crazy to testify against them in their trial for Morley's murder.

The coast is clear. Superman and Jimmy attempt to bring Perry to his senses, but they soon discover that he is too far gone from sheer exhaustion. Superman has a plan and tells Jimmy to get ready with his tape recorder.

Superman flies off to Henderson's office for details on Morley, the dead gang leader, and then

Perry White *(John Hamilton)* is harrassed by "Great Caesar's Ghost" *(Trevor Bardette)*.

It's SUPERMAN to the rescue when "Great Caesar's Ghost" is exposed as a fraud.

quickly returns to Perry's house. He soon exposes the hoax by dressing up as Morley's ghost. He forces a confession out of the fake Caesar's ghost and his accomplices just as Henderson and his troops arrive with the handcuffs.

Perry White makes a hasty recovery to reality and smiles at Superman in relief. The show closes to a final exclamation of "Great Caesar's Ghost" from the happy editor.

EPISODE 58

TEST OF A WARRIOR

directed by GEORGE BLAIR
written by LEROY H. ZEHREN

This could hardly be considered a classic episode, but it is the first of two attempts to add a little western flavor to the series. It also shares its title with an illustrated story appearing on the comic book pages of *Action #200*.

The story begins when Jimmy intercepts a tribesman named **JOHN TALL STAR** (George Lewis)

in the hallway of the Daily Planet. After exchanging the usual stereotypical Indian greetings, Jimmy leads him into Perry's office.

"Someone to see you, *Chief!*" says Olsen with a childish grin as if baiting the grumpy editor's reaction.

As Perry turns from his desk to face Tall Star, he replies, "Don't call me...!" Jimmy is quickly excused in spite of his plea to remain for the rest of the story.

After Perry politely offers him a chair, Tall Star explains his mission. He is delivering a message on behalf of his good friend, *Red Hawk,* also a former University student like himself. Red Hawk's father is *Great Horse,* and he has recently been elected Chief of their tribe. Customs dictate the old Chief must pass through a great ordeal— a test of a warrior. Red Hawk, however, fears his father is too long in years to survive it. Tall Star has been sent to the city to request the help of the legendary *Great White Bird* who is known to all in Metropolis as Superman.

Tall Star continues to explain the importance of the situation. If Great Horse remains Chief and is later succeeded by his son Red Hawk, he could ultimately bring to his tribe the benefits of his college education and modern progress.

Kent, the traditional contact of Superman, is presently away on assignment, but Perry promises to alert him of the situation. Meanwhile, Lois and Jimmy are dispatched to the Indian village to cover the newsworthy story.

It soon becomes apparent that the **MEDICINE MAN** *(Ralph Moody)* is the villain. He has set up **GREAT HORSE** *(Francis McDonald)* for an ordeal, knowing he will fail. His plan is to keep the tribe under his control and preserve the old ways and customs of his people.

When the ceremonies begin, Lois rushes off to the nearest telephone at the trading post. She eagerly waits on Kent's return call while Jimmy remains in the village with **RED HAWK** *(Maurice Jara)* to stall for time. Jimmy soon finds himself named honorary tribesman after impressing the assemblage with his uncanny power over lightning by setting off a series of photo flashbulbs. When Jimmy chokes on the ceremonial peace pipe, he is christened with an Indian name that translates to mean *Big Cough*.

Believing that Superman will never arrive in time, Jimmy volunteers to act as a second for Great Horse and face the challenges of the Medicine Man. Jimmy is blindfolded and sent into the Cave of the Bear. If he comes out alive, the honor of Great Horse will be upheld.

What follows is silly. Superman arrives in time to crash through the cave walls and prevent an **INDIAN** *(Lane Bradford)*, disguised as a deadly clawed bear, from harming Jimmy. The Indian emerges from the cave following Jimmy's victory. He is completely oblivious to Superman's intervention.

The Medicine Man's next instruction is for Great Horse to topple a mighty tree armed only with a small tomahawk. As Jimmy distracts the other tribesmen with a photo session, Superman cleverly assists Great Horse by taking a slice out of the tree trunk.

Now the Medicine Man smells a rat. He insists the *Great White Bird* show himself immediately. Superman walks a gauntlet and eventually flies away to bring rain by delivering a stick of dynamite to the clouds overhead.

The tribal intrigue is soon exposed, Great Horse is reinstated as the rightful leader, and the episode finally comes to a long-awaited end.

The closing scene is in Perry's office as the new Chief bestows a traditional head dress upon the editor. With it comes an Indian title that translates to mean *man who writes with thundering machine.*

"Gosh, Chief!" says Jimmy.

"Don't call me...!" replies Perry. He smiles and continues with, "All right, James. This is *one* time you may call me Chief."

The second attempt at a western theme comes a little later in this season as *The Bully of Dry Gulch.* Unfortunately, it isn't much better. While watching some of the color shows like this one, you really begin to appreciate the earlier episodes filmed in black and white.

EPISODE 59

OLSEN'S MILLIONS

directed by GEORGE BLAIR
written by DAVID CHANTLER

Based on an illustrated story appearing in the comic book pages of *Jimmy Olsen #3*, the title for this episode is a little misleading as it happens Jimmy becomes the unwilling beneficiary of only *one* million dollars. Anyway, the story begins as Jimmy drops by to visit with **MISS PEABODY** *(Elizabeth Patterson)* for an interview. It seems the eccentric old lady has accumulated quite a few alley cats and is known to have spent millions on the project.

To support the facts for his story, Jimmy agrees to take a look at Miss Peabody's records which she keeps in a safe. Jimmy accidentally causes the door to slam shut, trapping one of the curious kittens. When Miss Peabody rushes off to search the basement or the attic for the paper on which is written the combination to the safe, Jimmy puts a call into Clark Kent.

Within a moment, Superman arrives and rescues the trapped kitten by easily tearing the door off the safe. He is gone before Miss Peabody returns to discover Jimmy fondling the little critter. She insists that Jimmy accept her reward of a million dollars.

Production photo: Jimmy Olsen *(Jack Larson)* gets an ultimatum from Clark Kent *(George Reeves)*.

Of course, this news makes the papers and quickly draws the attention of **BIG GEORGE** *(George Stone)* and a thug named **STACEY TRACEY** *(Richard Reeves)*. They immediately wonder what it would be like to own a million dollars. Kent and Lois find out quickly when the dapper young millionaire arrives wearing a new suit and sporting a hat and cane. He is disappointed when both Kent and Lois refuse his generously offered cigars because he'll never get a chance to use his new gold lighter.

Jimmy gladly gives Perry his resignation. Then he retreats to his new and plush apartment where we are introduced to **HERBERT** *(Leonard Carey)*, who has arrived to apply for the job as butler. His

first duty for the young millionaire is answering the door to receive a visitor.

Kent stays long enough to see that Jimmy is doing very well for himself. Herbert brings them both an ice cream soda and accidentally remarks how he did a five year stretch behind the counter of a soda fountain. Before Kent has time to apply too much thought into the butler's use of prison terminology, the door bell rings again. This time, a **DELIVERY BOY** *(Tyler MacDuff)* makes several entrances carrying a variety of sporting equipment, including a small row boat, in from the local department store.

Meanwhile, Big George tells Stacey that it is time to move into action. Soon, the million

Production photo: George Reeves cooling off between takes.

dollars will be safely deposited into their own bank account.

Back at Jimmy's place, Kent is giving him a mild lecture on the dangers of trusting strangers as Herbert answers the doorbell to greet Stacey. The visitor enters with a mechanical gadget that he demonstrates will turn ordinary sea water into gold dust. All he needs is fifty thousand dollars to begin construction of a larger machine. Herbert exposes Stacey as a fraud and throws him out bodily. This act has been designed to reinforce Jimmy's trust in his faithful butler.

Later, when Lois returns with Jimmy to his new apartment, Herbert claims that Superman dropped by and left him a note. The instructions are to gather what is left of his million dollars and meet with him at some Pinehurst location where he will explain the emergency. Lois is curious

about the validity of the note, but Jimmy trusts Herbert and agrees to carry out the instructions. Before they leave, however, Lois does get a call through to the Daily Planet and leaves a message for Mr. Kent.

Soon, Lois and Jimmy are greeted by Big George. With him is Stacey who Jimmy recognizes to be the phoney gold machine inventor, but it is too late. Herbert pulls out a gun, and as usual, the two reporters are locked up. Lois cleverly remarks how this time the butler really did do it.

But all is not lost. Jimmy and Lois regretfully decide to use Jimmy's cash fortune as fuel for a signal fire. Superman is flying overhead. He is attracted by the smoke signals coming up from the chimney. He crashes through a wall in time to greet the greedy threesome.

In the final scene, Jimmy is sheepishly begging to have his status of cub reporter returned to him by Perry White in exchange for never calling him 'Chief' again. He exits after borrowing fifteen cents to tide him over until his next paycheck with a firm promise to Kent not to use the money to hire a butler.

EPISODE 60

CLARK KENT, OUTLAW

directed by GEORGE BLAIR
written by LEROY H. ZEHREN

Comic book collectors may wish to consult the pages of *Superman #98* for a comparative analysis of this adventure with the illustrated story of the same title.

Bullets are flying as the episode begins with Inspector Henderson directing an attempt to capture two desperadoes. As *FOSTER (John Doucette)* and *CURTIS (Sid Tomack)* return fire from inside a country shack, Kent drives up behind the police line in his sports car with Perry White. Tear gas finally forces Foster to give himself up as Kent slips away to become Superman.

While Curtis keeps the attention of Henderson and the police, Foster quietly slips a packet of money into the glove box of Kent's sports car. Curtis refuses to surrender and lights the fuse on a stick of dynamite. Superman crashes into the shack and covers the explosion with his invulnerable body, scaring Curtis into the waiting arms of the police.

However, things begin to look pretty grim for Kent when he returns to the scene. Foster identifies Kent as a member of the gang and sets out to prove it by directing Henderson to the hidden money in Kent's car. Of course, Kent claims that he is being framed, but Perry and Henderson act as if Kent really was a criminal, and he is put under arrest.

Kent is stripped of his honest reporter identity and fired from the Daily Planet. When Foster and Curtis are released from jail by Henderson, along with Clark Kent, they offer the outlaw reporter a job with their gang.

A clever scheme begins when the owner of a jewelry store, a man named *WINGATE (George Eldredge)*, wakes up to a telephone call in the middle of the night. The caller is Curtis, claiming to be a policeman. He tells Wingate to get down to his office right away as it has been burglarized. When Wingate exits his apartment, he is greeted by Curtis, and Foster knocks him out.

Wingate then wakes up in what appears to be a hospital room. A *NURSE (Lyn Thomas)* is standing at his bedside with *STODDARD (Tris Coffin)* pretending to be a government agent. Falling for the trick, Wingate confesses to Stoddard that the latest shipment of uncut diamonds is securely hidden in a safe at his apartment. Only his wife knows the combination, and she is conveniently out of town. So now Stoddard must find another way to steal the jewels.

Foster and Curtis have been watching the phoney hospital room scene through a special mirror. Kent is with them, and his criminal abilities are put to the test when he is sent to Wingate's apartment to recover the jewels. Lois and Jimmy stumble into the plan. They are held hostage in case Kent decides to double cross the gang.

Rather than commit a crime, Kent changes into Superman and flies to a diamond mine to borrow a few uncut stones. *BENNET (Pat O'Moore)* is the mining supervisor and he is very happy to meet Superman. He admits he has no uncut stones readily available, but he agrees most eagerly to let Superman enter the mine and dig for himself. After finding what he needs, Superman thanks Bennet and promises to return the borrowed stones in due time.

When Kent returns with the jewels, Stoddard is impressed, but not yet fully convinced of his intentions. Kent's next assignment is to dispose of Lois and Jimmy before the gang leaves town for good.

Curtis accompanies Kent to the Daily Planet where Lois and Jimmy are tied up and left to die in Perry's office. Kent dumps the contents of the trash can into Perry's reclining chair and touches it off with a match before he and Curtis make their exit.

Meanwhile, Stoddard has captured Perry White and has him in the phoney hospital room. Thinking Stoddard is really a government agent, Perry reveals the entire plan of having Kent pretend to be an outlaw in order to infiltrate the jewel smuggling gang. Stoddard believes this to be a good time to make an escape, so Perry and Kent are forced to take a sleeping pill. Perry drops off quickly, and after the gang exits for the getaway car, Kent switches to Superman and captures them. Henderson arrives with Lois and Jimmy. Superman turns the villains over to the police before he runs off to become Kent again before he is discovered.

In most of the color episodes, especially the later ones, Superman's takeoff was usually a running leap out of camera range. In this one, however, the viewers can see and hear quite clearly that he is in fact running along and then leaping off the springboard.

The wrap-up scene has Jimmy and Lois finding Kent asleep in the phoney hospital room. When they complain to him how he took a chance leaving them with a fire, he quickly explains how the chair was fireproof. Perry chimes in with a reminder of how the chair was a birthday gift from Kent because he was always worried that Perry would fall asleep with a lighted cigar.

"That's fine!" says Jimmy. "But what if something had gone wrong?"

"Well, in that case," replies Kent, "I guess Superman would have to show up in time as usual."

EPISODE 61

THE MAGIC NECKLACE

directed by GEORGE BLAIR
written by JACKSON GILLIS

An international adventure begins when *JAKE MORRELL (Lawrence Ryle)* and his two cohorts, *CLICKER (John Harmon)* and *LAZY (Frank Jenks)* enter the Metropolis Museum late one night to search through yet another crate of artifacts from the *Jody Expedition*. They are looking for an alleged magic necklace that is reputed to render whoever wears it invulnerable. Finding two possible pieces of jewelry that match the description of the necklace, Morrell orders his unusual method for testing their validity. His two

henchmen each take a turn wearing one while taking a sip of a poison solution. They do have an antidote, however, just in case the necklace proves not to be the genuine article.

When Jimmy and Lois arrive to interview the night watchman about the recent raids on the crates from the Jody Expedition, they meet up with the trio of crooks claiming to be members of the museum staff. Lois recognizes Morrell as a notorious gangster and lets it slip out that he is wasting his time because the magic necklace is still in Tibet with Professor Jody. Her foolish statement gets them kidnapped.

The next morning, Perry White crashes into Kent's office with a report of the previous night's museum burglary. When he inquires as to the whereabouts of Lois and Jimmy, Kent gets a phone call from the airport saying that Lois Lane's wallet has been discovered out on the runway.

Kent later learns from an airport *DISPATCHER (Cliff Ferré)* that the runway was used by a private airplane en route to Africa. When he returns to Perry's office, Henderson telephones a report that the airplane in question definitely belongs to gangster Jake Morrell and that it was last sighted on its way to Pakistan. They begin to wonder if a smart crook like Morrell could possibly believe the superstitious rubbish Professor Jody has been releasing about the magic necklace?

Meanwhile, *PROFESSOR JODY (Leonard Mudie)* is in his hut in Tibet. He is talking about his latest discovery to a *CORRESPONDENT (Ted Hecht)*. Jody's assistant, *AKBAR (Paul Fierro)*, rushes in to report that a plane has landed nearby with visitors. Superman makes an unnoticed landing outside.

Kent walks in as Jody is about to perform a demonstration of the magic necklace draped around his neck. Akbar is about to fire a gun at Professor Jody when he proclaims that Kent would make a more convincing subject. Jody removes the necklace and places it around Kent. As Lois, Jimmy, and Morrell enter, Akbar's gun accidentally drops to the floor, sending a bullet at Kent, convincing the correspondent that the necklace is indeed magic!

The entire party is moved inside a cave where Professor Jody gives a lecture about the ancient gods of the magic necklace. Morrell succumbs to the hype and offers a sachel full of a million

Production photo: George Reeves diving off the set and onto a waiting matress.

dollars in cash in exchange for the treasure after watching Jody survive a sword strike and a gunshot from Akbar. Kent, of course, sees through the fake demonstration.

Then comes the double cross. Morrell decides to take the necklace and the money, knocking Akbar unconscious. Lois and Jimmy are escorted away by Morrell. Kent manages to get trapped in a landslide with Jody and Akbar.

As Morrell attempts to lead his group out of the winding caverns, Kent listens to Jody confess to the fraud, but only because he wanted to raise money for his scientific discoveries.

Meanwhile, near the mouth of the cave, Morrell has Jimmy and Lois tied up. His men are about to set off some dynamite. Kent fakes an accidental knocking out of the torch light leaving him free to become Superman under cover of darkness.

Superman crashes through a wall and manages to round up the escaping crooks. Jimmy assures Lois that the dynamite will not harm them because he managed to grab the magic necklace from Morrell in the confusion. Lois, of course, is much more comfortable when Superman returns in time to throw the exploding dynamite up through the roof of the cave.

When Jimmy insists that the magic necklace he is wearing would have saved them as well as Superman, Lois kicks him in the shin to prove otherwise. Realizing that he is feeling pain in spite of the necklace, he faints away as Lois and Superman get a laugh at Jimmy's expense.

Finally, the fade out.

EPISODE 62

THE BULLY OF DRY GULCH

directed by GEORGE BLAIR
written by DAVID CHANTLER

Viewers of this episode may find it interesting to compare the story to the adventure illustrated in the comic book pages of *Jimmy Olsen #3*. Yet another example of how Producer Whitney Ellsworth maintained the connection between the television series and the family of comic books that I remember rushing to collect from the local drug store when I was a kid.

Lois and Jimmy are on a road trip when they happen upon a quaint little western town. They are immediately greeted with gunfire! The local bully, who cleverly calls himself **GUNNER FLINCH** (*Myron Healey*), is forcing an old cowboy, **SAGEBRUSH** (*Raymond Hatton*), to dance rather than be shot in the foot. A few of the locals have gathered around to watch the show, but no one bothers to stop it, except Lois and Jimmy.

Gunner makes eyes at Lois and tries to intimidate Jimmy, but the two city dwellers fail to take this low budget Liberty Valance too seriously. In fact, Jimmy decides to take on some local color by outfitting himself in a dude ranch costume.

In the town eatery, Gunner approaches Sagebrush and **PEDRO** (*Martin Garralaga*) to deliver their pay sacks. Then he proceeds to win it all back in a quick, single-deal card game with a handful of five aces. We begin to get the picture, and Sagebrush and Pedro have obviously been through all this before.

Gunner throws Jimmy into jail, and Lois gets on the phone to make a plea to Clark Kent. At first, he seems not to want any distractions and strongly suggests they should rely on their own resources. But when Lois finally explains that this town bully has been making googoo eyes at her, he realizes the seriousness of the situation and announces that he is on his way.

Superman makes a speedy flight to Dry Gulch and executes a grand entrance through the wall of Jimmy's jail cell. He is so excited to see Superman that he doesn't bother to protest the shower of bricks and mortar from what is now a new doorway to the jail. In fact, he can hardly wait to confront Gunner, but Superman swears him to secrecy and tells Jimmy that Clark Kent should be along shortly.

Kent arrives to meet Lois. She easily accepts his reply to her curiosity about his almost instant appearance when he flatly says he *flew*. Jimmy joins them and almost gives away the secret Superman told him of Kent's expected visit. Lois asks how Jimmy managed to get out of jail.

"The same way I got in," he replies with a smile. "Accidentally!"

In the cafe, Kent is unimpressed with a show of gunfire from Flinch that all but destroys the glassware behind the bar. Ordered to drink and play cards by the boisterous bully, Kent responds by requesting a glass of milk. Kent sends Gunner's marked deck of cards up in smoke with a little heat vision in what appears to be an accident while lighting Gunner's cigar. Then Kent gets a new deck from the **BARTENDER** (*Eddie Baker*).

After some exaggerated camera work on Kent's speedy handling and dealing of the cards, he manages to win from Gunner the two pay sacks he just cheated away from Pedro and Sagebrush with another handful of one too many aces. When Gunner protests, the two cowhands are quick to remind him that he recently did the same. Flinch is publicly humiliated by this city slicker with his own tricks.

Wise enough not to threaten Kent, who he will attempt to figure out later, Gunner reminds Jimmy that his time in town is rapidly nearing an end. To punctuate his intent, Gunner shoots Pedro in what appears to all but Kent as a cold-blooded killing. Deciding it's time to exercise the greater part of valor, Kent elects to do nothing. Lois is disgusted as they watch Sagebrush drag the apparently dead Pedro out of town and off to a grave on Boot Hill.

Outside of town, Pedro, confesses to Sagebrush that he's had enough of these fake killings designed to make Gunner look like a tough guy. The charade is finally clear to every viewer who has not yet figured out what is going on.

Out on Boot Hill, Jimmy, Lois, and Kent are paying their last respects to the fresh grave of Pedro. Jimmy notices and reads the inscription on a tombstone near an open hole.

"Here lies Olsen, the dude... to Gunner he was very rude."

To Kent, this is the last straw. He makes a quick exit into the countryside. Sagebrush remarks it's a good thing he left because he would make a much bigger target for Gunner than Olsen.

Superman appears from the rocks and makes a running leap toward and over the camera (the same shot is used again in the Seven Souvenirs episode). Pedro is walking along the road away from town when he is intercepted by Superman. Together, they conspire to put an end to Gunner's fake show of villany.

In a showdown on Mainstreet, Pedro refuses to back away from Flinch's threatening fast draw and all too easily forces a confession out of him. Superman appears at the final moment, as if having waited in the wings just in case this silly plan went sour, to reaffirm the lesson of why it's not nice to be a bully. If only world diplomacy were as simple.

EPISODE 63

FLIGHT TO THE NORTH

directed by GEORGE BLAIR
written by DAVID CHANTLER

In this adventure, Superman is introduced to a very likable competitor. This far-fetched episode begins when bumpkin **SYLVESTER J. SUPERMAN** (Chuck Connors) comes to Metropolis from his hometown of Skunk Hollow with his travelling companion is a mule named *Lilly Bell.* He checks into a flea-bag hotel wearing bib overalls and a red undershirt. Sylvester soon convinces the hotel **MANAGER** (George Chandler) that he is the real superhero by bending an iron bar.

Meanwhile, Superman has returned to the Daily Planet building where, as Clark Kent, he is greeted in his office by **LEFTOVER LOUIE LYMAN** (Ben Welden), fresh out of the penitentiary. He makes it clear to Kent by grabbing his lapels that he knows about the nasty stories he wrote about his escapades and tells him to mind his own business. Kent agrees, but only if Louie stays out of trouble.

Louie returns to his apartment to meet with **BUCKETS** (Ralph Sanford) where they discuss the

$50,000 stashed from an old bank heist and how they must keep a low profile until the heat of Louie's parole is off. When asked what he missed most while doing time in the big house, Louie confesses lemon meringue pie. Buckets insists his Aunt Tilly makes the best in the world, but Louie claims his old neighborhood girl friend, Margie as the title holder. They each bet their respective half of the stolen loot on their claims and agree to meet next Thursday with pies for an impartial judge.

Sylvester is reading the newspaper classified section when he happens on an urgent plea for the services of Superman. He's not quite sure how anyone knows that he is in town, but he tells Lilly Bell that it wouldn't be polite to turn his back on a cry for help.

Louie pays a visit to **MARGIE** (Marjorie Owens) and confesses how he has always dreamed of her famous baking talents. She is flattered, but unfortunately cannot satisfy his request because of her promise to her fiancé that she will never bake for anyone else.

As disappointed Louie exits, Sylvester arrives in answer to her advertisement in the newspaper. She also finds it difficult to believe this strange character is Superman until he lifts her piano. When Kent arrives to investigate, he is introduced to Superman. Margie explains that she has requested Superman to deliver a fresh lemon meringue pie to her fiancé stationed at an airforce outpost in Alaska. Sylvester accepts the duty and vows no one will touch the pie except the intended recipient.

In the hallway outside, Louie attempts to bribe Sylvester for the pie, but he is unsuccessful. Kent sees the crook and warns him to stay away or he'll be writing more nasty newspaper stories about him that will get him in trouble with his parole officer.

Before long, Sylvester and Lilly Bell arrive in a snow storm to deliver the goods to a very bewildered **STEVE** (Richard Garland) and are rewarded with a meal that consists of two weeks worth of airforce rations. Then Louie arrives with a gun. After he steals the pie, Louie exits.

"If there's anything lower than a mule thief," says Sylvester, "it's a pie stealer."

Margie's fiancé tells Sylvester not to worry, figuring it is the thought that counts. When the *real* Superman enters looking for the pie stealer, Steve feels he is definitely on the edge of a nervous breakdown. A radio message comes in reporting that Louie's plane has crashed and he is holed up in a nearby ice cavern. Superman excuses himself and makes a hasty exit.

Shivering Louie is very happy to see Superman crash through a wall of ice to save him. Together, they return to Steve's outpost with the pie. Sylvester agrees to take Louie for a ride back to Metropolis aboard Lilly Bell. Superman asks Steve for a taste of the lemon pie, assuring him that he is not losing his mind.

"Arctic solitude can sure do funny things to a man," says Steve.

In the final scene, Buckets comes to visit Louie. He is recovering from his frozen journey to the North by sitting with his feet in a pan of hot water, wrapped in a blanket, shivering. Aunt Tilly wouldn't even speak to him, let alone bake him a pie. The bet is called off.

Kent and Sylvester stop to see how Louie is doing. He and Buckets agree to live honest lives. Sylvester announces that he will return to Skunk Hollow where he can be just plain Superman. Kent shakes his hand and wishes him the best. Metropolis is not big enough for both of them.

EPISODE 64

THE SEVEN SOUVENIRS

directed by GEORGE BLAIR
written by JACKSON GILLIS

This episode marks a high point seldom reached by the color shows. The story is actually a clever mystery with an interesting twist ending. It begins with Superman arriving in time to head off some escaping crooks. He secures their capture by bending an iron crowbar around their arms until Inspector Henderson arrives to make the arrests. Jimmy decides he'd like to have the bent crowbar as a souvenir, but it cannot be found anywhere.

Later, Jimmy sees the crowbar in the window of a curio shop and goes inside to investigate. Here he meets **MR. WILLIE** (*Phil Tead*) offering the item for sale at a price of twenty-five dollars. In fact, he has an entire collection of Superman souvenirs in stock and sells to Jimmy a brick with a special thumb print for a mere three dollars and a quarter.

Jimmy returns to Kent's office to show him and Lois his newly discovered find. Miss Lane shares his enthusiasm. She also happened on the shop of Mr. Willie the day before and picked up a little dagger with a blade that was reputedly bent when a foreign spy tried to stab Superman.

Suddenly, **MR. JASPER** (*Arthur Space*) stumbles into the office begging for help. He has just been attacked by a dreadful man with a scar across his face. Moving to his office down the hall where he controls the Jasper Engineering Company, he discovers that his payroll has not been stolen, but his Superman souvenir dagger is missing. Lois shows her's for comparison and Jasper explains how Mr. Willie assured him that he had purchased the only one of its kind.

Kent arrives at Mr. Willie's curio shop to inquire about a Superman souvenir dagger. Mr. Willie claims to know exactly what Kent is looking for, and he excuses himself to retrieve it from his stock room. With his x-ray vision, Kent watches as Mr. Willie takes an ordinary knife, fixes it into a vice grip, and then manually bends the blade to appear much like the two he already sold to Lois and Mr. Jasper.

Kent interrupts the embarrassed Mr. Willie and lectures him on the selling of fake souvenirs. He warns that Superman may also frown on his little practice. Mr. Willie confesses he never meant any harm and tells how he just sold a souvenir dagger to a lady just before Kent entered the shop.

With that information, Kent rushes out of the shop, changes into Superman, and soon arrives at the site of a car wreck. He rips off the door to free the **LADY** (*Louise Lewis*) driver. She tells him about a scarfaced man who was hiding in her back seat. He took her souvenir dagger and ran away.

The **SCAR MAN** (*Rick Vallin*) runs into an alley out of sight and quickly compares his recent acquisition to another dagger from his pocket. He is apparently collecting the souvenirs from everyone on a list who has purchased from Mr. Willie's shop. After Scar Man takes the one from Lois at gunpoint, however, Superman decides it is time to figure out what is going on.

Production photo: Jimmy Olsen *(Jack Larson)* and Clark Kent *(George Reeves)* get the phone call announcing another season of episodes.

Kent intentionally walks into an ambush carrying another fake souvenir dagger. He gets hit in the head by Scar Man. Kent falls to the ground, but he will not let loose of the dagger. *LOUIE (Steve Calvert)* helps Scar Man gather up Kent's limp body and put him into the car.

A country drive brings Scar Man, Louie, and an unconscious Kent to the house where the Boss is waiting to pay off on the collected souvenirs. When Kent lets go of the dagger, they dump him out of the car and drive away. He is now free to become Superman, and then he executes an impressive outdoor take off running toward and over the camera *(watch for the same shot used in the "Bully of Dry Gulch" episode)*.

After putting in a call to Henderson and watching Scar Man and Louie come out of the house with their payoff money, Superman intercepts their getaway car and knocks them out as Henderson arrives with Lois, Jimmy, and several policemen. When they return to the house, which belongs to Mr. Jasper, Superman sees the seven souvenir daggers through a wall layed out on a table in the next room. With his x-ray vision, he examines each of the knives, but finds nothing unusual hidden inside any of them. Jasper claims no knowledge of the two mysterious men, and when one policeman finds another seven souvenir daggers hidden upstairs, it seems Jasper is telling the truth.

But Superman knows better. The entire affair was designed by Mr. Jasper to trick Superman into using his powerful x-ray vision to convert the special alloy of the fabricated souvenir daggers into a million dollars worth of pure radium. Henderson arrests Jasper for fraud.

Superman returns to give a final warning to Mr. Willie, but finds his curio shop has been converted into a bakery. He vows never to sell another phoney souvenir and offers to bake Superman a wedding cake whenever he decides to take the plunge. After Superman exits, Mr. Willie imagines how valuable his red cape would be as a Superman souvenir.

EPISODE 65

KING FOR A DAY

directed by GEORGE BLAIR
written by DWIGHT BABCOCK

Years ago, the baby prince of Burgonia was smuggled into the United States after his father was assassinated. Now, young **PRINCE GREGORI** (*Chet Marshall*) is an international front page story. In this episode, Perry White wants Jimmy to get an interview, feeling the Prince may speak more freely to someone his own age. Kent will go along to keep Jimmy out of trouble.

While Kent paces the sidewalk outside the exclusive brownstone apartment building, Jimmy is with Prince Gregor discussing what it is like to be a member of a royal family. Kent glances up and then quickly ducks into an alley.

Within seconds, Superman arrives through an open window just in time to shield the two young men from the blast of a planted explosive device. Superman then offers his protection, but Gregor declines because he has friends who will soon secretly smuggle him back into his country to regain the throne and restore democracy.

After Superman leaps out the window, Gregor gives Jimmy his family ring to pass on to Superman as a token of his appreciation. Preferring that Jimmy call him Greg, the Prince also gives him permission to wear the royal ring until he sees Superman again.

Because the interview was a success, Kent and Jimmy are assigned to cover the new king's coronation in Burgonia. When they arrive at the airport of the foreign city, they are observed by two spies, **MARAL** (*Phil Van Zandt*) and **RIGOR** (*Jan Arvan*). They conclude that Jimmy is the real Prince sneaking into the country because they recognize the ring he is wearing.

Later, while Kent is off visiting with **COLONEL GUBECK** (*Stephen Bekassy*), Jimmy is visited by the two spies. In spite of his protest, they address him as Prince Gregor and escort him to the summer palace. Here, Jimmy meets with his intended bride, the **BARONESS** (*Carolyn Scott*), who also believes him to be the long lost Prince Gregor.

Anyway, Prime Minister **VALLIN** (*Leon Askin*) and his two spies prepare a poisoned ice cream soda for Jimmy, but Kent arrives in time to prevent this tasteful attempt on his life. The three assassins are very surprised when Kent sucks down the soda by himself and remains standing. After the three make their exit and Kent excuses the Baroness, he tells Jimmy in private that Colonel Gubeck has requested he keep up the appearance of being the Prince so he and his men will have time to sneak the real Gregor into office.

Valance enters and maneuvers Jimmy near a draped doorway. Kent intervenes in time again to keep Jimmy from being stabbed by Rigor.

Jimmy is then asked to smoke a royal cigarette made from Burgonian tobacco. Kent overhears about an explosive planted in the cigarette. He takes it away from Jimmy and throws it out the window to save him one more time.

Finally, the prime minister **MARCEL** (*Peter Mamakos*), who is the real brain behind the attempt to overthrow the government of Burgonia, meets with his three assassins. He insists they stop fooling around with bungled attempts on Gregor's life. He orders them to take Gregor and shoot him as a traitor.

Jimmy stands before a firing squad. Superman crashes through a brick wall in time to stop the execution. After he quickly disarms all the puppet soldiers, the real Gregor arrives with Colonel Gubeck and his guards to assume his rightful place as leader. Jimmy then gladly turns over the ring to Superman.

For comic book collectors who might be taking notes, a similar story appeared in the pages of *Jimmy Olsen #4*.

The Episodes of
1955

BUDGET CUTS CAUSED THE PRODUCTION VALUES TO DIMINISH SLIGHTLY FOR THE 1955 season. *Harry Gerstad* directed seven of the episodes and *Phil Ford*, nephew of the great John Ford, directed the other six. Whitney Ellsworth was beginning to depend more on fewer writers, *David Chantler* wrote most of the stories for this season, and fresh location changes were kept to a minimum.

PRODUCTION CREDITS

producer . . . . Whitney Ellsworth
production manager . . . . Eddie Donahoe
director of photography . . . . Joe Biroc ASC
production co-ordinator . . . . David S. Garber
film editor . . . . Sam Waxman
assistant directors . . . . Gene Anderson, Sr.
Grayson Rogers
special effects . . . . Thol Simonson
story editor . . . . Mort Weisinger
sound engineer . . . . Earl Snyder

George Reeves —
his memory will live in our hearts forever!

1914 — 1959

CONTRIBUTORS: JAMES L. NOLT • GAIL L. NOLT • LISA K. NOLT • DR. DON RHODEN • RANDY GARRETT • ROBERT HARVEY
DANNY FUCHS • JANEEN C. CHRISTENSEN • LOUIS KOZA • JEFF HAYNES • MORE FUN COMICS & COLLECTIBLES
DOUGLAS ALEKSEY • JOYCE COPE • CARLOS RAMOS • WILLIAM M. COBURN • MIKE ROSE • JIM LONG • RICHARD BANDONI
ANDREW J. KLYDE • PAUL MORIN • MICHAEL E. MIGALSKI • ROBERT FALCONE • MITCHELL MAGLIO • JIM HANLEY
EMIL MOSORA, JR. • STEVEN ROMANO • ROSS D. PETERSON • DAVE DEL GREGO • STEVEN L. HERSH • JOHN M. O'NEILL
SAMUEL J. SYLVESTER • JEFFREY W. FANT • DONALD R. SMITH • MAURICIO ARAUJO • RICHARD SPECTOR
RICHARD C. POTTER • MIKE KORCEK • JIM HARRINGTON • STEVEN R. JACOBS • MICHAEL FORBES • MILTON P. STORY
TERRY REYNOLDS • PAUL LEONE PETERS • JOHN ANTOSIEWICZ • KERRY L. GAMMILL • WILLIAM P. MILLS
SCOTT BLEIBERG • ROBERT RESTELLI • JOHN TITSWORTH, JR. • MARIE FERRARA • JOHN CARFIZZI • GARY L. COLABUONO
CHARLES A. WAGNER • ALLEN KRETSCHMAR • JAN ALAN HENDERSON • STEVEN HADDER • ROB GOTTFRIED
WILLIAM KENNETH MITCHELL, JR. • ANGEL ALBINO • ROBERT PRESTIFILIPPO • GARY F. GLAZER
VINCENT SALTALAMACCHIA • MORRIS MYER • WILLIAM DAVID BROWN • STEPHEN ALEKSEY • CAPT. STEPHEN E. LENOIR
GLENN KEENAN • JAMES M. BOWERS, JR. • ROBERT BURDGE • ROBERT VANN • HILTON GARCIA • DANIEL H. FOGEL
FRED FARLEY • RICHARD HADLEY • PAUL SCANNAPIECO • JEFF MCLAUGHLIN • PAUL MANDELL • ROGER HILL
MICHAEL KLEINMAN • BRIAN MCKERNAN • ROBERT MARESCA • CURTIS JAMES • GEORGE RYAN • MICHAEL A. RAMEY
ANDY, GRACIE, & MICHAEL BIFULCO

GEORGE REEVES MEMORIAL FUND C/O JAMES L. NOLT • 222 MARION TERRACE • EPHRATA, PA 17522

This tribute to George Reeves occupied all of page 46 in the June 14-20, 1989 issue of the *Variety* newspaper. Fans collectively contributed $1700 to finance the purchase.

EPISODE 66

JOEY

directed by HARRY GERSTAD
written by DAVID CHANTLER

This sentimental tale begins when Perry White learns that **PETE THOMAS** *(Tom London)*, an old friend, is about to lose his ranch. Heart strings are further tweeked when we discover that Pete's grand-daughter, **ALICE** *(Janine Perreau)*, will be forced to give up her favorite horse named *Joey*. It turns out that Joey is a race horse, and in a jesture of friendship, Perry decides to buy the animal in the name of the Daily Planet as an investment.

Any profits realized from winning races will of course go to charity.

Meanwhile, a race track hustler named **LUKE PALMER** *(Mauritz Hugo)* is busy placing a fortune on a fixed-to-win horse named *Rover Girl*. His cohort, **SULLEY** *(Billy Nelson)* has witnessed Joey's workout at the track and advises Palmer to reconsider the wagers.

Joey's heart, however, is not into running any race. When Palmer and Sulley show up at the stables one night, they find the Daily Planet staff lamenting over the fallen horse, apparently sick from the absence of Alice. Perry decides Lois and Jimmy should drive out to the ranch and return with the young lady before the race begins

Production photo: *George Reeves, Mauritz Hugo, Billy Nelson,* and *John Hamilton* on the set of the "Joey" episode.

Noel Neill, Jack Larson, Janine Perreau, George Reeves, and *John Hamilton* at the racetrack.

After learning of this development, Palmer dispatches Sulley to intercept them.

While on their drive in the country, Lois and Jimmy believe they are lost and stop for directions to the Thomas Ranch. They meet with Sulley who has a shotgun. He informs them that Pete Thomas has sold the ranch. The new owner does not want any visitors.

Lois and Jimmy return to the office with news of their failed mission. Perry White is confused. Why did Pete Thomas sell the horse if he intended to sell the ranch anyway? Kent smells a rat. He puts through a telephone call only to learn that everything is status quo at the Thomas home, no sell out, and no new owner. Is it too late to gather Alice for Joey's morale before the race begins? Kent suggests Superman and excuses himself to start searching.

Here, Lois gets an idea, the one for which we've all been waiting. They should follow Kent and see how he always manages to contact Superman in the nick of time? But they are too late. By the time they get out into the hallway, Kent is already in the storage room. By the time they check out the storage room, Superman is already out the window and on his way toward the ranch.

His surprise visit startles the half asleep Sulley and he manages to knock himself out cold by running into a tree. Superman's next order of business is to pick up Alice and fly her back to Metropolis Raceway in time to revive the homesick horse.

When they gather at the stable and witness the plan has worked, Perry sends Joey out to win the race as if he were Knute Rockne addressing the team at halftime. The following scenes are comprised mostly of stock footage from Hollywood Park. Detroit area television viewers may recognize the race track announcer as character acter *Bill Kennedy*, who later became a matinee movie host on channel 50. He also appeared in the first season episode *Crime Wave*.

When Joey loses the race to Luke Palmer's

Production photo: *Jack Larson, John Hamilton, Noel Neill,* and *George Reeves* posing for a color test.

Rover Girl, Kent immediately excuses himself to the office. Within seconds, Superman lands in the winner's circle. He informs the officials that Rover Girl is equipped with a saddle capable of receiving electric shock signals from the grandstand. After cornering the escaping villains, he returns to the stables as Kent just in time to hear Perry White return Joey's ownership back over to Alice.

EPISODE 67

THE UNLUCKY NUMBER

directed by HARRY GERSTAD
written by DAVID CHANTLER

This is a rather contrived tale of mistaken identity that begins when Lois and Kent are walking down the street. Vic's Lunch Room is sponsoring a contest where the prize is a $15,000

dream home for anyone who can guess the number of jelly beans in a quart jar. When Kent recognizes a known confidence man by name of *SLIPPERY ELM (Russell Conklin)* entering the diner, he decides to lend fate a hand by rapidly counting the beans in the jar with his x-ray vision. When a little old lady, *CLARA EXBROOK (Elizabeth Patterson)* remarks how she has always dreamed of owning a new home, Kent gives her the lucky number and encourages her to enter the contest.

Inside the diner, Kent and Lois wait while the beans are being counted by *MR. KELLY (Alan Reynolds)*. At the finish, Slippery comes forward confidently with his supposed winning guess that is within three of the correct count, but Mrs. Exbrook claims the prize with the exact number.

Lois stays with Mrs. Exbrook for a story while Kent positions himself to overhear a conversation between Slippery and another crook named *BOOTS (Jack Littlefield)*. The rigged contest has been ruined. They suspect the only other member of the gang who knew the correct count, a man named Dexter.

That evening, **DEXTER** *(John Berardino)* arrives on the porch of the Exbrook rooming house where he is greeted by **BOBBY** *(Henry Blair)*, who tells him the news about his grandmother winning the contest at Kelly's diner. Within moments, several gunshots are aimed at Dexter's chest from a swift passing automobile, but Dexter remains standing. Bobby is amazed, but Dexter tells him to forget what he just witnessed and then goes inside the house.

In his room, Dexter removes the bullet proof vest and puts it away in the closet just before Bobby enters with his revelation that Dexter is really Superman. To avoid having to answer a lot of complicated questions, Dexter allows Bobby to believe that he *is* Superman.

Later, Bobby is sitting on the porch when Inspector Henderson drops by to investigate a report of gunfire. Bobby answers his questions politely and tells him that a man named Dexter Brown rents a room in the house.

In Kent's office, Lois reads a story about the

George Reeves waits patiently while director *Harry Gerstad* reviews the shot with *John Berardino.*

Noel Neill, Henry Blair, George Reeves, and *John Berardino* rehearsing a scene for "The Unlucky Number" episode.

shooting incident at the Exbrook home, the same Clara Exbrook who won the jelly bean contest. Kent is particularly interested when he hears Lois mention the name Dexter. He quickly excuses himself to run an errand.

Down the hall and into the storage room goes Kent. Out the usual window goes Superman. When he meets with Bobby on his porch, Superman is barraged with questions. What is he doing back here? Why does he look different? Why does he talk different? Superman is certainly confused. When he asks about the shooting, Bobby figures he's being tested by his friend, Dexter, so he plays along and offers Superman no concrete information.

Lois and Kent have a new assignment. They are to investigate the crooked lotteries and raffles plaguing the city by buying tickets as an excuse to

snoop around. Lois follows through by purchasing a lottery ticket from a news **VENDOR** *(Tony DeMario)* just before Dexter arrives to collect the proceeds. He is upset when he learns the ticket fixed to win has accidently been sold to a reporter named Lois Lane. Bobby has followed Dexter and is watching from around the corner.

Dexter arrives at the Contest Headquarters to tell the **COLLECTOR** *(Alfred Linder)* of his intentions to break away from Boots and the gang. He invites cooperation from any of the boys who wish to join up with him, but first they have to take care of Lois Lane. Bobby is at the window listening to everything unnoticed.

Dexter returns home to an obviously disappointed Bobby who tells about how he has discovered that Superman is really a crook. Dexter attempts to justify his illegal activities as

Production photos: *George Reeves* demonstrates to *Jack Littlefield* the penalty for someone who pulls a gun on Superman.

being the only way to finance his operations as Superman, and that Bobby should not try to judge him.

Later, Dexter kidnaps Lois at gunpoint and returns her to the house to force the winning ticket away from her. Bobby returns unexpectedly as Boots and the gang show up. Dexter hides in the closet, but Bobby gives him away. Boots shoots several holes in the closet door, and then Superman comes out to make the capture.

Bobby is really surprised when Dexter appears from inside the closet. Dexter confesses to deceiving Bobby for the wrong reasons and vows to go straight after paying his debt to society. Bobby's respect for both Dexter and Superman has been restored.

Apparently, Superman believes that Dexter is sincere in his claim to accept the notion of rehabilitation.

"Then my work here is done," says Superman, borrowing the well-worn phrase from the Lone Ranger. He asks Bobby if he would be kind enough to open the window so he may leap off into the sunset.

EPISODE 68

THE BIG FREEZE

directed by HARRY GERSTAD
written by DAVID CHANTLER

This episode is an attempt at serious crime drama which falls short of the mark because the villains are not quite believable. Although the scientific theory behind the threat to Superman is solid, its execution is sloppy and strained. The story opens in the apartment of **DUKE TAYLOR** (*George E. Stone*) as he explains his plan for controlling city politics to his bumbling associate, **LITTLE JACK** (*Richard Reeves*).

With an army of hired thugs positioned at the major voting sites, Taylor believes the populace will be sufficiently threatened to cast their ballots in favor of his candidate for city mayor. When Little Jack inquires as to how Superman will be kept out of the situation, a knock at the door provides the answer.

In walks a double-talking genius named **DR. WATTS** (*Rolfe Sedan*) with a report to Duke that all the preparations have been completed for the elimination of Superman. You may recognize the eccentric doctor as the mailman who was continually devastated by Gracie on the long running *Burns and Allen Show*.

The four Daily Planet regulars are gathered in Perry White's office as he explains how the city will be overrun with racketeers if the incumbent Mayor Wilson is defeated by the crooked candidate Buckley. How could Superman allow such a thing to happen? Kent suggests they fill the newspaper with strong editorials and cautions that "it is not wise for people to depend on Superman to keep their own house in order."

Duke and his accomplice enter the laboratory of Dr. Watts, a room that appears to Little Jack like the inside of a television set. The are eagerly greeted by the scientist who explains how he has constructed a special room that is capable of sustaining a temperature of 2000 degrees below zero. Dr. Watts proceeds to demonstrate the power of his invention by holding a rubber ball with a pair of tongs just inside the freezing chamber through a little sliding door. Of course, when the rubber ball is extracted and dropped on the table, it shatters like a glass Christmas tree ornament.

An important ingredient in the tried and true formula that makes up most of the episodes is the villains most often worked in pairs, one always being noticeably more intelligent than the other. This made the process of moving along through the story much easier by providing a dialog of exposition. Little Jack takes us another step into the plot by asking how Duke plans to get Superman into the refrigerated room?

Kent is in his office banging on the typewriter. As he finishes up an editorial on the voters' responsibility to maintain a clean city, he sees an envelope shoved in under the door. It is an invitation from Duke.

Jimmy is with Lois in her office as she completes an editorial appealing to the women voters of the city. They also receive an invitation slipped under the door. In neither case does anyone bother to get a look at who might be the mysterious messenger.

Duke and Little Jack escort Kent to the laboratory where he makes a comment on how the place looks like the inside of a television set.

Duke explains that Lois and Jimmy are locked up behind the iron door and if Superman doesn't show up by 2PM to rescue them, a bomb will go off. He further warns that the arrival of police will also set off the bomb. Kent agrees to get word to Superman and let him decide how to deal with the obvious trap.

The next scene has Superman crashing into the laboratory. He lifts the heavy iron door off the freezer vault and rushes inside, calling out for Lois. The room instantly clouds up with white smoke. When Duke and Little Jack enter the room, they are greeted by a totally white figure of Superman. "He looks like a snowman," remarks Little Jack as Lois and Jimmy arrive to discover a powerless Superman.

After a failed attempt to fly, the frozen figure of Superman makes his way down a back alley and changes into his Clark Kent wardrobe. If you watch carefully, you may notice the "King Chemical Company" sign on a building in the alley which was used in *The Lucky Cat* episode.

Anyway, Kent somehow manages to enter the Daily Planet building unnoticed in his rather pale condition and into the office of Lois Lane. With the help of some cosmetics found in her desk, Kent succeeds in adding some needed color to his head and hands just before Perry White and Lois interrupt him. Perry makes a casual remark about how Kent appears to be unseasonably tan, but all are more concerned about how the election will fare due to Superman's weakened condition.

With his contractual duties complete, the meek Dr. Watts arrives at Duke's apartment to collect his $50,000 fee. Instead, Duke orders Little Jack to show him the door. Dr. Watts threatens to get even. Little Jack laughs and reminds him to vote for Buckley.

The principal players are gathered once again in White's office as if assembled for a funeral. With the voting stations staffed by Duke Taylor's thugs, the incumbent mayor doesn't stand a chance unless Superman can somehow make a timely recovery.

Almost as if on cue, Kent answers the knock at the door to find Dr. Watts insisting he must talk with Superman. He confesses to being responsible for Superman's condition. Kent quickly insists on hearing what the Doctor has to say. When it is explained how sudden intense heat could either destroy or cure Superman, Kent makes a hasty exit.

"Jeepers, maybe we'll never see him again," frowns Jimmy.

"Who? Clark?" asks Lois. "He'll be right back."

"No," replies Jimmy. "I mean Superman."

Kent arrives at the Metropolis Iron Works. The **GUARD** (*Eddie Baker*) is kind enough to let the reporter through the gate for a look around. Kent changes to Superman, and then walks into the blast furnace. In a moment, he exits totally revitalized.

Superman makes an encouraging appearance at a voting station and inspires a concerned **CITIZEN** (*John Phillips*) to throw a punch at Little Jack. When asked how he now intends to vote, the citizen reminds Superman that privacy is still his privilege.

"I hope it always remains that way," says Superman to punctuate the moral of the story.

When Kent returns to Perry's office, it is very clear by the reports coming in over the wire service machine that the voting has taken a turn for the better. Another episode closes on a high note.

EPISODE 69

PERIL BY SEA

directed by HARRY GERSTAD
written by DAVID CHANTLER

Superman returns to the Daily Planet to assume his identity as Clark Kent, and to continue his temporary duties as editor. He enters Perry White's office where Lois and Jimmy are waiting to file their report on how Superman just prevented a bank robbery. We learn that Perry has been away from his desk for two months. Kent announces that Perry has invited all three of them out to his cottage by the sea to find out what he has been secretly doing all this time.

Inside a submarine, noted smuggler **ACE MILLER** (*Claude Akins*) is watching a cottage on the coast through the periscope. He explains to his accomplice **BARNEY** (*Julian Upton*) that it is time they came up with a new gimmick to supplement

their smuggling operation. He tells Barney that this cottage is guarded like Fort Knox, but he doesn't know why.

Kent, Lois and Jimmy are allowed to pass the inspection station by the security **GUARD** (*Ed Penny*) to visit Perry in his cottage. It has been converted into a laboratory, complete with a walk-in safe for guarding something very important. Jimmy is surprised to learn that Perry White is an accomplished scientist. Because his hobby is studying ancient scientific documents, Perry has been commissioned for some top secret development project by the government. He has just completed a formula for extracting a rare form of uranium used in medical research called U183 from ordinary sea water.

Jimmy is proud of Perry's humanitarian work and suggests the whole world should know about it. However, Kent and Perry caution that publicity is the last thing they need. Jimmy feels otherwise.

Soon, Ace is reading all about the newspaper editor turned scientist who has been working on one of history's greatest experiments. Barney remarks that this new formula could be worth more than turning lead into gold. As they have been looking for a new gimmick, Ace points out that this might just be it.

Back at the office, Kent is giving Jimmy a lecture on why he should never send stories down to the composing room without first clearing them through the editor. With his story, he has not only broken security, but perhaps jeopardized the entire project and maybe even Perry White's life. Jimmy says he feels like jumping out the window and drinking poison on the way down. Kent has a more fitting punishment in mind. He sends Lois to escort Jimmy back out to the cottage where he can tell Perry what he has done in person.

While driving out to the cottage, Jimmy tells Lois that he would rather do anything than tell Mr. White what he has done. Suddenly, Ace and Barney pop up from the back seat. With a gun, they insist on being taken to see the secret laboratory.

Henderson tells Kent how Jimmy's story has given him a lot of trouble. It seems he was partially responsible for security around the secret project and the government is on his case.

Kent sends him to the cottage to lecture Jimmy in person if anything is left of him after Perry White gets finished.

Pretending to be fellow scientists with the unwilling help of Lois and Jimmy, Ace and Barney gain access to White's laboratory where they force Perry at gunpoint to turn over the secret formula. Perry, Lois and Jimmy are locked up in the walk-in safe. After welding the door closed, Ace and Barney escape to the submarine where they get ready to torpedo the cottage to eliminate the witnesses.

When Kent fails to make contact by telephone, he changes to Superman and flies to the coast. Ace fires a torpedo, Superman dives into the sea to intercept it in time to save the cottage. Seeing Superman's face in the periscope persuades Ace and Barney to give themselves up to the authorities.

Superman rushes into the laboratory past Henderson and lifts the door to the safe off its hinges to rescue the captives. When Lois asks how they might ever be able to thank him, Superman smiles and suggests they get back to the office and help Clark Kent. He will never be able to get the newspaper out by himself.

Although this is a better than average color episode, there are a few minor flaws that are difficult to overlook. When Jimmy and Lois are en route to the cottage, it's hard to believe that Ace and Barney could remain hidden in the back seat of the convertible for so long. And Superman streaking under water to intercept the torpedo is obviously an above ground flying shot superimposed on water with the sound of flying through the air. However, the villains play it straight and all in all, it is an enjoyable show.

EPISODE 70

TOPSY TURVEY

directed by HARRY GERSTAD
written by DAVID CHANTLER

Borrowing an unsettling effect experienced in Gotham City as illustrated in the adventure called "The Machines of Menace" appearing in the comic book pages of *Batman #80,* it is quite clear that something strange is happening in Metropolis. When a **MAN** *(Charles Williams)* who has endured one hundred and three days of sitting on a platform constructed high atop the flagpole of a tall building suddenly believes he is hanging upside down, Superman arrives to investigate.

Soon after, Lois rushes into Kent's office to tell him how Superman saved the flagpole sitter from going crazy. He removes the finished story from his typewriter and tells her he knows all about it. As she is about to query his jump on the event, **PROFESSOR PEPPERWINKLE** *(Phil Tead)* arrives with a box he claims to be his latest invention, the *anti-magneto gravitational register.* He explains how its inner workings produce invisible waves that have a rather peculiar disorienting effect on the human ear. He also explains that it took him three years to invent this device, which Jimmy describes as a science fiction pinball machine, but he has absolutely no idea for what good it could be used.

When the Professor activates the device, the room suddenly appears to be upside down. Everyone is caught off guard, especially Jimmy, who comically clings to an open file cabinet drawer to keep from falling to the ceiling.

Then a character named **CARNEY** *(Ben Welden)* rushes into the room prepared to give Kent a lecture. He is so disoriented that he yells "Hey, Rube!" and stays only long enought to hear Kent introduce Prof. Pepperwinkle before he makes a quick exit.

The machine is reactivated and the room returns to normal. Kent immediately makes the connection between the previous testing of this machine and the frightened flagpole sitter.

Carney returns to the carnival office and tells **YOYO** *(Mickey Knox)* how he was about to give Kent a warning against writing negative articles about their operation when he happened into a weird demonstration that made him feel like the room was upside down. YoYo suggests how such a machine, if it existed, could facilitate bank robberies. Carney remembers the Professor's name and gives him a telephone call requesting a private demonstration.

Lois informs Kent that she and Jimmy are going over to see the Professor about a possible use he may have discovered for his new contraption. Kent wonders why the old genius

Superman calms the fearful effects of Professor Pepperwinkle's latest invention upon a flagpole sitter *(Charles Williams)* in the "Topsy Turvey" episode.

cannot invent something more practical such as a better mousetrap. Lois remarks that he'd probably rather invent a better mouse.

Anyway, YoYo and Carney have secured the device, letting the Professor believe they have set up several remote devices in other carnivals as a new amusement attraction. Actually, they have strategically placed them along an escape route from a bank. When Lois and Jimmy arrive as guests of the Professor, they figure out what is really going on. The Professor then refuses to go through with the demonstration, but YoYo threatens harm to Lois and Jimmy if he does not cooperate.

Carney pulls off the robbery on schedule, using the diversion of the demonstration to escape. When Kent hears what several witnesses report at Henderson's office, he immediately arrives at the most logical conclusion—it's Professor Pepperwinkle's machine. Then he recalls how the character in his office yelled "Hey, Rube," a phrase used by carnival people during an emergency.

Back at the carnival, as YoYo and Carney are busy counting the bank loot, Jimmy coughs up a diversion as Pepperwinkle activates the machine. The room turns upside down as Superman arrives. After YoYo fires several bullets, Superman renders the two crooks unconscious and secures their capture by bending a barbell around them as the machine returns the room to its upright orientation.

If only there had been a few more minutes, the Professor is confident they could have captured the villains without Superman's assistance. This gives him an idea for a machine that could freeze time. The show closes after Jimmy invites everybody over for his mother's favorite desert, pineapple upside-down cake.

EPISODE 71

JIMMY, THE KID

directed by PHIL FORD
written by LEROY H. ZEHREN

Most likely inspired by "Jimmy Olsen's Double," an illustrated story from the comic book pages of *Superman #93*, this episode provides another showcase for performances by *Jack Larson* in a dual role. Some opening scenes establish that Clark Kent is working overtime on a story to expose another big time crook.

When two **THUGS** (*Rick Vallin, Steve Conte*) return to the office of and report to **J. W. GRIDLEY** (*Damian O'Flynn*) of their failure to remove evidence against him from Clark Kent's office, Gridley introduces his trump card. Waiting in the next room is **KID COLLINS** (*Jack Larson*) with his girl friend, **MACEY** (*Diana Darrin*). The girl is told to get lost before Gridley outlines his plan to substitute Collins for Jimmy Olsen. On the Daily Planet staff, the duplicate Jimmy can easily retrieve the incriminating evidence gathered by Clark Kent.

Larson's performance as the gangster is well developed when he is put to the test. The two thugs interrogate Collins regarding details of being a Folsum Penitentiary resident. With his sarcastic wit and tough way of speaking, the two thugs are finally convinced that this character is really not Olsen, and so are the viewers.

The first thug arrives to find Jimmy in Kent's office, and at gunpoint, orders him to take a ride. When he resists, the thug insists he try nothing tricky because he can shoot his gun right through his pocket without even making a hole. Jimmy has to ask, and the thug quickly points out that he already has a hole in his pocket from the last time he did this routine.

At Gridley's office, Jimmy is introduced to Collins to exchange identification and clothing. When Collins appears as Jimmy at the Daily Planet building, he whistles at Lois in the hallway, puts his feet up on the desk in the city room, and starts to puff on a big Havana cigar. Then Perry White enters the room with word of a serious forest fire. He orders Kent to the scene and to telephone the story back to Jimmy, who is really Collins, as soon as possible.

Our hope of seeing Superman in some spectacular action sequence is quickly let down. All we get is the usual flying shot, an aerial view of a newsreel forest fire, and then a dull recap of what Superman actually did when Kent gives the story to Collins by telephone. He punctuates the story with a brief Smokey the Bear editorial and he instructs Collins to write up the story based on that theme. Collins inquires about the security of the Gridley evidence. Kent tells him to mind his own business and merely dismisses the interest to youthful eagerness.

Collins delivers the following account to Perry White in his office. "A forest fire tried to muscle into Metropolis today... It was hotter than the hot seat at Sing Sing... along came Superman just in time like the FBI... any crumb but Superman would have blown his top, but Superman blowed out the fire, it was duck soup for him."

Perry explodes in a fit of disgust, telling Collins that firing him would be too easy, and orders him to get out of his office. Collins takes a cigar from Perry's pocket before he leaves the room smiling.

In the hallway, Lois watches Collins enter Kent's office. She walks in on his attempt to break open the filing cabinet. When she warns him to

Production photo: *Jack Larson* studies the workings of a press camera with *George Reeves.*

wait for Kent, he exits with a snappy referral to Lois as *Honey.*

Meanwhile, Collins' girl friend returns to Gridley's office and finds Jimmy tied up in a chair. Believing Jimmy is really Collins, she turns him loose.

After Collins turns Kent's apartment upside down, he again takes a crack at the filing cabinet in his office. When Lois walks in this time, Collins tells her she should mind her own business. She informs him that she was working late to rewrite his fire story. When he claims to know nothing about her newspaper terminology, she finally figures out that he isn't really Jimmy Olsen. His gun tells her to sit down and keep quiet.

Upon returning home, Kent learns from the landlady, **MRS. COOPER** (*Florence Ravenel*), that she didn't think he would mind if Jimmy Olsen was allowed to enter. Kent discovers that his secret closet is open, and then he quickly becomes Superman. Remember, he has spare costumes now.

Collins is getting nowhere on cracking the lock on the filing cabinet. Lois is so interested in the Superman costume that he found in Kent's apartment that she accidently lets out that Perry White also has a key to the cabinet. When they go to Perry to get the key, Jimmy shows up and is knocked out by Collins. Perry hands over the key.

As Collins rejoins Gridley and the gang, Superman arrives through the window of Perry's office. Jimmy wakes up to tell what happened to him. Superman has Lois call the police to meet him at Gridley's office.

When the gang arrives at Gridley's office, Superman appears from inside the walk-in safe. He takes some gunshots, and then finally knocks everyone out on the floor.

The closing scene in Perry's office has Kent explaining that he borrowed Superman's costume for a detailed description that will appear in his feature story for the Sunday edition. Once again, everyone accepts his explanation, and his secret remains secure.

EPISODE 72

THE GIRL WHO HIRED SUPERMAN

directed by PHIL FORD
written by DAVID CHANTLER

In the plush living room of the Van Cleaver estate, **JONAS ROCKWELL** *(John Eldredge)* sits leisurely reading the newspaper as **ORRESTO** *(Maurice Marsac)* paces uncomfortably back and forth. Three times, Superman has ruined their operation and Orresto demands to know what Jonas plans to do about it. Jonas assures the visiting dignitary that everything is under control. He has sent Mara to the Daily Planet where she will set his plan in motion.

Meanwhile, **MARA VAN CLEAVER** *(Gloria Talbott)*, a wealthy young socialite and ward of Jonas, is in the middle of dictating her intentions of placing a full page ad in the Daily Planet to **MILLY** *(Lyn Guild)*. Kent happens to overhear her strange request to hire Superman and informs Mara that Superman is not for sale. She explains how a party is being staged to entertain a diplomat from South Argonia, and she offers $10,000 to any charity if Superman will agree to make a personal appearance.

Later, Lois and Jimmy arrive at the estate to cover the event for a feature story. Jonas introduces Orresto as a diplomat with a mouthful of names *(Orresto Di Minia La Scala La Cuesta El Centro Jones)* just before Superman makes a spectacular appearance by crashing in through a large window.

Superman tears apart a stack of telephone books in a command performance.

With Superman certainly providing adequate security for the foreign visitor, Jonas decides it would be okay to dismiss **CASPER** *(George Khoury)*, Orresto's personal bodyguard for the evening. While Superman is busy earning his charity donation by performing various super tricks, Casper steals some engraving plates for printing paper money.

After crushing Mara's diamond into powder and back again, tearing two telephone books in half, and twisting up some fireplace tools, Superman receives a subtle round of applause as Casper returns and secretly slips the stolen goods to Jonas.

It is suggested that Jimmy take a group photograph featuring Orresto with Superman, after which Jonas cleverly slips the engraving plates into the film holder of Jimmy's camera. When Superman agrees to fly the film back to

Production photo: *Noel Neill* and *George Reeves* on the set used in the "Dagger Island" and "The Jolly Roger" episodes.

Argonia as a jesture of friendly international relations, Jonas and Orresto know their plan for smuggling the goods is complete.

When they return to the office, Jimmy discovers that something is not right with his photographic supplies. Lois insists they return to the estate and get the truth from Jonas.

As Jonas and Orresto are leaving for Argonia, Lois and Jimmy arrive. Pressed for details on what Superman has been tricked into smuggling out of the country, Jonas informs Lois and Jimmy that they have accidently stumbled into serious danger. He instructs Casper to lock the

two nosey reporters away in the lead lined bomb shelter where they will be left to die.

Then Kent arrives to inform the crooks that the police are aware of their counterfeit operation and should be arriving soon. Casper pulls a gun and shoots Kent, but he is luckily carrying the printing plates in his pocket that deflects the bullets. When Mara tries to pass a secret note to Kent revealing the location of Lois and Jimmy, her betrayal is discovered by Jonas and the two are also thrown into the bomb shelter trap.

Mara apologizes to the others for the trouble

she has caused, and Kent tells her that Superman knew she was innocent of Jonas's activities. The expression on her face when he crushed her valuable diamond was a clue that she had no idea the jewel was a fake. Jonas must have stolen the original diamond to finance his operation.

"Miss Lane actually thinks you're Superman," says Jimmy to Clark Kent, sensing a hopeless situation. "So why don't you just bust out of here?"

"If I did that now, she'd be sure," says Kent, smiling.

Then they hear a big lightning storm brewing outside. The bomb shelter is furnished with a radio, but the battery power supply is dead. Kent gets an idea, but insists that the others leave the room while he tries something dangerous. Then he uses his body to channel a lightning bolt from a water pipe into the dead power supply. They use the radio to call Inspector Henderson, and Jimmy is amazed that they managed to get themselves out of trouble without any help from Superman.

In the last scene, Mara appears in Kent's office as a newly hired copy girl. She explains how she lost her entire fortune due to the poor management of her estate by Jonas. When Kent offers to return the charity donation, she refuses and insists on changing her appreciation for life by working for a living. Kent thanks her and tells her that a lot of kids will be able to go to summer camp due to her generosity.

EPISODE 73

THE WEDDING OF SUPERMAN

directed by PHIL FORD
written by JACKSON GILLIS

In a dreamy imaginary tale as illustrated in "Superman Marries Lois Lane" appearing in *Action Comics #206*, Lois opens the episode by addressing the viewers with a plea for understanding. She explains the following story may seem insignificant to most people (*it does*), but to her it is very important. While the regular woman's page editor is on vacation, Lois has assumed the duties of sorting and responding to the bags of mail addressed to the "advice for the lovelorn" column.

The Public Defender, **MR. FARADY** (*Milton Frome*), is waiting in Perry White's office with Inspector Henderson to discuss the current crime situation. When Lois enters to tell Perry that the additional work load is more than she can handle, he tells her it will have to wait. Superman arrives to discuss plans for finding the leader of the latest crime wave, currently the number one project of the Daily Planet. Lois is told she will just have to deal with the bags of love advice letters herself.

The next morning, Lois wakes up buried in mail she has been attempting to read when a knock at the door brings a flower delivery. The attached note is signed by Superman, and he apologizes for being so busy lately with the current crime wave. He wants ask her an important question. Lois gets a burst of energy and decides to work on solving the mystery of who is behind the crime organization herself.

At the office, Lois receives a call from **MABEL** (*Julie Bennett*) claiming to know the identity of the criminal ringleader. Kent overhears the call and follows Lois to Poole's Jewelry Store. Mabel and **POOLE** (*Doyle Brooks*) have just been kidnapped by Farady's gang. When Lois walks in on some dynamite, Superman arrives in time to save her from the explosion. Then a black sedan drives by and Superman protects her from a shower of bullets.

In a mushy display of affection, Superman asks Lois to marry him. He takes a handful of diamonds from a nearby display case and squeezes them into one large engagement stone.

Farady reads the headline in the newspaper about Superman's wedding. He explains to his **ASSISTANT** (*John Cliff*) how he plans to marry Lois before Superman has the chance so she won't be able to testify against him as the criminal mastermind of Metropolis.

Hoping to trick Superman into rushing off to the Swiss Alps for a while, Farady's assistant assumes the identity of a fashion consultant. He advises Lois to have Superman bring her some edelweiss to compliment her new hair style.

Farady arrives with a **JUSTICE OF THE PEACE** (*Nolan Leary*) to quickly perform a shotgun marriage ceremony, but when they hear the familiar sound of Superman landing outside for a quick return, Farady runs away. Superman greets Lois with googoo eyes and edelweiss. He explains that Clark Kent cannot be their best man in the wedding because they are one in the same.

Soon, the wedding is about to take place in Perry's office as the camera moves in on the wedding cake. A bomb has been planted by Farady, and it is ticking away inside. Then we see the alarm clock as Lois wakes up to the sound of someone knocking at her door. She opens it to the greetings of Henderson and Farady. As she begins to accuse Farady of being the criminal leader, Kent arrives. When Lois throws her arms around him and addresses him as Superman, everyone is surprised, especially Kent. She finally realizes it has all been a dream.

EPISODE 74

DAGGER ISLAND

directed by PHIL FORD
written by ROBERT LESLIE BELLEM

Assembled in Perry White's office are the three surviving heirs to the estate of James Craymore. In the opening scene, we are introduced to **MICKEY** *(Dean Cromer)*, the taxi driver, **JEFF** *(Ray Montgomery)*, the college instructor, and **PAUL** *(Myron Healey)*, the lazy playboy. They have all gathered to hear the reading of Craymore's last will and testament, which has been handed over to Perry White. Another of Perry's hidden talents is the law degree he attained in his younger days, long before he became editor of the Daily Planet.

The estate consists of a million dollars in perfect diamonds. The three potential heirs are to assemble on Dagger Island in the Caribbean, where a fourth relative and heir, Jonathan Scag, has lived most of his adult life. Here, they will be given clues for a treasure hunt. The winner will become the sole owner of the estate. Kent and Lois will attend as umpires and Jimmy as the official photographer. Perry hands over the clues to Lois in a sealed envelope and instructs her to keep them until the group reassembles on the island one week later.

Kent is at the airport confirming their flight reservations when he calls Lois at the office. She is attacked by an unknown assailant and put to sleep with a handful of chloroform. Kent quickly changes to Superman and is on his way to the rescue. Before he arrives, the intruder grabs the sealed envelope from Lois' purse, leaving a poison gas bomb smoking on her desk.

Superman arrives in the smoke filled office. Quickly, he inhales all the poison gas. Seeing that Lois is okay, he bids her goodbye and jumps out the window.

Here, the sharp eyed viewer will note the chair in the foreground near the open window. When Superman makes his immediate return to the building, he arrives through the very same window. Okay, so little kids won't notice, but I'm sure that professional adults were paid good wages for editing this film. Somebody goofed.

Lois discovers the envelope is missing from her purse. She goes into Perry's office and announces that she has been attacked, but saved thanks to Superman. Obviously, says Kent, someone wanted a head start in the contest. The good

Promotional advertisement for the "Dagger Island" episode as it appeared in the television listings of the Los Angeles area newspapers.

George Reeves clowning on the set of the "Dagger Island" episode.

news is that the envelope in her purse was only a decoy. The real one is locked up in the safe. The bad news is that a killer would be in attendance on Dagger Island.

The group is now dressed in safari clothes left over from a Jungle Jim movie and walking through the foliage of Dagger Island. They are greeted by gun toting **JONATHAN SCAG** *(Raymond Hatton)*. Kent explains to him that old man Craymore is dead and he has directed a treasure hunt that will begin in the morning.

The next day, it is discovered that all the drinking water has been stolen. Scag informs the group there is no way to communicate to the outside world, and they all know the boat will not be back for a week. Kent manages to slip away long enough to become Superman. He gets a flying start and dives down into the ground. This shot of Superman crashing into the earth will later be used in another episode, *Divide and Conquer*. Within moments, a fresh spring is

gushing good drinking water and Kent calls it to the group's attention.

Kent reads the clues that have been written in poetry. "My arm is steady, my hand is calm... To find my treasure, look for my palm." They all agree the clue is in reference to a palm tree. The question is, which one?

Kent continues, "It's twenty feet from base to treasure, on a line as straight as the eye can measure."

Jimmy conjures up an old legend of a white palm tree, called the Captain's tree. Old man Craymore was indeed a Captain. Scag says he knows of such a tree and leads the group to it for the reading of the final clue.

"The line is straight, but which direction? The answer is up to your own selection."

Within moments of splitting up, Mickey returns yelling how he found the diamonds. When the group asks to see them, he says no way and runs off toward camp. Jimmy decides to follow him, hoping to get a story. When a masked man attacks Mickey and finds no diamonds, he continues the chase after Jimmy.

Jimmy is hiding down in the ruins of an old pirate defense bunker. The masked man starts to drop cannon balls down hoping to hit Jimmy. Superman uses his heat vision on a cannon ball causing the masked man to burn his hands, drop the hot ball, and then run for cover. Superman remains totally out of sight.

Later, after Mickey admits to faking his find, the group reassembles at the white palm tree. Paul suggests that the diamonds are hidden up the tree in a cocoanut. Paul is awarded the prize and Kent exposes Scag as really being the not quite dead James Craymore. He confesses to orchestrating the contest so he could see what kind of characters were waiting in line for his estate.

Paul decides to share the treasure and Jeff is exposed as the dangerous criminal because he

has burn blisters on his hands. Jimmy points out they have solved a mystery and saved themselves without any help from Superman.

EPISODE 75

BLACKMAIL

directed by HARRY GERSTAD
written by OLIVER DRAKE
& DAVID CHANTLER

As the title suggests, blackmail is the aim of a master criminal by the name of **ARNOLD** (*Herburt Vigran*). He has just arranged an armored-car holdup that nets his gang a half million dollars. To assure no interference from Superman, an accomplice named **BATES** (*George Chandler*) leads him off on a wild-goose chase. Superman crashes through the wall of Bates' hideout, confiscates

Inspector Henderson *(Robert Shayne)* explains to Clark Kent *(George Reeves)* how he is being framed by gangsters in a complex robbery scheme.

Superman arrives in time to remove the phoney evidence against Inspector Henderson.

his thirteen thousand dollars worth of loot, and then flies him to jail to face questioning by Henderson.

Henderson appears at Kent's office to tell him the money found on Bates was not from the robbery. They figure he was paid to be a decoy. Since the police have nothing to hold him on, Kent suggests Henderson should let him escape and then trail him to the leader.

Arnold is playing scrabble with **EDDIE** *(Sidney Tomack)* in their bomb shelter hideout when Bates calls from a telephone booth to report his escape. Arnold reminds him that he was paid to stay in jail, but when Bates sees that he is being followed, Arnold realizes the escape was a setup and figures a way to turn the tables on Henderson.

Eddie pays a visit to Henderson and demands he turn over all the evidence against Arnold and the Benton robbery. If not, they will expose the fact that Henderson let Bates escape for twenty thousand dollars in bribe money, which has already been carefully planted on his behalf.

After Eddie makes an exit, Kent arrives to hear how Henderson cannot arrest the crooks behind the Benton robbery without ruining his career. Kent seems to understand without having heard the whole story, almost as if he was listening outside to Eddie with his super hearing. Henderson fails to pick up on this clue that Kent is Superman. It is difficult to decide whether Henderson is just too wrapped up in his pending blackmail, whether the story editor was sleeping on the job, or whether a critical scene was edited from the story to make more room for commercial messages.

Eddie returns to the hideout. He tells Arnold that he delivered the message and Henderson will probably come through with the evidence file because he was scared. When he tells Arnold that Kent was at the police station, he fears that Superman might get involved. Eddie says no matter, they can always use the new anti-Superman weapon. Arnold reminds him that the device has not yet been tested and to play it safe, they decide to get Kent out of the picture.

Lois and Jimmy arrive at Kent's empty office to discover a note on his desk. It says that Bates is ready to give himself up to the police if Kent will meet with him at the hideout where he was originally captured by Superman. Lois and Jimmy decide to meet with Bates themselves and scoop Kent on a good story.

When they arrive to meet Bates, they instead are greeted by Eddie pointing a gun. He orders the two nosey reporters to sit still until Kent arrives. Soon, Eddie starts complaining about back pains. It seems he is a hypochondriac, and Jimmy takes advantage of the opportunity by claiming to be a student of medicine. When Eddie allows Jimmy to approach him, he slugs the villain and knocks him cold.

Kent is in Henderson's office when Lois and Jimmy rush in to announce they have captured Eddie. The last thing Henderson wants to do now is arrest Eddie because of the blackmail scheme, but duty calls. After his arrest, Eddie tells the **COMMISSIONER** (*Selmer Jackson*) that Henderson has the bribe money. He will be glad to show where it is hidden with concrete proof that it belongs to the crooked Inspector.

Luckily, Kent discovers a locker key hidden inside the fender of Henderson's squad car. He changes to Superman and quickly arrives in time to remove the planted money before Eddie and the Commissioner arrive. Fearing he has been double-crossed, Eddie spills the beans and gives away the location of Arnold's hideout.

When Superman arrives to capture him, Arnold decides its time to test his new weapon. He turns it on Superman, but it blows up in his face. Once again, the point is made very clear that no invention of man will ever harm Superman.

EPISODE 76

THE DEADLY ROCK

directed by HARRY GERSTAD
written by JACKSON GILLIS

Under the opening title is a close shot of a gloved hand placing a glowing rock into a travel bag. Some stock footage of a commercial airliner establishes a flight to Metropolis airport. Inside

the terminal, **GARY ALLEN** (*Robert Lowery*) is using the telephone to announce his arrival to Clark Kent when the **BAGGAGE MAN** (*Jim Hayward*) sets the travel bag on the counter. Suddenly, Gary feels weak and dizzy before he drops to the floor.

Kent quickly changes to Superman and goes to the airport via a shortcut that few people are able to use. Gary wakes up as Kent helps him to a nearby bench. Jimmy arrives, surprised to see Kent, and is introduced to Gary Allen. Insisting he has never fainted before, Gary believes his condition has something to do with where he was standing. Kent suggests he is still feeling the effects of his plane-crash experience back in Africa, but when they return to the baggage counter, Gary starts to fall again. As Jimmy moves in to catch him, Kent also shows signs of weakness, but Jimmy is too busy helping Gary to notice. Back at the bench again, Kent sends Jimmy after a drink of water in order to buy time to compose himself.

Meanwhile, a funny little man named **VAN WICK** (*Steven Geary*) arrives to claim the travel bag. When the baggage man inquires about what is so heavy, Van Wick replies it is something that will harm nobody except one person. He giggles and then moves away as the baggage man scratches his head.

Later, a **DOCTOR** (*Vincent Perry*) reports to Kent and Jimmy that Gary's blood test indicates he has been exposed to some kind of metallic radiation. Gary explains the plane crash he had back in Africa was at the same time Superman tangled with the *panic in the sky* and he was caught in a shower of meteor fragments.

Kent tells Gary a man named Van Wick from Africa claimed a very heavy travel bag at the airport, but Gary doesn't know him. Jimmy believes the travel bag must contain kryptonite, but Kent tells him to keep that theory a secret for the time being.

Van Wick presents his scheme of using kryptonite to expose Superman for a price to **BIG TOM RUFUS** (*Bob Foulk*), a notorious and wealthy gangster with a secretary he calls **THE DUTCHESS** (*Lyn Thomas*). He agrees to pay eight million and sends **SNORKEL** (*Ric Roman*) to accompany Van Wick to the Daily Planet where Superman is known to appear.

Van Wick and Snorkel are loitering around the

hallway of the Daily Planet when the elevator doors open. The sharp-eyed viewer may notice the woman wearing a red skirt, a plaid jacket over a white blouse, and white gloves is the same lady that arrived at the airport just before Gary. The production budget of the series not only required the repeated use of the same extra players, but also could not afford them a change of wardrobe.

Anyway, Gary comes out of the elevator intending to meet Kent for lunch when he falls faint again because of his proximity to the deadly rock. Van Wick and Snorkel push him back into the elevator for a getaway.

Jimmy finally confides in Lois his worry about a possible threat to Superman. He tells her how a taxi driver friend reported taking a crazy man named Van Wick out to the house of Big Tom Rufus. Lois convinces Jimmy to investigate. They leave Kent a note and drive out to the Rufus country home.

Meanwhile, Gary sits unconscious in a chair as Van Wick explains to Rufus and group that Gary must be Superman because of how he reacts to kryptonite. Superman is watching unnoticed from the window as Snorkel fires three bullets at Gary. When the shots fail to harm him, they conclude that Superman is caught at last.

Jimmy and Lois are captured outside by another *THUG* *(Sid Melton)*. They are tied up and left with unconscious Gary while Rufus and the gang makes an escape.

The house is set to blow up any minute. Superman appears at the window with a flame thrower he found in the garage. He tells Jimmy to kick the rock into the fireplace. After Superman torches the kryptonite, he crashes through the window and prevents the bomb from going off.

Production photo: Investigative reporter—Clark Kent *(George Reeves)* is holding the pigeon that begins the next mystery of "The Phantom Ring" episode.

Lois and Jimmy are waiting with Gary in Kent's office. Gary explains how the kryptonite knocked him out while at the same time making him impervious to any mortal danger. All of this probably due to the effect of his plane crash in the meteor shower when Superman destroyed the asteroid back in 1953.

When Kent arrives, they all ask where he has been during all the excitement.

"Why, looking for Gary, of course." Kent replies with a smile. "We were supposed to have lunch."

An illustrated adventure entitled "Superman's Last Hour" in the comic pages of *Superman #92* may have inspired this episode.

EPISODE 77

THE PHANTOM RING

directed by PHIL FORD
written by DAVID CHANTLER

In this episode, writer David Chantler borrows from an idea that had already been perfected in the second Columbia serial. In *Atom Man vs. Superman*, Lex Luthor equipped his gang members with special coins that allowed them to not only become invisible, but actually teleport to and from their secret hideout.

Lois and Jimmy rush into Kent's office to deliver a package that is later discovered to be the work of *The Phantom*. Inside the box is a homing pigeon and a note to Kent proposing a secret meeting to discuss the recent string of robberies. If Kent wishes such a meeting, he is to reply by attaching a note to the pigeon. He is warned to try no tricks with the police and the message is signed, *Spectre*. Kent explains the pigeon is a clever idea because it cannot be traced like the mail or a telephone call.

After sending Lois and Jimmy away, Kent changes to Superman. He gives the bird a toss out the window and then follows after it.

Somewhere out in the country is a shack serving as the hideout for **THE SPECTRE** (Peter Brocco) and his gang, **AL** (Lane Bradford), **ROSEY** (Paul Burke), **JOE** (Ed Hinton), and **LUKE** (Henry Rowland). They are discussing their latest

gimmick for pulling off robberies when they are alerted to the approach of the pigeon and a UFO on their radar screen.

By pulling a lever, the gang disappears and a lead lined panel covers the radar screen and control panel hidden in the wall. When Superman arrives after the pigeon, he finds only an empty room.

Later, Kent is in Henderson's office discussing a warehouse robbery that took place in broad daylight without any witnesses. Kent jokingly suggests the obvious answer is the crooks are invisible.

Back at the hideout, it is time to make one of the gang members invisible by remote control. Outside the Apex Jewelry Store, Luke suddenly becomes invisible. Luke enters the store unnoticed and steals a tray full of gems.

When Kent and Henderson arrive to investigate, The **CLERK** (George Brand) tells how all he noticed was the door mysteriously opened and closed. Henderson looks at Kent when once again he proposes the obvious, yet impossible answer.

When Luke returns to the hideout with the stolen gems, he reports that Clark Kent is on to them. The Spectre decides that Kent must be eliminated.

Lois and Jimmy are in Kent's office when a voice orders them to go for a ride. When a gun appears to be suspended in thin air, and Jimmy feels the push of an invisible arm, they agree to the instructions.

Meanwhile, The Spectre is explaining the theory behind radar and their invisibility machine to one of the gangsters. As radar waves detect objects by bouncing off objects, so does the eye view things by reflected light waves. When they are under the influence of the invisibility machine, they cannot be seen nor detected by radar, a fact which later ironically contributes to their capture.

Then Lois and Jimmy arrive with the invisible Luke. The Spectre refers to them as cheese for the trap, ready to spring on Mr. Clark Kent.

Acting upon instructions from The Spectre, Kent is flying a chartered airplane when two voices from the back seat inform him that this is his last trip. When they appear, they remind him how he could have joined the group, but because

The Spectre *(Peter Brocco)* holds a gun on Clark Kent *(George Reeves)* while Rosey *(Paul Burke)* sneers in "The Phantom Ring" episode.

he double-crossed them by sending Superman with the homing pigeon, he ruined any chance he had to stay alive.

Knowing that Kent will soon be a dead man, The Spectre spills the entire scheme about the invisibility machine. Each member of the gang carries a special coin that acts as a receiver to the machine. They also tell Kent about how Luke is waiting right now at the Metropolis Bank to become invisible and pull off a robbery. Then Kent is hit on the head and thrown out of the airplane.

Clark Kent becomes Superman and flies to the Metropolis Bank. He takes the special coin away from Luke and tells him to give himself up to the police. After becoming invisible, we hear the sound of Superman taking off and then see a panning shot of an invisible Superman flying through the sky.

At the hideout, the visible gangsters are gloating about how they tossed the nosey Kent out of an airplane. Then the phantom Superman crashes through the wall and begins to clean up

the room in a nicely orchestrated fight scene. When Lois and Jimmy break out of the locked room, they see the unconscious bodies of the gang laying around in the debris of broken furniture, obviously the work of a hurricane named Superman.

"Poor Clark. He must've been scared to death," says Lois, thankful that Superman was able to save Mr. Kent.

"Oh, I think he took it rather well," Superman replies, "for Clark Kent, that is."

EPISODE 78

THE JOLLY ROGER

directed by PHIL FORD
written by DAVID CHANTLER

Comical dialog and a silly plot make up this episode. It is rather enjoyable, however, if you don't take it too seriously. Lois is waiting in Perry's office when Kent and Jimmy rush in to get

Production photo: *Noel Neill, Jack Larson,* and *George Reeves (out of character)* taking a break on the set of "The Phantom Ring" episode.

their next assignment. Perry says he has an idea for a Sunday supplement story and he wants Kent, Lois, and *Flashbulb* Olsen to cover it. Jimmy incites the group, ready to go, but Perry suggests it might be a good idea to hear the details before dashing away.

A deserted island in the Pacific is scheduled to be the next target for some special Navy artillary practice. Perry wants the reporters to visit Island Able and take pictures. A protest is expressed.

"I just hope there's a Monday supplement telling how we gave our lives for the Sunday supplement!" says Jimmy emphatically.

Perry glares at Jimmy. "Don't tempt me."

The idea is to get a photo layout showing the before and after. The fate of the island will demonstrate the power of the Navy fleet.

Stock footage of a commercial airliner dissolves into a view of a lush tropical island. Kent, Lois and Jimmy have arrived by seaplane,

wearing the appropriate safari clothing. If the jungle set and a few of the extra cast members appear familiar, you probably remember *Dagger Island* from just a few weeks earlier.

Within seconds of saying how peaceful and quiet the island appears, they are suddenly surrounded by a band of pirates. Kent finds it difficult to keep from smiling as the pirate **CAPTAIN BLOOD** *(Leonard Mudie)* introduces himself and his mates *(Myron Healey, Patrick Aherne, and Eric Snowdon).*

"I'm Capt. Blood, this is Capt. Thud, Capt. Scud, Capt. Mud, and Lieutenant Schultz."

From here on in, you must throw logic to the wind. The parody of shipwrecked pirates living on this island for generations continues when the reject buccaneers try to decide which method of capture and punishment to use on the intruders. Lois makes a request for some pirate songs, but they have never learned any.

Captain Blood *(Leonard Mudie)* with Clark Kent *(George Reeves)*.

At the camp, we meet **TYLER** *(Ray Montgomery)* and **RIFFLES** *(Dean Cromer)*. They were washed ashore three years ago when their plane crashed and have been stranded ever since. They immediately make plans to steal the visitors' seaplane and escape when the time is right.

Captain Blood announces that the only charge he knows about is mutiny. The visitors are sentenced without trial to be strung from the yardarm. But they don't have a yardarm. "Then they shall walk the plank!" But their forefathers ran out of planks two hundred years ago. The only alternative is to lop off their heads.

Kent has had just about enough and demands proof that these raggedy braggards are really pirates. Tyler and Riffles become attentative when Captain Blood uncovers a chest full of

treasure. In fear of the limited time remaining, Lois blurts out the reality of the approaching Navy fleet with designs on the island's destruction. Having never heard of modern navy strength, the pirates are spirited to defend their home with one rusty old cannon.

Seizing an opportunity, Tyler sides with Captain Blood and convinces him to restrain Kent and his two friends while he and Riffles scout the island for other invaders. Fortunately, the three are tied up and blindfolded, giving Kent the perfect chance to slip away.

Superman flies out to the bridge of the leading destroyer and tries to convince the **ADMIRAL** *(Pierre Watkin)* to call off the maneuvers. The **LIEUTENANT** *(Chet Marshall)* and the Admiral find his story as difficult to believe as we do, though

George Reeves on the set of "The Jolly Roger" episode, where he might have been quoted to say, *"Last episode of the season and I have my contract for thirteen more."*

you would expect they would know by now that Superman never tells a lie. Anyway, the officers insist that without proof, the attack must go on as scheduled.

Back at the island, Superman has Jimmy photograph the pirates and he quickly develops the negative with his x-ray vision. Remember, you were asked to throw logic to the wind.

The Navy cannons begin to open fire and Superman takes to the sky. Several flying shots of Superman in every direction are intercut with stock footage of giant cannons blasting away. No sharp eyes are required to notice the insignia on Superman's chest is reversed in the shots of him flying toward camera right. Other episodes display this error, but only in brief clips not nearly as obvious.

Seeing that the shells are all bursting in mid air, the Admiral orders a cease fire and a return to port. Kent captures Tyler and Riffles trying to steal the seaplane and returns to camp. In the confusion, the pirate treasure has been lost to quicksand and twenty fathoms of water.

Back at the office, Perry finishes reading the report. "Great story, beautiful pictures. Do you think anyone will believe it?"

"You believe it, don't you, Chief?"

"Oh, I believe it. But I'm not very bright."

Jimmy smiles, "That's the first time I heard him admit it."

As Perry attempts to get out of his chair, Jimmy races for the door. "Get out!" yells the frustrated editor as he throws a book at the fleeing photographer.

The Episodes of
1956

IN THE JANUARY 21, 1956 ISSUE OF *THE BILLBOARD,* A CONTEMPORARY INDUSTRY TRADE magazine, a column entitled *Films to Watch* featured a current ratings review of the series.

> *SUPERMAN—Flamingo Films*
> *Another long running national spot deal, "Superman" has been playing well over 100 markets for Kellogg's for over three years. It still pulls super ratings. In the breakdown of syndicated adventure shows appearing in this week's "scoreboard," "Superman's" November national average Telepulse of 13.7 is tops. It is tied for top adventure among teen-agers. Among all syndicated shows, it stands sixth, according to average weighted ratings. It always ranks among the top 10 syndicated shows in New York, where it has all this time been entrenched in the Monday, 6-6:30 p.m. slot on WRCA-TV. In the December Telepulse, it was the second ranking syndicated show in New York.*

However, when the Superman production entered its fifth year, it seemed the momentum was winding down. There was a variety of story ideas from which to attempt a fresh look, but the temptation to keep the violence light and focus on the humorous villains was too much for conservative Ellsworth. The producers and the sponsors were happy. There was no incentive to tamper with a winning formula.

Two veteran directors returned to make sure everyone made his entrance and exit on cue. *Harry Gerstad* directed eight shows, and *George Blair* handled the other five. Writer *David Chantler* knew so well the formula for a safe storyline and scripted nearly half the season, and he shared credit with sister *Peggy* on number eighty-five.

This was also the year Superman made a guest appearance on the "I Love Lucy" show. Actor George Reeves was drafted by Ricky Ricardo to attend a birthday party for his son, little Ricky. The usually mixed-up Lucy attempted to convince the gathering children that she was Superman when she learned mistakenly that Mr. Reeves' busy schedule would not allow him to show up. But like most of the *Adventures of Superman* series, he arrived in the nick of time to save the party and bring Lucy in out of the rain.

PRODUCTION CREDITS

producer . . . . Whitney Ellsworth
production manager . . . . Eddie Donahoe
director of photography . . . . Harold Wellman ASC
film editor . . . . Sam Waxman
art director . . . . John Mansbridge
set decorator . . . . Jerry Welch
assistant director . . . . Louis Germonprez
assistant director . . . . Dick Dixon
special effects . . . . Thol Simonson
sound engineer . . . . Robert Post

EPISODE 79

PERIL IN PARIS

directed by GEORGE BLAIR
written by DAVID CHANTLER

Opening to the sound of the French national anthem and a view of the Eiffel Tower, this episode begins with Clark Kent and Jimmy Olsen waiting in the office of the Prefect of Police. When **INSPECTOR LANIER** (*Robert Shayne*) enters, they are very much amazed and amused at how much this man looks like their own Inspector Henderson. But this little irony has nothing to do with the story.

Lanier has received a letter addressed to Superman. It is from a stage actress named Anna Constantine, living in a 'less fortunate country behind the iron curtain.' It is a plea for Superman to meet with her. The welfare of many people is at stake. Kent agrees to deliver the message.

Back at their hotel, Kent sends Jimmy off to file their news stories at the Press Bureau while he runs a few errands. After Jimmy leaves, Kent becomes Superman and leaps out the window. **ANNA CONSTANTINE** (*Lilyan Chauvin*) is waiting at a theatre. Superman arrives backstage to meet with her. He immediately hears a ticking bomb. Quickly, he locates it and shields Madame Constantine from an explosion.

GREGOR (*Peter Mamakos*), an old family friend, comes running to see what happened. Together, they explain how they have recovered the fortune in jewels that was stolen from the Constantine family during the war. They wish for Superman to fly the jewels to France, fearing a customs inspection, where they will sell them and use the money to help their people begin a new life in freedom. Superman agrees, but warns them that he will investigate their claim on the jewels and also check up on how the money is spent. They are most grateful and arrange a meeting place in France for that night.

Later, when Superman arrives to deliver the smuggled jewels to Anna and Gregor, they are confronted by officials **INSPECTOR LAMONT** (*Albert Carrier*) and **OFFICER GERARD** (*Charles LaTorre*). Anna and Gregor are placed under arrest as known smugglers and the jewels are confiscated.

As the two accused thieves are escorted to jail, Lamont warns Superman not to interfere or he will be reported as an accomplice. Confused, and unwilling to strain our relations with France any more than they are already, Superman reluctantly agrees.

The next day, Kent storms the office of Lanier and demands to see Anna and Gregor. When Lanier claims no knowledge of their arrest or of an officer named Lamont, Kent begins to sense a ruse.

Lanier tells Kent that a master jeweler named DuCray has just been released from prison. He suggests the phoney policemen may attempt to contact DuCray for cutting and fencing the Constantine jewels.

Kent pays a visit to **JACQUES DUCRAY** (*Franz Roehn*) at his curio shop. Kent enlists his help in recovering the stolen jewels and bringing the thieves to justice. DuCray agrees to start a rumor in the underworld that a young American named Olsen is looking to purchase the stolen gems and to contact Kent when the thieves approach him.

Back at the hotel, Kent explains the plan to Jimmy. He is to pretend to be a jewel expert and set up a meeting with the crooks in their hotel room when they contact him. After Kent leaves, Jimmy is unexpectedly visited by the thieves and taken away to their hideout.

Kent stops in to visit the curio shop, but DuCray is not around. When Gerard enters, no longer dressed as a policeman, he tells Kent that DuCray has recently sold the shop. Gerard orders Kent to leave immediately.

Jimmy is at the hideout, doing his best to maintain the identity of an American gangster. He examines the jewels with an eyeglass that keeps falling from his eye. He is nervously waiting for Superman to make an appearance. Anna and DuCray are being held captive and Gregor is in on the robbery scheme with Lamont. Jimmy drops his disguise when he rushes to meet Gerard at the door thinking he is Superman coming to the rescue.

As the crooks are about to push the three captives down into a pit under the hideout, Jimmy stalls for time by yelling to Superman who he hopes to be outside. When all seems lost, the cement wall explodes as Superman makes a spectacular entrance. Bullets fly, but the villains soon give up by jumping down into the pit. When Jimmy asks how he managed to find them, Superman tells DuCray how it was a good idea to send Gerard back to the curio shop to get his tools.

"But it was Mr. Kent who was to meet me at the shop," remarks a confused DuCray.

"How do you explain that?" asks Jimmy, smiling.

"You're not the only one I have to keep track of," replies Superman. "Sometimes I'm very close to Clark Kent." He winks at the camera as the show fades out.

EPISODE 80

TIN HERO

directed by GEORGE BLAIR
written by WILTON SCHILLER

Perry White has called a meeting to complain about not having any sensational crime stories to publish in the Daily Planet. The Mayor seeking re-election and gardening events on the front page does not sell newspapers! Certainly, criminal activity is taking place, and Perry instructs his reporters to find out about it.

FRANK SMULLENS *(Carl Ritchie)*, a Lou Costello type character is walking down the sidewalk working a loop of string into a cat's cradle. He accidentally stumbles into an escaping bank robber. Jimmy happens to be nearby with his camera as Smullens wrestles the villain to the ground. He snaps a picture of the daring capture.

The picture ends up on the front page with a headline describing how a private citizen has foiled an armed bank robbery. When Perry begins to reprimand Jimmy for not bringing the hero in for an exclusive interview, Jimmy opens the door to introduce Smullens to the editor.

Smullens explains how he was on his lunch break from his bookkeeping job when he had a feeling that he should be in the vicinity of the bank. He tells how he has witnessed other interesting events like shootings, a man jumping out a window, and a no hitter at the baseball park.

White believes Smullens to be a natural news hound and offers him a job at twice his current salary. After discussing it with his girlfriend, CELIA *(Paula Houston),* he agrees to become a crime busting reporter.

Smullens has a hunch. He and Kent are watching the bank when they see the bank president get his pocket picked by a crook who Kent recognizes as FINGERS DANNY *(Sam Finn)*. When Smullens moves in to stop him, Fingers pulls a gun. Kent quickly takes it away from him, but Smullens faints and drops to the sidewalk.

The crime busting reporter myth is perpetuated when Smullens happens upon a robbery in progress. Gangster MARTY *(Frank Richards)* is about to clean out a walk-in vault when he is interrupted. Once again, the sight of a gun causes Smullens to pass out. Marty locks him in the safe with a stick of dynamite.

Superman arrives in time to lift the door off its hinges, grab the dynamite, and throw it out into the sky before it explodes. He congratulates Smullens on preventing another robbery because gangster Marty has escaped without stealing anything.

At the hideout, BIG JACK *(Jack Lomas)* explains that Smullens must be eliminated if they are to have any hope of successfully pulling off eight jobs the next day. Marty asks how they are going to capture Smullens if Superman is watching him all the time? Big Jack says they will get to Smullens by capturing his girlfriend.

In Perry White's office, Jimmy intercepts a telephone call. Pretending to be Smullens, he is directed to Celia's house at 37 Maple Street. Lois enters as Jimmy rushes off on his hot tip. When he arrives at Celia's house, he finds that Marty and Big Jack are holding Celia captive.

Perry and Smullens arrive at the office. When Lois mentions the address of Jimmy's hot tip telephone call, Smullens recognizes it be his girlfriend's house. He rushes out of the office, Lois follows after him, and Kent makes an excuse to stay behind so he can run to the storage room to become Superman.

At Celia's place, she and Jimmy are tied up and Big Jack decides to turn on the gas jet of the fireplace. As he and Marty are about to exit, Superman arrives to turn off the gas and knock out the crooks. Rather than release Celia and

Lois Lane *(Noel Neill)* attempts to jog Superman's memory by showing the listing for last season's "The Wedding of Superman" episode.

Jimmy, he empties the guns and positions the two thugs on the couch. He apologizes for not untying Celia and Jimmy, and then he leaps out the window.

Within seconds, Smullens bravely rushes into the room, sees the two thugs on the couch, and then he attacks. He quickly takes the two guns away from them and bashes their heads together, unaware that they have already been dispatched by Superman.

"That will teach you to fool around with my girl," says Smullens.

Lois enters to see the results of another crime busting reporter adventure.

Later, in Perry's office, Smullens announces that he is giving up his job as reporter. He humbly reports that his old boss took notice of the stories about him in the newspaper and has offered him his old job back along with a raise and promotion. Perry is disappointed, but Kent reminds him that he did get a good series of articles just when he thought the crime situation was getting dull. Jimmy remarks that now they will have to go back to meetings of the "Better

Babies League" and cover gardening stories for the front page.

Perry White scowls.

EPISODE 81

MONEY TO BURN

directed by HARRY GERSTAD
written by DAVID CHANTLER

When the Daily Planet warehouse catches fire in the opening scenes, Lois and Jimmy rush to investigate along with their editor, Perry White. On the scene is a lunch truck operated by two shady characters who identify themselves as the "Firemen's Friends." Appearing to provide much needed coffee and sandwiches to the firemen on duty, *SLIM* (*Mauritz Hugo*) mans the serving counter of the truck while his *PARTNER* (*Dale Van Sickel*) goes into the burning building dressed in a fireproof suit to clean out the payroll vault.

Superman arrives unaware of the robbery. He takes a nearby fire hose and rushes toward the building. We know from the remarks of the witnesses that he leaps over the building and dives into the flames. Inside, we see him rush around at super speed spraying the fire with water. Within seconds, the danger is over, and Jimmy takes credit for turning on the water.

Later, Perry returns to his three reporters waiting in his office. He tells how he has just been interviewed by the insurance investigator. Perry had delivered a payroll to the warehouse just before the fire started and he is suspected of stealing it. If he puts in a claim for damages to the warehouse as a leading stockholder, he will be charged with fraud. Kent suspects foul play and offers to investigate. Perry insists on doing it alone.

Perry decides to question the two lunch truck operators regarding the fire. When he later enters their truck to snoop around, he finds the asbestos suit, but he is caught and stashed away in the vault of the burned out Daily Planet warehouse.

When Lois reports to Kent at the editor's office, they realize Perry has not checked in yet. Kent rushes off to follow his trail. He questions the *FIRE LIEUTENANT* (*Richard Emory*) and becomes very concerned when he hears that Perry never

stopped to talk with the fire department official. Then a fire alarm rings out, and Kent rushes off to become Superman.

At another blazing fire, the lunch truck is again on the scene. Superman comes crashing in through a brick wall to confront the man in the fireproof suit. The man makes a deal to reveal the location of the missing Perry White if Superman will allow him to escape. Superman reluctantly agrees, but warns the man not to let anything happen to Perry.

"I give you my word, Superman," says the unknown burglar. "He's in the safest surroundings possible."

The man laughs at the humor of his statement as he walks away without any interference from our hero. Much like *The Riddler* of the later Batman series, there is a hidden significance to the crook's clever remark.

Later, Kent is on hand to talk with the two lunch truck workers. They claim to remember seeing Perry at the warehouse fire and serving him some coffee. This and a witty remark by the second truck worker proves to be their downfall because Jimmy later reminds Kent that Perry doesn't drink coffee.

Kent soon figures the scheme is operated by the lunch truck workers and realizes the "safest surroundings possible" for Perry must be the warehouse vault. He rescues the editor and rounds up the two villains after Perry reveals their address. The show closes with the usual clever dialog which is beginning to wear thin after eighty-one episodes.

"I wonder what Clark Kent will say when I show up with this story?" says Perry as he telephones the police.

"Well, strangely enough," replies Superman, "I don't think he'll be surprised."

EPISODE 82

THE TOWN THAT WASN'T

directed by HARRY GERSTAD
written by WILTON SCHILLER

Jimmy is off on a vacation. A story breaks about a missing truck full of pharmaceutical supplies, and the production moves to some nice

Production photo: *George Reeves* is about to crash through a carefully prepared doorway.

countryside exterior locations. Jimmy is caught in a speed trap by a phoney **POLICEMAN** *(Charles Gray)*. He is escorted to see the **JUDGE** *(Richard Elliott)* in the courthouse of a very small town called Ackport.

A stiff fine leaves Jimmy with no more vacation money, so he returns to Metropolis. We soon learn from conversations between the policeman and the judge that they are operating in a portable town that serves as a front for their hijacking racket.

When Jimmy returns to the office with serious intentions of writing a story about his speed trap experience, Perry lectures him about using the

Production photo: *Noel Neill* waiting to write down *George Reeve's* latest inspiration.

newspaper to air his own private grievances. He instead assigns the angry young reporter to work with Kent on the hijacking story, unaware that the two subjects are related.

We see the phoney town in action again when a **TRUCK DRIVER** *(Phillip Barnes)* arrives and stops for lunch at the town diner. The **WAITER** *(Jack Littlefield)* pushes a secret button to alert another phoney **POLICEMAN** *(Terry Frost)* waiting nearby to inspect the parked truck and discover faulty brakes. The truck driver is cited and jailed.

The news arrives at the Daily Planet of another missing truck. Lois is assigned to follow the known route of the missing truck, and she finds her way into the phoney town. She is quickly arrested on suspicion of impersonating a newspaper reporter. When she fails to call into

the office on schedule, Kent, Jimmy, and Inspector Henderson follow up on her disappearance.

Out on the country road, Jimmy recognizes the old location of his previous experience in Ackport when he trips over a rock that was once obstructing the steps to the courthouse. When they find a few loose nails on the ground, Kent begins to realize what is happening.

As they continue their drive, they are soon stopped by a policeman who fails to recognize Jimmy. The three are dragged into the phoney court to see the judge. When Henderson identifies himself as an official from Metropolis, the three are led at gunpoint into jail where they meet up with Lois.

After the villains leave to watch for a soon to

arrive armored truck, Kent manages to unlock the jail cell door. But before anyone else can get out, he pretends to accidentally lock it again and uses the opportunity to make a change into Superman. The highlight of the episode is a nice outdoor, running takeoff from a carefully placed springboard. This camera footage also shows up later in *The Stolen Elephant* episode.

Superman collects the bad guys and returns them to confinement in their own jail cell. Lois inquires as to what ever happened to Clark Kent?

"He must've gotten a lift back to town," says Superman. "You know how he is when there is a story to be written."

After Superman makes a hasty exit, Lois turns to Jimmy and says, "Let's try and beat him back to Metropolis!"

"Who? Superman?" asks Jimmy.

"Of course not, Silly," replies Lois. "Mr. Kent."

"Nothing doing," says Jimmy. "We're gonna take it nice and easy. Don't you know that some of these towns are speed traps?"

When I was a kid, this was one of my favorite episodes. It impressed me to the point that I was always on the lookout for phoney little towns whenever the family would go out for a Sunday drive. However, as I got older, the logic began to break down when I realized that State Policemen patrol all the highways at one time or another and such a clever scheme would never be practical in real life.

When I confessed my disappointment for this story flaw to my younger sister, she added a new insight to the plan. If a real policeman came along, the crooks could easily fake shooting a television show until they went away. With that, even today, I worry when driving out on a secluded stretch of country road.

EPISODE 83

THE TOMB OF ZAHARAN

directed by GEORGE BLAIR
written by DAVID CHANTLER

The criminals in Metropolis take a back seat in this episode of international adventure. Perry has ordered his three favorite staff members to appear in his office for a new assignment. There is a clever scene in the beginning to fill out the full half-hour which has Lois and Jimmy dropping in on Kent as he appears to be typing with his eyes closed.

When Perry asks if either of the three knows anything about the secret cult of *Zaharan*, Jimmy responds with, "whatever it is, I didn't do it." They soon learn of a scheduled visit of two foreign dignitaries with the names **ABDUL BEN BEY** *(Ted Hecht)* and **ALI ZING** *(Jack Reitzen)*. They are on a world tour and rumor has it they are members of this ancient cult. The reporters are to greet them at the airport in search of an interview. To help them get the visitors' attention, Perry has borrowed an ancient scarab necklace from a professor friend for Lois to wear.

Stock footage of an airliner sets the stage for the airport sequence. The three reporters arrive at the terminal and see two sinister characters waiting nearby. Kent excuses himself to check with security and instead ducks into a nearby room to change into Superman.

When Abdul and Ali arrive, an airport **ROBBER** *(Jack Kruschen)* makes a dash for Lois and grabs her necklace before he escapes. Then another **VILLAIN** *(Gabriel Mooradian)* holds the two visitors at gunpoint until Superman crashes through the wall to confront him. After emptying his gun on Superman, he decides foolishly to attempt a running head butt at the colorful costume only to knock himself out. This must have brought back memories for George Reeves of his old wrestling days.

After the confusion is over, Abdul and Ali are talking with Lois and Jimmy when Kent arrives with the scarab necklace retrieved by Superman. The two visitors recognize it as once belonging to an ancient queen of Zaharan. Their interest in the necklace leads them to invite Lois and Jimmy back to their home city of Beldad. Perry agrees to let them go, but Kent is forced to stay behind and help the editor with the special anniversary issue of the newspaper.

Kent is concerned with the mysterious circumstances regarding a secret excavation in Beldad. Jimmy says not to worry, if there is any trouble, he will be there. Perry responds quickly with, "you'll not only be there, but chances are ten to one that you will have started it!" Perry's confidence in Jimmy is further weakened when he almost leaves without his camera.

Anyway, Jimmy and Lois soon find themselves kidnapped as usual and taken to an ancient temple. They are forced into costumes of the ancient people of Zaharan and sealed in a throne room where a poison smoke from burning incense will soon bring about their deaths. It seems that Abdul and Ali believe Lois to be the reincarnated queen because she is in possession of the sacred necklace.

Meanwhile, Kent and Perry get a telegram from Beldad, but they reason that it wasn't written by the two veteran reporters because it didn't sign off with the traditional newspaper -30-. Kent rushes around on an investigation that leads him to the Beldad equivalent of Inspector Henderson *(George Khoury)*. Here he learns of the Zaharan temple location.

Superman arrives before the police and moves a giant granite block to gain entry to the tomb for the rescue. Later, Abdul and Ali return to find the open tomb, and they believe that the prophecy has been fulfilled.

The closing scene in Perry's office has Lois and Jimmy making an entrance costumed in the ancient garb to help prove their outrageous story. This is just another example of how the series had been reduced to stories where danger is wildly fabricated for Superman to come to the rescue, strictly played for laughs.

EPISODE 84

THE MAN WHO MADE DREAMS COME TRUE

directed by GEORGE BLAIR
written by DAVID CHANTLER

In the opening scene of this episode, Lois Lane calls attention to an interesting advertisement in the newspaper. A man calling himself "The Dreamer" at 819 Half Moon Road claims an ability to make good dreams come true, and he assists clients in avoiding the consequences of bad dreams. Kent isn't too interested in what he calls a cheap, but probably legal, racket. Perry orders the three reporters to get an interview with the visiting King of Sartania.

We soon learn that **KING LEO** *(Cyril Delevanti)* is superstitious enough to carry a rabbit's foot and a collection of other good luck charms. He rules his country based on what he dreams. Coincidentally, Rutherford Jones, also known as **THE DREAMER** *(Keith Richards)*, has confided in his girlfriend, **RUBY** *(Laurie Mitchell)* that all his scheme needs now is a testimonial from some honest citizen to boost his popularity and lead them to the riches of the bigtime.

NANCY BOYD *(Sandy Harrison)* pays a visit to the Dreamer's special effects equipped parlor to confess her recurring dream to meet Superman. The Dreamer predicts she will meet the man of her dreams at her favorite ice-cream shop.

The Dreamer, disguised as an ordinary citizen, drops in on Clark Kent to make an innocent request. He claims to have a young lady friend whose shyness and unpopularity would benefit greatly from a visit by Superman. Kent is in a charitable mood and becomes Superman to pay a visit to Nancy. However, after talking with Nancy and **MIKE** *(Hal Hoover)*, the man behind the soda counter, Superman realizes that Nancy is very popular, and more importantly, she has recently seen the Dreamer.

Back at the office, Kent becomes more interested in the newspaper advertisement quoted earlier by Lois. He convinces her on a hunch to pay a visit to this mystic in search of a story. It finally develops when King Leo's passion for immortality collides with the scheme of the Dreamer to fleece him of his fortune.

Lois drops in to pay a visit to the Dreamer where she meets King Leo. Worried that his plan may be foiled, The Dreamer captures Lois and locks her away for safe keeping.

King Leo's bodyguard, **BRONSKY** *(John Banner)* is concerned for his ruler's safety, but is helpless when two attempts are executed to eliminate King Leo. The Dreamer has convinced him to tempt fate by standing in a bathtub with a live electrical wire, and then later by driving backwards down a curving mountain road. Superman intervenes both times, providing a spectacular crashing entrance through a glass window and a glaring oversight by the special effects department.

After he prevents King Leo's automobile from going over a cliff in broad daylight, Superman

Production photo: *NO ONE CAN PLEASE EVERYBODY, BUT WE TRY!*

moves around to the car to have a word with King Leo. In the background we see nothing but black. Somewhere on the cutting room floor is where the background footage ended up.

Superman eventually cures King Leo of his superstitious beliefs and captures the crooked Dreamer. Bronsky performs the final knockout as Superman stands back with his arms folded. All in all, a rather boring affair.

EPISODE 85

DISAPPEARING LOIS

directed by HARRY GERSTAD
written by DAVID CHANTLER
& PEGGY CHANTLER

Perry White has called a meeting of his three favorite reporters to discuss the story of the day. A notorious criminal named Lank Garrett has just been released on parole after serving a seven year sentence for robbery. The million dollars he is believed to have stolen was never recovered. The police feel Garrett is going to wait out the statute of limitations and eventually reclaim the loot to build a new crime empire.

Perry offers an extra month's salary to the reporter who gets an exclusive interview with the criminal boss who is known for his reluctance to speak with any members of the media. Lois decides to team up with Jimmy in order to get the story before Clark Kent can beat them to it. She invents a scheme to make Kent believe she has vanished, hoping to keep him occupied while she and Jimmy set out to get the interview with Garrett.

Kent offers to give Lois a ride to her new apartment. Then she puts her plan into motion to make him think she lives somewhere else. When Kent returns later with her forgotten purse, he finds the apartment refurnished along

Production photos: *George Reeves* posing with a series of props.

with a new occupant, **SARA GREEN** (*Yvonne White*). Kent launches a quick investigation only to learn the landlady and the janitor both claim to have never heard of Lois Lane. But they, of course, are all part of Lois' scheme.

Meanwhile, Lois and Jimmy disguise themselves as cleaning people to gain access to the apartment of **GARRETT** (*Milton Frome*) and his sidekick, **LEFTY** (*Ben Welden*). When Lois asks too many questions and Jimmy makes the mistake of saying Lois has three grandmothers to support, Garrett gets suspicious. He soon discovers they are reporters, but he admires their clever method

of getting in to see him. He is also quite willing to give them an interview when he learns that they are in competition with Kent for an exclusive. He was never crazy about how Kent treated him in the newspaper.

Garrett leaves Lois and Jimmy to clean up the apartment while he goes off on an errand and promises to consider talking when he returns. Superman shows up at the apartment unaware that Jimmy and Lois are watching him from the next room. They watch as Superman takes note of something in the floor. When he leaves, they lift the rug to find Garrett's secret hiding place for his million dollars. However, Garrett makes a timely return to catch them, and then he orders Lefty to escort them to a hideout cave in the country.

Lefty turns out to be a typical bumbling fool, so common in the criminal world of producer *Ellsworth*. Lois finds it easy to convince Lefty to strike out on his own and defy Garrett. He soon appoints Lois to be his new gun moll and Jimmy to be his chief henchman.

Kent has convinced Henderson to search Garrett's apartment, but he is surprised to find the money has been removed from the hiding place in the floor. Garrett laughs the whole thing off as a crazy idea of Kent seeking revenge.

Kent and Henderson are then called to Lois' apartment *(now back in order)* just in time to meet the arriving Lefty. They get the drop on him, but the tables are soon turned when Garrett shows up to discover that Lefty has double-crossed him. In the confusion, Kent gets himself shot and left for dead as Garrett leads everyone away at gunpoint.

Out at the country cave we know so well, Lois, Jimmy, Henderson, and Lefty are about to be buried in a forced landslide by Garrett's getaway car when Superman arrives in time to save them. Garrett and Lefty are captured, and Lois and Jimmy have their exclusive story.

In the final scene in Perry's office, we see Kent wearing his arm in a sling. Lois is concerned about his pain, but he confesses that it doesn't hurt at all, as if the bullet never touched him. Perry White offers the bonus to Lois for a story well done.

EPISODE 86

CLOSE SHAVE

directed by HARRY GERSTAD
written by STEVEN POST
& BEN CROCKER

In this episode, it seems that *TONY* (Richard Benedict), the barber, has a unique gift for bringing out the best in people. While waiting to get a haircut, Jimmy watches with great interest as Tony tries to convince an old friend, *RICK SABLE*

(Rick Vallin), to give up his career as a gangster and start to lead a good life. In fact, Tony's conversation is so hypnotic that Rick almost calls the police to alert them to a jewelry company robbery.

Back at the office, Jimmy relays what he witnessed at the barber shop. Kent finds it difficult to believe that a noted gangster would betray his own men, but when he hears that Lois is on her way to the same jeweler to pick up her wrist watch, Superman decides to play a hunch and investigate.

When Superman arrives at the jewelry store, he confronts *HARRY* (Donald Diamond) and *LEFTY* (Harry Fleer) coming out with their guns drawn. Lois is taken hostage, but Superman melts their firearms with his heat vision, and Lois knocks them out cold with a swing of her purse.

Jimmy decides to return to the barber shop and get a story about Tony. When Rick Sable returns to the shop to confirm how he almost turned in his own men, Tony hides Jimmy in the closet. He overhears how Rick is scared that he may be losing his grip on reality. Tony assures him that he is only suffering from guilt and really wishes to become an honest person. After Rick leaves, Jimmy sits in the barber chair and allows Tony to give him a pep talk on how he should be more aggressive toward his boss with his own ideas on how to be a good newspaper reporter.

In Perry White's office, Jimmy explains how he believes Tony has a unique power of influence. He tells Perry that he has an idea for a story. With Tony's help, Jimmy will get the scoop on Rick Sable's gang with details on all the crooked schemes they may be planning. Perry orders him to forget the idea and cover the garden club meeting as he was assigned.

Jimmy decides to follow his own idea. When Tony and Jimmy are almost at the home of Rick Sable, Lois pops up from hiding in the back seat. Before Jimmy can abort the dangerous assignment for the sake of Lois, *TRIGGER* (John Ferry) and *MICKEY* (Jack Littlefield), two members of the Sable gang, escort Tony and the two reporters into the house.

Later, Jimmy, Lois, and Tony are sitting around the kitchen table, each tied to his chair. Trigger and Mickey are waiting for the boss to return and decide how to deal with the intruders. Tony talks the two crooks into a hypnotic sleep, but before the captives can get loose, Rick Sable arrives.

As the two thugs wake up, Rick is in the process of untying his friend, Tony. He announces that he is disbanding the organization and turning himself in to the police. Mickey, however, announces that the organization now belongs to him. Rick calls him a coward and advises that he also turn himself in and take what is coming to them.

A deal is made. With a bomb set to go off at some unknown time within the next several minutes, whichever gang member remains in the room the longest will become the new leader and make all the decisions. Trigger exits first, then Rick runs away. Mickey claims the title of new boss, and then he leaves Jimmy, Lois, and Tony to die in the explosion.

When it looks like the end, Rick comes rushing back in the room. He only faked cowardess to get Mickey out of the house. But something is wrong! It is too late to stop the automatic timer before the explosion!

Superman arrives crashing through the wall in time to shield everyone from the blast. Mickey and Trigger return to witness the bravery displayed by Rick. He is still going through with his plan to go straight. Mickey and Trigger are so impressed, they agree to face the music with the boss. Tony offers each of them a job in his barber business as soon as they get out of jail. The show closes with Mickey and Trigger arguing over who will get the shoe shine concession.

EPISODE 87

THE PHONEY ALIBI

directed by GEORGE BLAIR
written by PEGGY CHANTLER

This episode begins when Kent gets a telephone tip from Inspector Henderson. Ed Crowley's gang has just robbed the Wentworth jewelry store and Schultzy Garfield is in a getaway car headed out of town on highway 201. The police have no chance of catching him. Kent quickly makes a change in the storeroom and Superman flies out to catch the escaping villain.

While Lois waits patiently for Kent to return to his office, **PROFESSOR PEPPERWINKLE** (*Phillips Tead*) arrives to explain his new invention. It proves to be a method for transporting real objects over the telephone lines, an idea which was recycled much more seriously in *The Fly*, 1986. Anyway, Lois takes him not so seriously and suggests he would better spend his time inventing a pick-proof lock. To that he claims he already has, unfortunately he has yet to invent the key to unlock it.

Meanwhile, **BENNY** (*Frank Kreig*) is standing by as **ED CROWLEY** (*John Cliff*) is attempting to set a new record with a yoyo. Then **CLIPPY** (*William Challee*) rushes in to report the fate of Schultzy at the hand of Superman. Clippy is scheduled to pull a job the next day, but he confesses to having cold feet. Crowley, the boss of the gang, decides it would be wise to lay low with any new jobs until he can think up a way to better establish good alibis. Clippy is relieved and quite content to go home and wait. He lives at the Pepperwinkle boarding house.

When Clippy arrives to check in with Pepperwinkle to see what is cooking for dinner, the professor decides to try an experiment. Clippy claims to have a friend in Kansas City he would like to visit. The professor explains how his new invention can squeeze the air from between the atoms of Clippy's body, start him vibrating, and send him down the telephone lines for a surprise visit to Kansas City. Clippy decides to humor the old man in the interest of hurrying dinner.

Before long, **MOE** (*Harry Arnie*) sees his telephone about to shake off the wall just before Clippy appears in a cloud of smoke. A new idea for establishing alibis occurs to Clippy and he rushes back to Metropolis to inform the boss. Clippy soon pulls off a robbery and has the machine send him off to San Francisco for the perfect alibi.

A gloomy Henderson arrives at Kent's office to report how Clippy Jones was seen robbing the Fifth Street Bank at a quarter to three. The problem is that at five past three, Clippy paid a visit to the Chief of Police in San Francisico. A similar operation takes place the next day with Benny when he turns up in Chicago.

While Kent is off to visit Henderson, Lois tells

Jimmy about the crazy idea she heard from Professor Pepperwinkle. They decide to investigate.

As usual, Jimmy and Lois discover what is going on just as the villains arrive. To silence the nosey reporters, Crowley has them forced into the chamber and telephoned to the Yukon. When Kent discovers the two are missing, he stops in to see Pepperwinkle.

When Kent learns about how the professor routinely takes his daily nap at the same time that Crowley's gang executes their fully witnessed robberies, he puts in a call to Henderson. Another quick call to the long distance operator tells him that a call to Alaska was recently generated from the professor's telephone.

Superman follows the telephone lines to intercept Jimmy and Lois. Later, Henderson reports to Kent that all the Crowley gang members have been captured. Pepperwinkle arrives to tell how he had to destroy his new machine. It seems his long distance telephone bill was incredible.

EPISODE 88

THE PRINCE ALBERT COAT

directed by HARRY GERSTAD
written by LEROY H. ZEHREN

If you like morality lessons delivered in small doses of subtlety, then this episode may be a little too much to bear. If, however, you don't mind having them served up like a slap in the face, then you must see *The Prince Albert Coat*. No one will come away from this show without a clear understanding of the differences between right and wrong, because Superman clearly restates the virtue of kindness and self-sacrifice just before the final fade out.

The plot begins in the home of elderly **MR. JACKSON** *(Raymond Hatton)* that he shares with his great grandson, **BOBBY** *(Steve Wooton)*, and his dog, **BUTCH.** There have been floods in a nearby area and a plea is being issued for volunteers to donate any old clothes for the now homeless people.

Young Bobby searches the house for a bundle of old clothing, including a ragged old Prince Albert coat folded neatly away in trunk. The Flood Relief Committee dispatches two unlikely characters in a truck to pick up the donation. Before going inside, **CUEBALL** *(Phil Arnold),* reminds **MIKE** *(Daniel White),* that they have a fine racket in this volunteer job and to be careful not to blow their cover when they pick up the goods.

Later, Jackson returns from a checker game boasting of how he blasted his opponent away like General Lee did to the Blue Boys at Bull Run, our first hint that his allegiance has always leaned to the Confederacy. When Bobby tells him about his good deed, Jackson realizes that he has lost his life savings that are tucked away in the lining of the old coat.

In search of the missing coat, Bobby and Mr. Jackson rush down to the Metropolis Department of Relief and explain their plight to **MRS. CRAIG** *(Claire DuBrey).* She is very sympathetic, but finds it difficult to understand why Mr. Jackson is so much against putting his money in a bank. He replies that he likes to keep his money where he can get it when he wants it. Jackson explains that he has been saving this money for Bobby's future. When later in the show it is announced that the life savings consisted of confederate currency implying that Jackson must have been saving it for a long time, we cannot help wondering why he never released the cash to his son or grandson before young Bobby was born.

Anyway, Mrs. Craig tries to keep an optimistic face and tells Mr. Jackson that she will see what can be done about locating the missing garment. Mr. Jackson can think of nothing other than going home to get some rest. Bobby, on the other hand, has something else in mind.

At the offices of the Daily Planet, Bobby gets an audience with Lois and Jimmy to listen to his appeal for Superman's help. Lois suggests they put a story out in the next edition and enlist the help of the good citizens of Metropolis. What better way is there to locate a missing coat than to announce to the entire city that a fortune in untraceable cash is sewn up inside its lining?

Of course, Mike and Cueball read the Daily Planet. They also remember where in the flood district they sent the missing coat. So, they're off to catch a fast freight train to Levee City.

Meanwhile, Kent volunteers to find out from the Relief Office where the two drivers who collected the Jackson donation may have sent the load of clothing in question. Within moments, Superman leaps out of his favorite window and zooms across the Metropolis skyline. Then, a telephone call from Kent sends Lois and Jimmy on a motor trip to Levee City. On the way, they stop off at the Jackson home and attempt to cheer up "Great Gramps." They agree to take Bobby and his dog whistle along for the ride.

The plot thickens at Levee City when **MR. MCCOY** *(Ken Christy),* the dispatcher at the Emergency Clothing Department, hands over the Prince Albert coat to a vaudeville performer by the name of **MORTIMER VANDERLIP** *(Frank Fenton).* His entire costume collection washed away in the recent flood.

Lois, Jimmy, and Bobby arrive at the Emergency Clothing Department. As McCoy recalls how he gave away the coat, Cueball and Mike arrive just in time to overhear McCoy say that it is on its way to Ivesville. They offer to assist in the search by driving the group to meet with Mortimer VanderLip.

On the way to Ivesville, a slight detour ends with Lois, Jimmy, and Bobby locked away in a brick smoke house. With a concrete floor at their feet and a slate roof over their heads, they remain helpless while the undesirable twosome closes in on the Prince Albert coat.

Having learned the two drivers are known criminals, Kent arrives in Levee City just in time to witness an evacuation. The nearby dam is about to burst. Superman executes one of the best springboard liftoffs of the season by leaping off the warehouse loading platform.

Several remaining minutes of what has promised to be a rather dull episode are *genuine Superman!* There are flying shots in every direction. There is a daring reconstruction of a failing dam with a couple of strategically placed steel girders, and finally, after picking up the sound of a dog whistle with his super hearing. There is an impressive entrance through the brick wall of the smoke house to rescue Bobby and his friends. After brushing the dust off his costume, he admits that he could have used the door, but that would not have been nearly as spectacular.

With two minutes to tie up the loose ends, Superman captures the crooks, borrows the coat from VanderLip, and returns to the Jackson home to witness Grampa Jackson's disappointment when he discovers the worthlessness of his life's savings.

The story comes to a close with the last minute arrival of **TOM SUMMERFIELD** *(Jack Finch),* a bank officer. He has been trying to locate Mr. Jackson for years, probably a duty he inherited from previous bank officers, in order to deliver the accumulated interest on a deposit of gold left by Jackson's father when Jackson himself was only a baby.

The flood area has been saved, VanderLip is able to do his show, and we assume the bad guys have been brought to justice. Lois and Jimmy have an exclusive story, Grampa Jackson's faith in banking has been restored, and Bobby's financial future is secure.

EPISODE 89

THE STOLEN ELEPHANT

directed by HARRY GERSTAD
written by DAVID CHANTLER

News is made when Clark Kent learns from **MR. HALEY** *(Thomas Jackson),* the owner of the circus, that the star attraction of a benefit performance is missing. A baby elephant named *Suzie* has been kidnapped and is being held for ransom. Superman's honor is at stake because he promised a whole bunch of underprivileged children that the circus would perform with Suzie at the picnic.

Meanwhile, we learn young **JOHNNY WILSON** *(Gregory Moffett)* has just moved to a remote farm in the country with his **MOM** *(Eve McVeagh).* It happens to be his birthday, and when he discovers a baby elephant hidden in their barn, he assumes it is a gift. Mom is as surprised as Johnny and neither realizes it is the hijacked elephant stashed by **BUTCHER** *(Gregg Martell)* and **SPIKE** *(I. Sanford Jolley).* Mom makes the mistake of telling Johnny he can keep the elephant, which only makes it more disappointing for him when the two villains return to claim legal ownership of the animal.

Production photo: *"Please, remember your lines so we can go home!"*

Mr. Haley drops into Kent's office to report that he has been contacted by some sleazy voice on the telephone demanding a ten-thousand-dollar ransom for the return of Suzie. Kent tries to convince him it is a matter for the police, but Mr. Haley would rather go to the bank and pay off the kidnappers because he is concerned for the elephant's safety.

Spike soon discovers the deserted barn in which they stashed the stolen elephant is not deserted at all. He rushes to tell Butcher of this new development. Butcher is busy at work on a plan to assure no interference from the ever present Superman with the construction of a model airplane.

Spike and Butcher pay a visit to young Johnny and convince him that they are the rightful owners of the elephant. Butcher shows Johnny an official-looking document which he claims to be an elephant registration. Johnny notes the number, J24197, for later reference, and then willingly gives up the elephant to the two men.

Johnny is heart-broken, but understands his mother's apology in the form of a lecture on how people often hurt the ones they love. All is not lost, however, when Johnny reads in the newspaper about the missing elephant. He immediately gets on the telephone to bring Clark Kent up to date.

Within a moment, Superman arrives at the barn to meet Johnny and his mom. Johnny relays what he knows of the two men, including the number he saw on the official document. Superman tells Mrs. Wilson to take Johnny into town to see Mr. Haley at the circus. He then excuses himself for a great outdoor take-off that you will recognize from the earlier episode entitled *The Town That Wasn't*.

Lois and Jimmy are already at the circus when Superman arrives. Jimmy has a model rocket airplane that someone gave him on the midway with instructions to turn it over to Mr. Haley right away. Superman quickly reads the instructions for depositing the ransom money inside the airplane and setting it loose in a northernly direction.

Lois remarks how it is a foolproof scheme for recovering ransom money. There is no time to notify police with a waiting helicopter. With Superman on hand, however, what else do they need?

As the rocket airplane takes to the air, Superman runs along side and executes a liftoff to the sound of his feet hitting the springboard. Here is where what could have been a predictable plot takes a delightful turn. Butcher directs the rocket by radio control to a site some 300 miles away. While Superman is off on a wild goose chase, the two villains drop in on the circus and collect the ransom money.

Superman finally recovers the elephant, captures the bad guys, and saves the day by tracing the villains through the Department of Motor Vehicles. The registration number that Johnny fortunately remembered so accurately was indeed Butcher's car registration number.

EPISODE 90

MR. ZERO

directed by HARRY GERSTAD
written by PEGGY CHANTLER

In Perry White's office, the editor tells Kent, who is making paper helicopters, that a *UFO* has been sighted over the desert. So begins what I initially labeled as the worst episode in the series in 1988. However, in the last decade, I must confess to a change of heart, as I have been forced to review it through the eyes of my own children. In retrospect, I may have enjoyed this episode in my early days even more than I remember. And *Billy Curtis* does bring a certain level of charm to

his role that some might consider infectious. Watch it with younger kids and then judge for yourself.

According to a report from General Thompson of the defense department, they cannot find the unidentified flying object. They hope Superman may be able to assist. At first, the episode promises to be an interesting science fiction drama, but we are quickly let down when a little *MARTIAN* (*Billy Curtis*) arrives to greet Jimmy in Kent's office.

"Take me to your leader," says the mysterious little visitor.

Kent arrives and Jimmy is quite relieved to hear that Kent also sees the little man with green hair. The Martian begins to cry as he tells how he has been banished from Mars because he is short. All Martians are exactly four feet, two inches tall. He identifies himself as *zero zero zero minus one* and confesses to being only four feet, one and three quarter inches tall. They decide to call the visitor Mr. Zero and his strange power is demonstrated when Lois arrives and gets paralyzed momentarily by Mr. Zero's pointed finger.

Jimmy takes Mr. Zero to a clothier to get fitted for some earthly garments. *GEORGIE GLEAP* (*Herburt Vigran*) enters and gets a finger pointed at him quite by accident as Mr. Zero motions for the store *CLERK* (*Leon Alton*) to trash his old Martian space suit.

Later, Georgie stops in to see Kent and meets Mr. Zero who he recognizes from the clothing store. He offers to take the new visitor out and introduce him around town as a jesture of hospitality. Georgie introduces Mr. Zero to his sidekick, *SLOUCHY MAGOO* (*George Barrows*) and together they convince him that the bank where lovely Miss Lane keeps her money is full of evil people who won't give her money back. They set out to rescue the money by pulling off a robbery while Mr. Zero puts the freeze on all the witnesses. The two villains swear Mr. Zero to secrecy.

Mr. Zero returns later to Kent's office and is surprised to hear Lois offer to lend Jimmy some money. He confesses to working with Georgie and Slouchy when he realizes he has been duped.

Anyway, based on information from Mr. Zero, Superman arrives at the hideout to capture the two villains and Mr. Zero arrives to put the freeze on them. When the **MARTIAN LEADER** (*George Spotts*) and the officials get word of how the mighty Superman was assisted by Mr. Zero, they offer to let him return to Mars with honor. The episode then comes to an end with Kent showing Perry how to make paper helicopters.

EPISODE 91

WHATEVER GOES UP

directed by HARRY GERSTAD
written by WILTON SCHILLER

Jimmy Olsen becomes a chemical genius quite by accident when he starts off to invent a better soft drink. While working in his ground-level apartment laboratory, he accidentally sprays some new concoction out the window and all over a passing pedestrian, ruining the man's pants. The irate fellow, **GANNIS** (*Milton Frome*), rushes into Jimmy's place to get revenge, but Superman arrives in time to prevent a fight. Gannis runs away and Jimmy admits that the mishap was all his fault.

During the next few minutes, Jimmy gives Superman a cook's tour of his lab experiments. As he demonstrates a new rubber compound, Superman realizes from the ingedients on a nearby shelf that Jimmy has created a very unstable chemical compound. He grabs the bouncing ball away just in time to prevent Jimmy from being harmed by an explosion. Superman strongly recommends that the young genius take up a less dangerous hobby like collecting butterflies.

Perry White gets a demonstration of Jimmy's new chemical discovery when he walks into his office and finds his paper weight floating around the room. Jimmy has perfected a new anti-gravity solution. The wise old editor convinces Jimmy that he must inform the government of his new discovery for the good of national defense.

MAJOR OSBORNE (*Tris Coffin*) arrives to get a look at the new discovery. The Major swears Perry and Jimmy to secrecy and suggests that Jimmy continue to work on the project in his own laboratory. As they discuss the details, the

"It's a wrap!"

bottle floats out the window, but luckily Superman happens by in time to save it.

Later, Jimmy is working in his laboratory. The real problem is that he has no idea what ingredients make up the secret formula. When Lois stops by to visit, he confesses that he happened on the formula while trying to invent a new chocolate cake mix. Lois suggests they recreate the accident.

Gannis returns and introduces himself as a government research agent. He catches Jimmy and Lois off guard with a gun and demands the sample and the secret formula. Jimmy offers him the sample, but when it floats out the window, Gannis is once again chased away by the arrival of Superman.

Word soon comes from Washington D.C. that the experts trying to analyze Jimmy's solution have discovered it to be very volatile when mixed with water. Major Osborne telephones Jimmy from Perry's office to warn him. When they get no answer, Kent sneaks away to become Superman.

Once again, Superman arrives just in time to save Jimmy and Lois from the threats of Mr. Gannis. However, Jimmy has poured his freshly brewed coffee into the last of the anti-gravity solution, and when Superman realizes the danger, he tosses the container to Gannis. It explodes and destroys the laboratory equipment, but in character with these non-violent episodes, Gannis only has his clothing and his pride ruined.

"Oh, no!" yells Gannis. "This time it's the whole suit!"

"Don't worry," replies Superman. "Where you're going, they'll furnish your clothes."

Jimmy sadly surveys his trashed laboratory as Lois tells him it's time to leave science to the scientists.

"Does anyone know where I can get a good, second-hand butterfly net?" Jimmy asks.

Jimmy must now accept that his status of chemistry genius must be exchanged for that of junior reporter. So ends the episode and another tired season.

The Episodes of
1957

ALTHOUGH THE FINAL SEASON BROUGHT NO MAJOR IMPROVEMENTS TO STORY QUALITY, THE variety was certainly improved, ranging from the silly *(All That Glitters)* to the serious *(Divide and Conquer)*. Some new energy was also injected by the producers with the recruitment of a record setting number of six directors for the thirteen episodes. Veteran *George Blair* returned to direct four of the shows, *Phil Ford* and *Lew Landers* each completed two, and *Howard Bretherton* directed one. Notable was the return of *Tommy Carr* from the black and white seasons to direct the first new episode, and *George Reeves* joined the ranks of the Directors' Guild to head up the production of the last three episodes of the series.

PRODUCTION CREDITS

producer . . . . Whitney Ellsworth
production manager . . . . Ben Chapman
director of photography . . . . Joe Biroc ASC
film editor . . . . Sam Waxman
art director . . . . Lou Croxton
set director . . . . Glenn Thompson
assistant directors . . . . Bob Barnes
Edward Haldeman
special effects . . . . Thol Simonson
make-up . . . . Gus Norin
sound engineer . . . . Herman Lewis

Lois Lane *(Noel Neill)* weighs in with an assist from SUPERMAN.

EPISODE 92

THE LAST KNIGHT

directed by TOMMY CARR
written by DAVID CHANTLER

Lois and Jimmy are on assignment at the museum. While in the room displaying relics of King Arthur and the days of knighthood, Jimmy accidentally drops a flashbulb. As he searches the floor for it, he finds an interesting cufflink at the foot of what appears to be a dummy dressed in a suit of armor. After closing time, the suit of armor begins to move and proceeds to a jewelry display case where it triggers an alarm.

Later, the security **GUARD** (*Thomas Dillon*) and Inspector Henderson are questioning Lois and Jimmy. Superman arrives to prove the jewel planted in Jimmy's camera case is only a fake. When Jimmy calls attention to the fact that the suit of armor that was standing in the corner is now gone, he insists that he and Lois didn't take it. Within a few moments, Superman discovers the real jewel is still in the display case. Lois and Jimmy have stumbled into another mystery.

Meanwhile, at a country castle, we learn the entire event was set up as a diversion while the leader of this secret society of knights made off with the suit of armor. The leader calls himself **SIR ARTHUR** (*Marshall Bradford*), and because of this daring exploit, he is nominated by the other three knights, **SIR GAWAINE** (*Paul Power*), **SIR LANCELOT** (*Pierre Watkin*), and **SIR HENRY** (*Jason Johnson*) to be king of the Society for the Preservation of Knights and Dragons. But all is not well as Arthur confesses to dropping a secret society cufflink at the museum. It is now in the hands of a reporter named Jimmy Olsen. They must recover the link before it leads to their exposure.

Eventually, the Knights capture Lois and Jimmy and throw them into the castle dungeon. They threaten Jimmy, but he refuses to return the missing cufflink. The problem is that he forgot what he did with it. Lois remarks how all they can do now is hope for a knight on a white horse. She is, of course, referring to the one we know who wears red and blue.

When Sir Henry is sent out on a quest for the missing cufflink, he is captured by the police at Kent's apartment. When Kent returns, he claims to know Sir Henry and convinces the officers to leave Henry in his custody.

In the following scene, Clark Kent's uncanny talent for searching out a story brings all the revealing facts from Sir Henry. Kent reminds the captured knight that he was probably betrayed by one of his own people.

"Just think it over," says Kent. "I'm sure you'll want to talk."

Henry removes his helmet. "My real name is Oliver Smith. I used to be in the lumber business. Since I retired, my only interest has been the S.P.K.D."

"SPKD?" asks Kent.

"The Society for the Preservation of Knighthood and Dragons."

Kent attempts to hide a smile. Henry continues by explaining why he was in Kent's apartment. He was looking for the missing cufflink taken by Jimmy Olsen bcause it might have exposed their secret organization.

"This is just a harmless club, Mr. Kent," Sir Henry explains. "Merely an unusual hobby. It's the secrecy that makes it exciting."

"It isn't harmless anymore," Kent insists. "There must be a reason."

Henry then goes on to explain how all the members are quite wealthy. They have put all their money into negotiable bonds at the castle to finance the society. It becomes obvious to Kent that any survivor would inherit all the money.

Kent suggests that he give up the silliness and return to leading a normal life. Henry agrees, leaves Kent the suit of armor, and tells of the capture of Lois and Jimmy before he makes his exit.

Kent quickly suits up as Superman inside the armor and leaps out the window. He arrives at the castle and by mimicking Henry's voice, he learns what is really going on.

Discovered to be an imposter, Superman is thrown into the dungeon. Here, Arthur tips his hand as the real villain out to collect on an insurance policy when he locks up the other knights. He then drops poison gas down into the locked room.

Superman finally reveals himself by shedding the suit of armor in time to save everyone and capture the unscrupulous Arthur. Jimmy finally

Production photo: *"Bring on the knights!"*

remembers where he put the cufflink for safe keeping—on his cuff. Superman asks Jimmy never to go near the prehistoric man exhibit because he shudders to think what might happen. Apparently, Superman has long forgotten the first color episode from a few years before.

This episode stands as a slightly better example of the series because it marked the return of director *Tommy Carr*. Although the story was weak, the action was well directed and it shows as a noticeable improvement.

EPISODE 93
THE MAGIC SECRET
directed by PHIL FORD
written by ROBERT LESLIE BELLEM & WHITNEY ELLSWORTH

When Perry White demonstrates the power of magic by levitating Lois Lane, we become aware of Jimmy's interest in the subject. This fact proves later to be the hook which draws him and Lois into the hands of the underworld.

The story moves quickly as Superman finds himself in pursuit of two escaping criminals, **KRAMER** *(Jack Reynolds)* and **BURNS** *(Kenneth Alton),* who are swiftly moving down a country highway in a speeding getaway car. Directing their escape by radio is the leader of the organization, a man named **GRIZWALD** *(Freeman Lusk),* along with his associate named **EDDIE** *(Buddy Lewis)* standing nearby.

Superman catches up to the criminals and lifts the getaway car off its wheels. When the two see Superman in the rearview mirror, they radio a report to Griswald before dropping the walkie-talkie and making a run for cover. After Superman watches the two knock themselves out by running into each other, he picks up the walkie-talkie and relays a message of his own.

Superman warns Griswald that he too will soon find himself behind bars along with his two accomplices. To punctuate his message, Superman sends a powerful signal through the radio transmitter with his x-ray vision that causes Griswald's receiver to burst into flames. Eddie is then quick to remind the boss that Superman has now spoiled their activities four times in a row.

Soon, **PROFESSOR VON BRUINER** *(George Selk)* drops in for a visit with a promise to rid Mr. Griswald of his worst enemy once and for all time. In exchange for this service, Griswald offers to make Von Bruiner a millionaire.

The Professor proceeds to restate the Superman legend of how he once lived on a planet that exploded. He invites Griswald and Eddie to tour his facility in the country where he has constructed a concrete hole in the ground that is sixty feet deep. Two miles away on a hilltop is the second part of the facility where a specially designed radar device collects particles of *kryptonite* from outer space. These particles will be transmitted to a special projector aimed down into the concrete hole. In order for the destruction of Superman to take place, they must somehow get him down into the hole.

Griswald proposes what he believes is an original idea. They will kidnap Jimmy, and then they will tell Kent about it with the hope that he will contact Superman for the rescue. To lure Jimmy into the trap, they will offer him secret magic lessons.

George and his mother, Helen Bessolo.

Jimmy sees an advertisement planted by Griswald in the newspaper. He borrows some money from Lois to pay for the magic lessons. She goes along with him to protect her investment.

Eventually, the two reporters are forced at gunpoint to lower themselves by rope into the concrete hole. Griswald then calls Kent, pretending he was once part of the kidnapping, but now wants no part of it. He reveals the location of their captivity and recommends using a helicopter to avoid any police interference. Griswald is certain that Kent will send Superman.

Superman drops down into the concrete cage to rescue Jimmy and Lois. He is subjected to a rain of kryptonite rays that looks very much like projector scratches on the film. Griswald watches the event through a pair of binoculars from a safe distance.

Down in the hole, Superman drops from his weakened condition. When the walls begin to close in on the three captives, Superman waves his arm and levitates Lois to a horizontal position that stops the walls from closing. Jimmy works his way to the surface and redirects the kryptonite projector toward Griswald. Superman is saved.

After the machinery of Von Bruiner is destroyed and the criminals are behind bars, the reporters meet in Perry's office. Lois explains how she hurts all over from keeping the walls from closing, especially her head. Perry offers a raise in salary to Lois and Jimmy as he asks where Kent was keeping himself during the episode. Kent smiles and claims to have been practicing his levitation skills. Lois says he should have been with them because Superman may have taught the trick to him.

"Why, Lois, what a wonderful idea," replies Kent. "As a matter of fact, I think he did."

EPISODE 94

DIVIDE AND CONQUER

directed by PHIL FORD
written by ROBERT LESLIE BELLEM
& WHITNEY ELLSWORTH

The first scene establishes the foreign country location. **HERNANDO OBREON** (*Robert Tafur*), the Vice-President of the Republic, listens to a report from **FELIPE GONZALES** (*Jack Reitzen*), about the arrangements for the assassination of the President. A briefcase containing an explosive device has been planted and is set to go off.

In the office of **PRESIDENTE BATEO** (*Donald Lawton*) are Lois, Kent, and Perry White in a meeting with the leader to discuss the possibilities of establishing a Latin American version of the Daily Planet in this country. White points out how Bateo is widely respected for his government that uses the revenue from the native mineral mines for the good of the people.

Kent hears a ticking noise. He sees the bomb in the briefcase with his x-ray vision. Kent then interrupts Perry in mid-sentence to insist that they must be on their way to visit the possible site for the construction of their new publishing facilities. After rushing Perry and Lois safely out of the President's office, Kent uses the old excuse of forgetting his hat in order to go back.

As Superman, he crashes through the wall, dives on the bomb just as it explodes, and manages to save the life of President Bateo. But when Obregon and Gonzalez enter to witness their failure, the Vice-President quickly refers to a national law. It requires anyone in the company of the leader during an attempt on his life must be confined to jail until an investigation can be undertaken. He firmly reminds the President that he may not override this law or he himself would be breaking the law and be forced to step down from the Presidency. Rather than violate the code of the land, Superman submits to arrest.

At his request, Superman is visited in his jail cell by his old friend, **PROFESSOR LUCERNE** (*Everett Glass*), to discuss the apparently hopeless situation. The **JAIL KEEPER** (*Jack Littlefield*) sits in a chair nearby and is eventually lulled into dreamland, probably from listening to the Professor's boring discussion of molecular theory. The Professor explains to Superman that if he could concentrate on pushing his tightly packed molecules apart in an orderly fashion, he could indeed become two people and therefore, literally be in two places at the same time. The danger, of course, is each of him would only be at half strength, and in that condition, it might not be possible to reverse the procedure. The Professor bids Superman farewell and good luck.

Within moments of the Professor's departure, Superman becomes two supermen, almost too easily. His weakness is graphically demonstrated when it takes the combined effort of the two supermen to pull the iron cage off the second-story window. And rather than leap into the sky to the tune of strings and horns music immediately, one Superman instead merely jumps to the ground below. He then gets a good running start before flying into the air. The remaining Superman carefully puts the window cage back in place just before the guard returns to check up on him.

In the President's office, Bateo announces to Perry and Lois that if it becomes necessary, he will dissolve his own government, leaving Obregon out in the cold, and he will insist on a new election. The Daily Planet people agree to meet with Bateo in the morning for a tour of the national mines.

The freed Superman returns to Kent's hotel room just in time to change clothing before Perry and Lois arrive at his door. They have apparently

George Reeves may have been asking *Phil Ford* for some directing tips.

agreed to let Kent skip the festivities and rest because he was shaken up by the explosion that rocked the President's office. A convenient excuse for Kent to remain a free agent for his duties as Superman.

After an interview with Lois, Obregon and Gonzalez discuss their plan for a mine-shaft accident during the President's tour with the meddling Americans. The scheme is successfully implemented after the two are certain that Superman is still confined to his jail cell. Together, they set off an explosion, filling the mine shaft with tons of debris. We see that all are still alive a mile down in the earth, but hopelessly trapped with a limited supply of breathable air. It appears that Obregon has won.

Kent wakes up in his hotel room to a news flash on the radio. The President has apparently been killed along with his American visitors and Obregon has been appointed as the new leader. He quickly changes into Superman and flies out

to the site of the mine disaster. His x-ray vision allows him to see the people below are still alive, but he is far too weak to do anything about it.

Obregon visits the other Superman in jail while an angry mob waits outside. A story has been leaked that it was Superman who killed the President. In a fit of frustration, the weakened Superman attempts to shake down the jail door, but he apparently fails.

Obregon smiles, believing now that the Superman stories are only legend. He orders the door unlocked so Superman may leave, pointing the way toward the angry mob waiting outside. Superman smiles, quickly removes the loose cage from the window and leaps out into the air just after feeling the sting of a bullet fired from the guard's rifle.

The two Supermen meet at the site of the mine. After exchanging a few clever lines of dialog, they successfully join together into one powerful Superman. Within seconds, he drills his way down into the ground to rescue Lois, Perry, and all the President's men.

Back at his office, Obregon and Gonzalez are gloating about their new control of the rich mineral resources when Superman arrives with Bateo. They have in their possession the explosive detonator box used to cause the mine disaster. The box has both Obregon's and Gonzalez' fingerprints, evidence to put the two away for a long time. The irony is when Superman rescued the President, he created a new tunnel that leads to even greater wealth for the country.

Superman once again returns to the hotel room just in time to become Clark Kent. When Perry and Lois enter, she confesses to have actually had the ridiculous notion that Kent might really be Superman.

"Why, Lois. It's very difficult to be two places at once, even for Superman," Kent replies at the final fade out.

EPISODE 95

THE MYSTERIOUS CUBE

directed by GEORGE BLAIR
written by ROBERT LESLIE BELLEM
& WHITNEY ELLSWORTH

This unusual story begins when we learn of a gangster named *PAUL BARTON* (Bruce Wendell). He is believed to be hiding inside a mysterious cube made of an unknown material that nothing can penetrate. Henderson and Kent are on the scene to discuss the situation with Paul's brother *STEVE* (Keith Richards) and his sidekick *JODY* (Ben Welden). The cube appeared about seven years ago, around the same time that Paul Barton disappeared from his career in crime. Several attempts have been made to gain access to the cube, one by a *MAN* (Joel Riordan) with a cutting torch, but none have been successful.

The subject of Paul Barton is being discussed in Perry's office by the usual group. He was a notorious criminal known to be guilty of every crime in the book including murder before he disappeared. They all figure he is waiting out the statute of limitations. Soon, his brother Steve will declare Paul Barton legally dead and he will be free from any prosecution.

With time running out, Kent slips away and changes into Superman for a visit to the mysterious cube. He tries to look through the walls of the cube with his x-ray vision, but he cannot do it. When asked about the material which makes up the cube, Steve confesses to not knowing and also claims that the famous scientist who perfected the formula is no longer alive.

When Steve gloatingly tells Superman his brother is really inside the cube, Superman throws himself against the wall only to bounce away. He vows to get Paul Barton out before the time limit is up, and then he leaps into the sky to visit a friend—*PROFESSOR LUCERNE* (Everett Glass).

The Professor proposes that Superman could move through a solid object if he could concentrate hard enough on vibrating the molecules of his body faster than the molecules of the solid object. After he successfully moves through the wall of the laboratory, the Professor warns that he may find the mysterious cube much more difficult than a concrete wall. He may even find himself forever trapped inside the strange material.

Just in case Superman does make good on his threat, Steve and Jody kidnap Jimmy and Lois for insurance. They set a trap where the two reporters could quickly be subjected to a poison gas if Superman appears to make trouble.

Anyway, Superman returns and begins his journey through the wall, but when he hears Steve communicating with Paul about the danger to Jimmy and Lois, he decides to back out. Steve is relieved, and believing that Superman has failed, decides to make a deal. If Superman will stay clear until noon and let Paul come out a free man, he will spare the life of Lois and Jimmy.

Steve accidentally makes it known to Superman that Paul has a clock inside the cube that is synchronized with the Naval Observatory in Arlington by radio signals. Superman gets an idea and flies away to speak with the *ADMIRAL* (John Ayres) in command. By word from the President, the Admiral agrees to Superman's request.

Well, Paul times his exit to happen five minutes after he is legally declared dead, but

A very telling production photo: On the set of "The Atomic Captive" it seems as if *George Reeves* is getting tired. . . the probable truth was that he was getting tired of posing for all these production photos. His enthusiasm in front of the motion picture camera never wavered.

when he walks out into the fresh air, Henderson arrests him for all crimes committed. It is soon revealed that he arrived in public five minutes too soon because his radio controlled clock was speeded up thanks to Superman.

Paul Barton is disgusted to learn he wasted seven years of his life and that Superman has saved Lois and Jimmy. Superman also demonstrates that his molecular ability would have allowed him to enter the cube if it had not been for his discovery that Lois and Jimmy were in certain danger. The final kicker is that Clark

Kent filed the story before anyone else had a chance.

Although based on an interesting premise, the story is full of holes and unanswered questions. Why did Superman wait until the last day to attempt a recovery of Paul Barton? Why didn't Paul Barton wait a few extra days? How did Superman rescue Jimmy and Lois? Expecting the viewers to ignore all of these items is a little too much for the producers to ask, but by now it was becoming an all too familiar theme of the series. Now we really begin to wonder how things would have worked out if *Robert Maxwell* had been still at the helm.

EPISODE 96

THE ATOMIC CAPTIVE

directed by GEORGE BLAIR
written by ROBERT LESLIE BELLEM
& WHITNEY ELLSWORTH

The cold war is evident in this episode when a nuclear scientist named *LATISLOV* (*Raskin Ben-Ari*) is visited by agents of a foreign country. *NICOLAI* (*George Khoury*) and *IGOR* (*Mark Sheeler*) tell Latislov that his two sisters will face certain danger if he does not return with them to their native land and work on their atomic energy project. We also learn that Latislov has recently been exposed to radiation, a fact the two agents are aware of because they are wearing radiation suits to avoid contamination.

Superman arrives in time to prevent the kidnapping and requests that Latislov works with him to help capture the real spy leaders operating in the country. Superman teaches Latislov to whistle at a specific frequency, a signal he should use to call for help whenever he feels the need.

To make a long story short, a nuclear explosive device is scheduled for testing in the area, and the Daily Planet reporters are on hand for the event. Jimmy and Lois believe an interview with Latislov would make more interesting copy so they set out to his desert home. Unknown to them, *MISS COLLINS* (*Elaine Riley*), known as agent x-29, and *ZARINSKI* (*Jan Arvan*), known as agent x-249, set out at the same time to attempt another kidnapping.

While waiting at the block house headquarters of the bomb test, the *GENERAL BARROW* (*Walter Reed*) informs Kent that the blast is set to go off and nothing can stop it. Almost on cue, Kent hears the whistle signal from Latislov who has taken off in a car with Jimmy and Lois. They forgot to get gasoline, and they are stranded somewhere near ground zero.

In spite of pleas from the General, Kent runs outside the protection of the block house and switches to Superman. He takes to the sky as the nuclear explosion creates a massive mushroom cloud. Waving his arms around in a very undramatic sequence, Superman forces the explosion back into the ground from which it came. He then finds Latislov and the two reporters unharmed even though the blast was strong enough to flip their car over on its side. They quickly point out that they are now contaminated because of close contact with Latislov. Superman only grins at their fear, pointing out that he just came from flying around in the nuclear cloud which makes him at least twice as contaiminated. He is not worried. A dull story deserves a dull ending, and that we get. Superman takes their hands between his and forces the radioactivity away with a flash of light.

The final scene in Perry's office has Superman returning the two sisters to Latislov. The episode finally fades to black.

EPISODE 97

THE SUPERMAN SILVER MINE

directed by GEORGE BLAIR
written by PEGGY CHANTLER

Visiting Perry White in his office along with Jimmy and Lois is a cowboy character calling himself *MR. PEBBLE* (*Dabbs Greer*). Superman arrives right on time to keep an appointment with Mr. Pebble who generously donates a piece of his country property for a children's summer camp. To fund the building project, he will use the proceeds from the silver mine which sits on the property.

A short time later, *BORIS* (*Charles Maxwell*) is in a coffee shop, reading a newspaper account of Mr. Pebble to his boss, *DAN* (*Dabbs Greer*). He recognizes the picture of Mr. Pebble as someone strangely familiar. It is Dan who points out how he himself is the spitting image of this charitable millionaire, and so the plot begins. Dan remarks about how he believes their bad luck is about to change.

Boris pays a visit to Mr. Pebble at his apartment to size him up. At gunpoint, he leads the friendly Mr. Pebble away.

Meanwhile, speculation mounts on the true intentions of Mr. Pebble as Henderson points out the striking resemblance between the cowboy millionaire and a known felon named Dan Dobey. The fact that Mr. Pebble failed to give the Daily Planet people a location for the alleged silver mine also contributes to the concern. Another interesting detail which later proves useful to Superman is that Dan Dobey once had an auto accident which fractured his skull. This required the surgical installation of a metal plate in his head.

Lois and Jimmy decide to investigate the mysterious Mr. Pebble. When they arrive at his apartment, they are greeted by the imposter, Dan Dobey. When they catch Dobey with his phoney mustache falling off, they are kidnapped and locked up with the real Mr. Pebble in a remote country cavern. Lois comments on how they are safe as long as Mr. Pebble refuses to give up the location of the silver mine.

Henderson arrives at Kent's office to tell how he got a call from Jimmy's mother reporting him missing. They soon discover Lois is also missing and figure it has something to do with Mr. Pebble.

Kent visits the apartment and is greeted by Boris who informs him that the millionaire is asleep and wants no visitors. Kent insists on speaking with him after he accidentally notices the phoney mustache on the table. Boris then tells the Boss to put on his disguise and get rid of the nosey reporter.

Using his x-ray vision, Kent sees the metal plate in Dobey's head. After a brief conversation, Kent makes an exit and goes to see Henderson.

When Dobey and Boris go out to give Pebble a last chance to reveal the secret location of the silver mine, Superman follows them. At the scene of the cave, Boris takes a few shots at Superman, but he is soon rendered unconscious. As he rescues the captured people, Dobey makes his running escape down the mountain toward his waiting car.

Now, in the good old days, Superman would have taken a flying leap and captured the escaping villain. This time, Superman takes a nearby iron pipe, bends it into the shape of a horseshoe, and magnetically charges it up with his x-ray vision. With the use of some reverse photography, the magnet brings the villain with the metal plate in his head rolling back up the hill into the waiting arms of Superman. Mr. Pebble

finally reveals the secret location of the silver mine. They have been standing on it all the time.

EPISODE 98

THE BIG FORGET

directed by GEORGE BLAIR
written by DAVID CHANTLER

No, the title does not refer to the entire last season, but rather a new invention by the whimsical **PROFESSOR J.J. PEPPERWINKLE** *(Phil Tead)*. This time, Superman bets his secret identity on the success of the new invention which is revealed to the reporters of the Daily Planet in Perry White's office. Reluctant to have a spray can aimed at her face, Lois takes the Professor's new creation, an anti-memory vapor, and promises him a full report in due time.

Later, we are introduced to the gangster **MUGSY MAPLE** *(Herburt Vigran)* and **KNUCKLES NELSON** *(Billy Nelson)*. They are two small time crooks hanging around in their hideout apartment plotting the course of their next job. Jimmy enters the room disguised as a window cleaner with a faulty hearing aid in hopes of getting a story. He straps himself to the window ledge as the two crooks discuss their plans for a robbery, but Jimmy blows his cover by speaking up when he should be listening.

As the two villains are about to take Jimmy on a one-way ride, he reveals the spray can containing Pepperwinkle's new invention. In an attempt to shower the villains with the anti-memory vapor, he accidentally aims the can at himself and totally forgets where he is or why he is there. Mugsy picks up on the effect of the spray, and after experimenting on Knuckles, decides to use the new invention in his next robbery scheme.

Assumed to be harmless, Jimmy is set free and returns to the Daily Planet to confess that he lost the Professor's new invention. When a report comes in that a robbery has taken place with no witnesses who can remember what happened, they immediately credit the infamous Mugsy Maple as the perpetrator.

Superman arrives through the window of Mugsy's apartment and finds it empty. He then

"I'm ready to direct!"

flies to Pepperwinkle's laboratory and finds it empty as well. A phone call to Henderson sets up a meeting back at Mugsy's apartment, but in order to fill out the episode to it's full half hour, Henderson claims he will be delayed.

Meanwhile, Mugsy and Knuckles return from their successful robbery to be greeted by Perry, Lois, and Jimmy. When they realize the reporters are suspicious of their association with Pepperwinkle, they are all taken away to Mugsy's secret hiding place out in the country.

When Superman reappears at Mugsy's apartment to meet Henderson, they find that Lois has left her purse behind. Superman figures the private telephone in Mugsy's desk must be a direct link to wherever Lois is being held captive.

While Henderson sits at Mugsy's desk reciting sequential numbers into the telephone, Superman leaps out the window to follow Henderson's voice along the telephone lines to locate Mugsy's secret hideout.

When Superman arrives outside the hideout, he overhears Lois saying she hopes Superman doesn't need to rescue them because then Perry won't give her and Jimmy a raise in salary for getting the Mugsy Maple story. Superman smiles and quickly changes into Clark Kent before he walks into the trap.

When all of the Daily Planet people and Professor Pepperwinkle are forced to enter a basement vault, Clark pulls the steel door closed behind him and locks it without being noticed.

Publicity photo, 1957.

Mugsy mixes a poison pellet with a bottle of acid and breaks it against the wall to silence the witnesses. He soon realizes that he and Knuckles are also trapped to face their doom.

With nothing left to do but reveal to all that he is really Superman, Kent quickly changes into his action suit and reverses the poison gas back into the broken bottle with a gust of super breath. After he helps Jimmy bust open the steel door, Superman sprays everybody with the anti-memory vapor and makes a quick exit.

In the final moments, Perry rewards Jimmy and Lois with the raise in salary, believing the only possible explanation for their rescue was the work of Jimmy. Pepperwinkle announces that he has forgotten the formula for his anti-memory vapor and Superman's secret is safe for the remaining six episodes.

EPISODE 99

THE GENTLE MONSTER

directed by HOWARD BRETHERTON
written by DAVID CHANTLER

With only five more episodes to be completed before the production closed its doors forever, story ideas were getting more difficult to locate. This episode is basically a rework of *The Runaway Robot* from the first season with a mechanical man appearing as another crazy invention of the whimsical **PROFESSOR PEPPERWINKLE** (*Phil Tead*). Once again, the best intentions of the lovable scientist, who never seems to get things quite right, are misdirected by the criminal minds of Metropolis.

Clark Kent is manning the night desk when he receives a threatening telephone call. A gangster named *DUKE* (*John Vivyan*) announces that his sinister trio is preparing to send a bottle of nitroglycerin to the Daily Planet. Kent dismisses the call as a prank.

The evil plan is outlined by the unscrupulous *SCIENTIST* (*Orville Sherman*) to Duke and *BLADE* (*Ben Welden*). A radio controlled hot air balloon will deliver the explosive device to the target. Duke gives the order to proceed.

Meanwhile, Kent receives another call from a lady claiming to have seen a weird iron monster prowling around her neighborhood. Jimmy and Lois decide to investigate.

When the two reporters arrive at the all too familiar address of Pepperwinkle, they soon discover a six-foot metal robot who the Professor has named *MR. MCTAVISH* (*Wilkie DeMartel*). Pepperwinkle explains that he invented the robot to keep him company. He doesn't wish any publicity. He assures the newspaper people the robot is quite harmless and that it responds to the sound of the Professor's voice. However, for the sake of a demonstration, the Professor reveals a special microphone that will convert anyone's voice to his special frequency.

When Superman arrives to witness the comical cause of alarm, he quickly becomes overpowered by something unknown. Lois and Jimmy help him outside where he regains his strength and insists on flying away. Lois and Jimmy soon discover that Mr. McTavish is powered by a small quantity of *kryptonite*. Of course, this entire scene has been witnessed by Blade, who quickly returns to report his findings to Duke.

Later, the three masked villains break into Pepperwinkle's laboratory home, and they steal Mr. McTavish. They also kidnap Lois for insurance against interference from Superman.

Using a geiger counter, Superman and the Professor drive around the city in a car hoping to pick up a signal from the kryptonite. As luck would have it, they soon discover the warehouse where McTavish is being ordered by remote control to construct the bomb and balloon assembly. Superman enters the warehouse. He is quickly overpowered by the kryptonite, and he fails to stop the bomb from floating away.

However, the Professor arrives in time to save Superman.

Superman recovers the bomb and flies it back to the criminal hideout by following the radio beam used to control the balloon. The gangsters quickly sign a full confession in exchange for Superman's removal of the device before it explodes. The episode finally fades to black as we see Kent, Lois and Jimmy being served dinner at the Professor's house by the now gentle monster.

EPISODE 100

SUPERMAN'S WIFE

directed by LEW LANDERS
written by ROBERT LESLIE BELLEM
& WHITNEY ELLSWORTH

The title of this episode promises a melodrama similar to *The Wedding of Superman* a few seasons ago. It is not a dream this time, but merely a fabrication to lure into a trap a criminal leader known only as *MR. X* (*John Eldredge*). The story gets underway immediately when Superman arrives at police headquarters where *DUKE BARLOW* (*Wayne Heffley*) is being questioned on a lie detector about his involvement in the Fifth National Bank robbery. Then Superman is introduced to lovely officer *HELEN O'HARA* (*Joi Lansing*).

"Inspector Henderson tells me you've been working on the case of Mr. X," says Superman with a smile as he takes her hand.

"Yes, but without much luck I'm afraid," replies O'Hara. "I've even been trying to get inside his organization, but I haven't been able to figure out a way yet."

"I see," replies Superman. "Sergeant O'Hara, will you marry me?"

With a new wife as bait, the trap for Mr. X is set that nearly backfires when Superman finds himself hundreds of feet under water in a bathysphere with Perry, Lois and Jimmy. Assuming that Superman is immobilized, Mr. X is free to have his way with the armored car business and the new Mrs. Superman.

As always, Superman's quick thinking in the face of danger overcomes the situation. He pulls the cable from the ceiling of the bathysphere and hauls it up to the surface before it fills up with water. The viewers are expected to ignore the physics of the rescue as Superman's feet remain securely attached to the floor of the ocean exploring vessel while they make their way up to safety. Once the three humans are safely back on the pier, Superman lets the bathysphere drop back to the ocean floor. He pushes open the door and flies underwater with the proper sound effects added this time, unlike *Peril by Sea* from a previous season.

Sgt. O'Hara is tied to a bridge that is about to explode when the armored truck arrives. Mr. X and his accomplices, *BLINKY* (*Harry Arnie*) and *DUGAN* (*John Bennes*), are watching from a safe distance. Superman, however, diverts the armored truck and saves O'Hara before the explosion. When he lands to round up the gang, Reeves looks and sounds like he is suffering from a cold as he slurs a line, "I'm sorry [*to*] disappoint you gentlemen."

Soon it is revealed that the wedding was only a hoax. "You're a brave man, O'Hara," says Jimmy and adds that he might like to ask the lovely sergeant to marry him if he were the marrying kind. However, she decides to wait for Superman to ask her again in spite of the friendly warning from Lois that she has competition. Kent remarks to Jimmy that these ladies don't believe there is anyone in the world but Superman.

"Well? Is there?" reply Lois and O'Hara in unison.

Everyone is laughing as the show fades out.

EPISODE 101

THREE IN ONE

directed by LEW LANDERS
written by WILTON SCHILLER
& WHITNEY ELLSWORTH

A bleak day for sawdust entertainment when a circus owner, *TEX DAWSON* (*Craig Duncan*) reports to Perry White that due to an unhealthy financial situation, he must close down the big top. In this show, we soon learn that two of the circus performers are working on the wrong side of the law. *PALLINI* (*Rick Vallin*), the climbing expert, scales a seventeen story building and drops a rope

to bring up *HARMON* (*Sid Tomack*), the escape artist to take a crack at a company safe. Pallini gets away just before Superman arrives, and Harmon is captured.

Kent and Lois visit the jail with Henderson. Harmon claims he was forced to the robbery scene by Superman for reasons unknown to him, and he refuses to give his name for fear of embarrassment to his family and friends.

Later, Harmon breaks out of jail by picking the lock and returns to meet Pallini at the circus. Together, they trick the not so smart *ATLAS* (*Buddy Baer*), the circus strong man, into joining up with their newly formed detective agency for a new assignment.

Soon, Pallini and Harmon are clearing out another safe. They convince Atlas that they have been hired to move the money because the owner suspects someone will be making a robbery attempt. They instruct Atlas to bend the bars on the iron door that is already open.

Kent is in Henderson's office when a report comes in about a robbery in progress at the Cityside Loan Company. Pretending to remain behind to call the newspaper, Kent switches to Superman and arrives at the scene just ahead of Henderson and his men. Seeing the bent bars and the empty safe, Henderson has no other choice but to arrest Superman.

Harmon and Pallini read the story in the newspaper and figure their plan to frame Superman is working. Even Atlas thinks Superman is really a crook. Now, with Superman out of the way, they will be able to pull off one big job and scram.

In jail, Superman proposes the obvious, some gang is trying to incriminate him just to clear a path for a series of robberies. Lois arrives to give a few encouraging words about how the Daily Planet is working overtime to help clear his name. That is everyone except Kent. He is nowhere to be found. Superman, hoping to flush out the criminals, suggests they plant a fake story about how the new Chapman Building will have a solid gold ball installed as a cap to its flagpole.

Pallini and Harmon take the bait. This will be their final performance. To enlist the needed help of Atlas, they convince him that Superman stole the gold from a bunch of widows and orphans and they have been hired to get it back.

While Pallini and Atlas are scouting the location around the Chapman Building, Jimmy arrives to interview Harmon, the great escape artist. During a demonstration of his straight-jacket trick, Harmon locks Jimmy up in a trunk and goes off to meet Pallini and Atlas.

While visiting Superman in jail, Lois blows the delivery of a line of dialog. She explains to Superman that with Clark missing, Mr. Kent (*rather than Mr. White*) is trying to locate Jimmy to work until Clark gets back. Superman finally gets the idea. The escape artist, the climbing expert, and the strong man are all grouping together to be Superman.

Back at the circus, Atlas is ordered to drop the trunk with Jimmy inside down into a tank of water. When Jimmy yells out, Harmon pretends to be practicing his new ventriloquist act and Atlas believes him.

Henderson allows Superman to escape from jail. He goes to the circus to save Jimmy from his watery grave, and then disguises himself as a night watchman at the Chapman Building. Pallini and Atlas are at the top to steal the gold ball. When Pallini goes back down the rope, Superman convinces Atlas that he is not a crook and together, they capture Pallini and Harmon.

In Perry's office, Tex Dawson sadly announces that he must still close the circus because the two best performers have landed in jail. Kent volunteers the services of Superman as a guest performer for a few days until the new circus acts can arrive from Europe. Lois suggests they all go to the circus, but Kent declines the invitation because he is going on vacation. Lois accuses Kent of being jealous of Superman. "Could be, Lois," says Kent, smiling. "Could be."

EPISODE 102

THE BRAINY BURRO

directed by GEORGE REEVES
written by DAVID CHANTLER

George Reeves makes his directing debut in this episode. While on assignment at a remote village in Mexico, our Daily Planet reporters meet in a cantina. Actually, Lois and Jimmy arrived first, and Kent has been dispatched by

Perry White to find out what they are doing. The usual insinuations are made by Lois regarding Kent's arrival at a time of no scheduled flights to the area, but all suspicions are dismissed, as usual, when a young local named **PEPE** (*Marc Cavell*) enters the cantina with a mule named Carmelita. The mule taps out answers to questions with a hoof to demonstrate her ability to read minds. Coincidentally, a couple of crooks, **TIGER** (*Mauritz Hugo*) and **ALBERT** (*Ken Mayer*), overhear this demo with designs on cashing in on it.

Outside the cantina, Tiger and Albert catch up to Pepe and offer two hundred pesos for a private demonstration of Carmelita's uncanny talent. They escort the unsuspecting Pepe and the mule to the inside of a bank to which Tiger happens to have the keys. When he sees **JAUN LUQUE** (*Edward LeVeque*), the bank president, tied up in a chair and blindfolded, Pepe becomes a little concerned about this nocturnal activity. No amount of money will persuade him to have Carmelita read the safe combination from Luki's mind, but the threat of an automobile accident for the mule convinces him otherwise. After Carmelita taps out the numbers to open the safe, Pepe and the mule are set free. Tiger threatens to expose Pepe as an accomplice if he goes to the police.

The next day, while meeting with Pepe outside their motel, Kent and his group meet police inspector **TOMAYO** (*Natividad Vacio*), inquiring about the previous night's bank robbery. They all agree to allow a search of their accommodations. While the police are inspecting one of the rooms, Kent watches with his x-ray vision as they discover a satchel of money under the bed. Tugging at his tie and glasses, Kent quietly slips away, leaving Lois and Jimmy to face arrest.

Superman visits with Tomayo in his office to discuss what evidence exists regarding the bank robbery. When told 10,000 pesos found in Señor Kent's bungalow, Superman requests permission to work on the case.

Meanwhile, Pepe and Carmelita visit Lois and Jimmy from outside their jail window. Pepe admits to having taken part in the robbery and tells them he is going to break them out. As Carmelita pulls away the wall of the adobe jail, Señor Luki, locked up with them as a suspect, proclaims his career as a trusted bank president is over indeed. As they exit the jail, they are greeted at gunpoint by Tiger and Albert.

Superman suggests to Tomayo the stolen money must've been planted on the visiting Americans. A knock at the door is followed by Carmelita's entrance to police headquarters. Superman questions the clever mule the way Chico Marx used to question Harpo. Lois and Jimmy are in trouble.

Out in the country, Lois and the group of escapees are all tied up against the rocks. They are faced with a small flame coming from a valve in a cross-country gasline. Tiger explains how he and Albert are going to increase the flow of gas from farther up the line. The flames will burn away the confining ropes and they will have a perfect alibi.

Superman and Tomayo arrive at the open hole in the jail with Carmelita. A few more carefully asked questions to the mule makes it clear that Pepe and the Americans were taken away by two thugs. They are located seven miles outside of town in a specific direction. Superman is off and running.

Superman arrives in time to blow out the gas fire and save everybody who is tied up. He then runs off camera to the sound effects of a take off, makes another landing off camera near the crooks, takes several bullets fired at him, and then he leisurely moves in for the capture. With a hundred and one adventures under his belt, George Reeves is obviously tired.

The final scene is pitiful. With the car all packed up for the return trip to Metropolis, Kent walks back alone to the trailer where Carmelita is caged. He whispers a proposition to the mule: he won't publish any stories about the only bank robbing burro if Carmelita will keep silent about Clark Kent and Superman.

EPISODE 103

THE PERILS OF SUPERMAN

directed by GEORGE REEVES
written by ROBERT LESLIE BELLEM
& WHITNEY ELLSWORTH

George Reeves takes on his second directorial assignment in an attempt to return the viewers to those thrilling days of the movie serials.

A man in a lead mask arrives at the Daily Planet. After confronting *ETHEL* (*Yvonne White*), the receptionist, the mysterious visitor makes his way upstairs to put Perry White and his staff on notice. He explains how Superman has ruined the best paying racket he ever organized by putting most of his gangster friends behind bars. He intends to get even with Superman by bringing harm to his friends.

When Perry informs the crook that he will never get away with his crazy plan, he responds by telling how his mask is locked on his head and that ten other men just like him are all walking the city streets. Superman will never be able to keep track of all ten at the same time. When the opportunity is right, the trap will close on Superman's friends.

Kent manages to slip away before the man in the lead mask says farewell. At the main entrance to the building, Kent watches as a parade of men wearing lead masks moves up and down the sidewalk.

Later, Lois and Perry are kidnapped and forced to drive to a remote shack outside the city. After tricking Perry into reciting the directions to the shack into a hidden tape recorder, they play back the words to Jimmy. He thinks it's actually Perry ordering him to meet them.

From Henderson's office, Kent tries to put through a warning call to Jimmy, but he's already gone. Henderson agrees to use Kent as bait to catch the crooks.

At the Daily Planet, Henderson and his men have all the entrances covered. However, a lead masked man with a gun is waiting for Kent in his office. He orders Kent to proceed to the roof.

As Henderson watches a helicopter take off from the roof of the building, he remarks to one of his men, "If anybody ever needed Superman, Kent needs him now."

In some secluded warehouse, Kent is hanging by his arms tied together above a boiling vat of acid. Pretending defeat, Kent manages to get a full description of the gloating crook's plan. Then Kent is lowered slowly down into the vat of acid as the crooks get away in their helicopter.

Within moments, Superman comes up out of the boiling acid. Alternating shots of Superman flying and Perry White strapped to a huge log headed for a spinning buzz saw conclude as

Superman crashes through the wooden wall and steps between Perry and the spinning blade. Here is a horrible example of sloppy film editing as we can easily see from this camera angle that Superman's chest is a good ten inches from the saw as the teeth of the blade go flying off.

After he unties Perry from the log, the cheap production values are even more obvious as Superman exits through the broken wall. Instead of countryside scenery in the background, we see only a studio wall with Superman's shadow on it.

Next, we see Superman come to rescue Lois from the tracks just before a train is to go speeding by. Here, we are treated to some nicely matched live action shots of a train with studio shots of a stretch of railroad track.

Meanwhile, Jimmy is in his car driving down a winding canyon road when his steering wheel and brakes quit working. Superman does not arrive in time to prevent the car from shooting over a cliff and smashing into explosive flames.

Jimmy is still alive, hanging from the top ledge of the cliff as Superman makes a lazy landing just in time to catch Jimmy before he falls to his death. If you watch carefully, you'll notice that Superman's cape isn't blowing in the wind, as if George Reeves merely jumped up so the camera could catch him coming down.

The wrap up scene takes place as usual in Perry's office. Henderson reports how Superman collected all the lead masked men. To pick out the leader of the gang, Superman used his x-ray vision to see which one had the key.

The last scene shows the two crooks *(Michael Fox, Steve Mitchell)* wondering how Kent could possibly be alive after they watched his almost certain death in the vat of acid. The obvious is dismissed as impossible and Superman's secret is safe for one more episode.

EPISODE 104

ALL THAT GLITTERS

directed by GEORGE REEVES
written by ROBERT LESLIE BELLEM
& WHITNEY ELLSWORTH

Assembled in Perry White's office are **MR. SALEM** *(George Eldredge)*, the Secretary of the Treasury, and **MR. CARTER** *(Paul Cavanagh)*, President of the World Bank. Standing between these two financial leaders is **PROFESSOR PEPPERWINKLE** *(Phillips Tead)* with a one pound gold brick in his hand. The meeting has been called to convince Pepperwinkle, who has developed a way to manufacture gold synthetically, to cease operation before the world economy is ruined.

The idea of Fort Knox becoming a ghost town does not appeal to Pepperwinkle. He agrees the secret formula will never be released to the public. Perry issues the order that no one is allowed to discuss this development outside the office, especially J. Blabbermouth Olsen.

Later, Jimmy and Lois are dining with the Professor when Jimmy starts talking about the gold making machine. In the next booth are **MITCHELL** (*Lee Hendry*) AND **BOOTS** (*Jack Littlefield*) listening to the conversation. They decide to pay a visit to the Professor.

At Pepperwinkle's laboratory, the two gangsters arrive and order him to begin working on a few tons of gold. They threaten to harm Lois and Jimmy if the Professor refuses to comply.

The Professor is not worried, as he explains to Lois and Jimmy, because when the crooks return to pick up their gold, he will be ready for them. He demonstrates his new automatic crook stopper by pushing a secret button. Two sandbags drop from the ceiling. Unfortunately, one of them hits Jimmy square on the head.

When Jimmy wakes up from his unconscious condition, his blurry vision comes into focus. He insists they contact Superman before the crooks return. The Professor again claims they don't need him because he has made an amazing discovery that unlocks the power of Superman. From a sample of kryptonite he retrieved from his backyard, he has discovered that positive charged kryptonite is good, and negative is bad.

"So what?" says Lois. The Professor then reveals his new machine that separates the positive from the negative to produce a special capsule. Whoever swallows it will be given super powers comparable to Superman.

After witnessing a mouse, charged with positive kryptonite, pulling a heavy cabinet across the floor, Lois and Jimmy volunteer to test the new concoction. Jimmy then easily bends an iron bar, and Lois straightens it. Jimmy crashes a hole in the wall, rather than turning a door knob. Then Lois and Jimmy leap into the air for a bit of flying along with Superman's theme music in the background.

Lois and Jimmy enter the office of the Fifth National Bank and talk with **MR. GOLBY** *(Richard Elliott)* and his **SECRETARY** *(Myrna Fahey)*. When Jimmy and Lois show some of the sequentially numbered money that was given to the Professor by the thugs, they learn from Mr. Golby that just such a withdrawal was made earlier by one of the bank's valued customers, a gangster named Bugs Morgan. Mr. Golby also tells them that Mr. Morgan is currently residing at the Acme warehouse.

Lois and Jimmy excuse themselves and then jump out the window. Landing at the warehouse, they use x-ray vision and super hearing to locate the two thugs inside. The two heroes kick down the door and take several bullets from the crooks before capturing them.

When Lois and Jimmy return to tell the Professor that he is no longer in danger, he instead is startled. He accidentally pushes the trigger button on the automatic crook stopper. Once again, the sandbag hits Jimmy on the head. He wakes up and realizes the past several minutes have been a dream.

The two thugs enter with guns and order the Professor to get to work. The machine is turned on and Pepperwinkle begins to drop in the magic ingedients. Scrap iron, apple cider, peanuts with shells, and a bar of platinum. When the crooks realize it takes $10,000 worth of platinum to make $5,000 worth of gold, they decide to get even by setting off some dynamite.

Superman arrives crashing through the wall just in time to grab the dynamite and drop it down inside the Professor's gold making machine. The explosion is contained, but the machine is destroyed. They look over at Jimmy to see he has fainted.

When they all gather in Perry's office for the last time, Jimmy explains that he didn't faint, but rather fell asleep from exhaustion after performing all the super activity in the dream.

"Golly, Mr. Kent," says Jimmy. "You'll never know how wonderful it is to be like Superman."

After a pause, Kent replies, "No, Jimmy. I guess I never will."

Fade out. With one hundred and four episodes complete, George Reeves and the others will live forever in syndicated reruns.

MADE IN HOLLYWOOD, USA

"Superman" costume is offered at auction in 1989

One of the "Superman" costumes worn by George Reeves during the production of the color episodes was offered to the highest bidder at an auction sale in Los Angeles by Camden House Auctioneers, Inc. in November, 1989. The costume, auction item #749, consisted of a long sleeve top section, the tights, the shorts, and the cape. Missing items that would have completed the outfit were the yellow belt and the red boots.

According to the catalog issued prior to the sale, which featured the costume on both the front and back cover, the source of the prized piece of memorabilia that was manufactured by the Western Costume Co. in Hollywood was the series producer, Whitney Ellsworth. In 1975, Ellsworth donated the costume to the library of California State University, Fullerton, where it remained until sold to a private party some ten years later.

In the decades following the time George Reeves labored under the stage lights in this sweat suit, moths had taken to feast upon it. Why it was allowed to deteriorate is anybody's guess. We can only hope that the new owner is taking proper care of it. According to the follow-up report issued to catalog buyers, the item was sold for $46,200. Included in the deal was an autographed script from the 1957 episode entitled "The Last Knight," and it was signed by George Reeves, Noel Neill, Jack Larson, and Robert Shayne. The script was reported in the auction catalog to have originally belonged to Pierre Watkin, the guest star who played *Sir Lancelot* in that episode.

Of course, any fan now has the opportunity to see another of the original color costumes, as well as one of the black & white season costumes at the Super Museum in Metropolis, Illinois.

Etcetera

LOIS and LOIS

THERE IS NO DENYING THAT BOTH *PHYLLIS COATES* AND *NOEL NEILL* WERE EXCELLENT actresses. Each had a distinct and different style, and each was well-suited for the role of **LOIS LANE—LADY REPORTER.** However, to review the television series without devoting some attention to the fact that there were indeed two Lois Lanes, would be like ignoring the fact that roughly half the time you order Coke in a restaurant, you indeed get Pepsi. The differences in the two performances of Superman's feminine interest are as subtle as the differences between Coke and Pepsi. While at the same time, they are as radically different as fire and ice.

Technically, only one can be first. Yet, in a way, both actresses can be awarded that status. Noel Neill first portrayed Lois Lane in the theatrical serials opposite *Kirk Alyn.* Phyllis Coates, on the other hand, was the first actress to fill the role of Lois Lane in a feature film which later became part of the television series. Therefore, neither can be given the distinction of being the best because they were the first. In fact, the purpose of this particular piece of writing is not to confirm or deny which of these two actresses was the best, but rather to pay attention to reasons why each made a notable contribution to the ensemble that made up the television Superman family.

Having more than one performer play a recurring role in a television or movie series is not unique to the *Adventures of Superman.* More often than not, it is a practice that has been easily accepted by eager audiences. Dick York was replaced, but hardly forgotten, from one season to the next by Dick Sargent as Darin Stevens on *Bewitched,* and Clayton Moore was similarly replaced by John Hart as the masked rider of the plains for several episodes of *The Lone Ranger.* Bea Benadaret had no fewer than four husbands named Harry on *The Burns and Allen Show* without altering the comic effect. This list could go on forever and would certainly include the character of Catwoman in the *Batman* series, Lieutenant Saavik in the *Star Trek* movies, 007 in the *James Bond* pictures, Miss Ellie on TV's *Dallas,* and the character changes on the daily soaps would fill a book by themselves. Ironically, the tradition continued in more recent years when *Gerard Christopher* replaced *John Haymes Newton* in the Superboy series of the late eighties, and finally, *Beverly Garland* replaced *Phyllis Coates* as Lois Lane's mom in "Lois & Clark, The New Adventures of Superman," after the series had already traded in one Jimmy Olsen for another.

It all started for *Phyllis Coates* back in 1951 when her agent told her to report to the RKO-Pathe studios for an audition with over ninety other actresses. Within forty-eight hours, she was signed for the role which would begin filming some two weeks later. The casting of Phyllis Coates in the role of Lois Lane was nothing short of genius on the part of producer Robert Maxwell. The two dimensional character of Clark Kent's female co-worker in the comic books was certainly a hard-hitting, no-nonsense, investigative reporter. Coates brought those features to life on the screen. From the first moment she came face to face with a new reporter by the name of Clark Kent, she was forever striking out on her own and refused to be upstaged by him.

This irrepressible Lois Lane played by Coates appeared as a key character in twenty of the first season episodes, with a brief appearance at the beginning of *Double Trouble,* and her absence in the others was quite evident. In addition to her sassy dialog, which was usually a series of insults directed at Kent, she had quite an attention-gathering scream.

In spite of the very tight parameters of a 50's television series, Phyllis Coates did very well at fleshing out what could have been a routine character. We are treated to several quick glimpses of this character that was Lois Lane. Although we know hardly anything of her interests outside of working at the Daily Planet, she was obviously a single career woman with no aspirations toward living a domestic life, and her wardrobe was rather limited, a true reflection of the fact that women were usually paid much less than their male counterparts.

Her interest in the preservation of antiques is brought out in *Mystery of the Broken Statues* as she happens upon a story in a knick knack shop while picking up a repaired piece of china. Lois was always expressing compassion for others in unfortunate circumstances *(except for Kent),* and we learn a little of her childhood origins in *The Deserted Village* when she and Kent return to her hometown of Cliffton by the Sea.

However, unlike her successor, Coates never showed more than a casual romantic interest in our hero. The only reference ever made in that direction was at the end of *Rescue* when she remarked to Kent how Superman had finally taken her out.

By the end of 1952, Phyllis Coates had to face the reality that she **was** Lois Lane. "Less than a week after the program went on the air, I had to change the color of my hair!" said Coates in an interview that appeared in *TV People* magazine. "I couldn't go anywhere without being mobbed... grown-up women wanted to know how it feels to be held in Superman's arms."

It became obvious to Coates that she, like Superman himself, had taken on a double identity. After playing in dozens of westerns where she was never quite sure if the hero would arrive in time to make a rescue, "...with Superman, it's different. The minute he comes on the scene, I can sit back and relax."

In the first season episodes featuring Phyllis Coates, Lois was usually appreciative whenever Superman stepped in on her behalf, but she never really appeared totally dependent on him as the Lois of later episodes. None of this, of course, was the direct doing of Coates, but more the result of the writing. We'll never really know for sure how she would have handled her performance interpretation in some of the more silly stories of the later episodes if Whitney Ellsworth had been able to convince her to come back. And we can only speculate how the series might have developed if Robert Maxwell had stayed on.

Noel Neill assumed the role of Lois Lane in 1953 when the series continued under the leadership of Whitney Ellsworth. She was already familiar with the character from her work in the two Columbia serials, and she was experienced in the rigors of action-adventure filming after having completed the Republic serials *Adventures of Frank and Jesse James (1948)* with Clayton Moore, and *James Brothers of Missouri (1950)* with Keith Richards and Roy Barcroft. Her first episode, *Five Minutes to Doom,* showed little alteration from the previous stories of 1951, and the second season was underway with a new and well qualified Lois Lane.

The most apparent contrast to the first season Lois was that Noel Neill smiled more often. She wasn't as hard on Clark Kent as Coates was, and many times she actually expressed an understanding when Kent didn't seem to act the man he should have been. In all fairness to the comparison, only the first fifty-two episodes should be considered. What the character of Lois Lane finally evolved into during the later color shows was more under the control of the writers *(or lack of writers)* and the producer than Noel Neill.

Lois and Jimmy eventually became bored with dangerous situations and often made light of them. This was the unavoidable fate of any long lasting series. The images of the inseparable pair facing certain death in *Night of Terror* and then so much later in *The Atomic Captive* are best summed up by a remark made by Jack Larson in a 1983 interview appearing in *Collectables Illustrated* magazine.

"The biggest memory I have of playing Jimmy is that I was always tied to a chair with a bomb at my feet, as was Lois, and George would break through walls to rescue us."

In a brief interview aired on *Entertainment Tonight* in 1987, Larson reminisced with the following remarks.

"Everyone would like to be saved by Superman the way I was week after week on the television series." He smiled as he went on to say, "No matter how bad you are, like Jimmy was. No matter how eager or how dumb you are, and the trouble you get into— you've got Superman to save you."

After leaving the Superman series, Phyllis Coates continued to work in front of the motion picture cameras with featured roles in two Republic serials. She played Carol Bryant in *Jungle Drums of Africa (1953)* with an unmasked Clayton Moore, and she played the title role in *Panther Girl of the Congo (1955).* In a 1989 interview that appeared in STARLOG Magazine, Phyllis Coates told writer Tom Weaver that she remembered the *Panther Girl* experience where she was required to wear a short-skirted costume which caused her legs to be rubbed raw from riding an elephant all day. The costume she wore was a duplicate of the one used by Frances Gifford in *Jungle Girl.* Between the two Republics, Phyllis filmed another serial with Jock Mahoney over at Columbia titled *Gunfighters of the Northwest (1954).* She also showed up on television shows occassionaly throughout the 1950s, and I remember recognizing her in the movie *I Was a Teenage Frankenstein (1957),* in spite of the fact that she had blonde hair. Phyllis Coates' most recent appearance on television was in 1993 when she introduced the character of *Ellen Lane,* the mother of the Lois Lane played by Teri Hatcher. In June, 1994, Phyllis Coates made personal appearances at the 16th Annual Superman Celebration in Metropolis, Illinois. Every year, *The Metropolis Planet* newspaper selects an outstanding community achiever to receive the Lois Lane Award.

Some years after the *Adventures of Superman* production closed down, Noel Neill perpetuated her public identity as Lois Lane by doing a series of college appearances. She has entertained new generations of Superman fans with screenings of her series work, by answering questions from the audiences, and by sometimes inviting a few of them up on stage to act out bits from the television scripts.

Much ado was created for the fans back in 1977 when it was announced that Noel Neill and Kirk Alyn would appear in the new Superman movie as parents of Lois Lane. However, when the film was released in 1978, you had to be careful not to blink as young Clark Kent *(Jeff East)* races a speeding train to a crossing. With hardly seconds of screen time, you might catch a glimpse of Noel sitting on the train with a little girl *(whom we are suppose to assume is Lois Lane).* It's even more difficult to recognize Kirk Alyn, sitting across from her with most of his face turned away from the camera. They both deserved more respect and far better treatment, but you must remember, this was at a time when higher powers would have liked us to forget there ever was another Superman.

In 1987, Noel Neill was still voicing her love and involvement in the Superman legend at a promotional appearance in Cleveland, Ohio. Thirty years after walking the soundstage sets of the Metropolis Daily Planet, Noel Neill was still signing autographs eagerly sought after by loving fans. The event was produced by Tim Gorman in an attempt to get a Superman statue, a Superman museum, and a comic book convention all to happen in Cleveland by 1988, the fiftieth anniversary of Jerry Siegel's and Joe Shuster's creation. The event happened as scheduled, and Noel Neill was there along with Jack Larson and Kirk Alyn, her co-stars from both the television show and the movie serials. And in June, 1997, Noel was in Metropolis for the 19th Annual Superman Celebration.

From *Superman and the Mole Men* to *All That Glitters,* the television series was continually changing. The stories evolved from hard-hitting crime dramas to silly plots wrapped around strange scientific inventions. Production leadership changed, directors rotated assignments, and Lois Lane actually had her face modified. Most evident was how George Reeves aged with the show, going from an energetic, no-nonsense crime fighter to a comfortable, super-human babysitter who always managed an appearance just in time to get everyone out of trouble.

Until the early 1990s, most of the episodes that appeared on television were those worn prints of those filmed in color and almost always in some poorly edited form to make way for more commercials. Because the color shows were most attractive to potential advertisers, viewers ended up with only a poor sample of the entire series. In 1987, only the feature version of *Superman and the Mole Men* was released to home viewers on videocassette. Although it sadly lacks the warmly familiar theme music and appearances by Jimmy Olsen and Perry White, this cassette does contain the original opening title and

Noel Neill and *Jack Larson* in Cleveland, Ohio (1988).

credits, and scenes never aired in the television episodes. At the time, we were hoping that Warner Brothers would release the entire series package on videotape. They have only released four double-episode cassettes to date. However, the series did enjoy a four year run on cable television's Nickelodeon network which sparked renewed interest in the series for old fans and introduced the show to a whole new generation. In 1995, I received an announcement from Terre Haute, Indiana, that Columbia House was putting out "The Collector's Edition" of the series. As of this printing, there are 20 triple episode volumes available. Call customer service at 800-457-0866 for an update if you haven't already signed up for this offer.

So, to quote the everlasting narrator's voice, "Don't miss the next thrill-packed episode in the amazing *Adventures of Superman!*"

NOTABLE GUEST STARS

The *Adventures of Superman* provided work for many established character actors and bit players. Many of them appeared in more than one episode, and some of them went on to become starring players in other television shows. Credit for the success of the *Adventures of Superman* must be partially attributed to the colorful performances of the guest starring actors and actresses.

The following performers are noted for having appeared in three or more episodes of the series. They are listed in alphabetical order along with the episode numbers in which they received credit at the end of the show.

Jan Arvan, *(45, 65, 96)*— **Sam Balter,** *(30, 33, 36, 37, 39)*— **Richard Benedict,** *(6, 44, 86)*— **Lane Bradford,** *(30, 58, 77)*— **Peter Brocco,** *(10, 42, 77)*— **Paul Burke,** *(41, 56, 77)*— **Steve Carr,** *(2-6, 8, 10, 15, 16, 22)*— **Tristram Coffin,** *(3, 4, 60, 91)*— **John Doucette,** *(7, 49, 60)*— **John Eldredge,** *(24, 31, 72, 100)*— **Milton Frome,** *(73, 85, 91)*— **Dabbs Greer,** *(1, 27, 97)*— **John Harmon,** *(17, 33, 61)*— **Raymond Hatton,** *(62, 74, 88)*— **Myron Healey,** *(62, 74, 78)*— **Sterling Holloway,** *(39, 51, 53)*— **Selmer Jackson,** *(16, 30, 75)*— **John Kellogg,** *(6, 27, 28)*— **Jack Littlefield,** *(67, 82, 86, 94, 104)*— **Leonard Mudie,** *(18, 34, 61, 78)*— **Billy Nelson,** *(35, 39, 54, 66, 98)*— **Richard Reeves,** *(11, 30, 43, 59, 68)*— **Frank Richards,** *(6, 31, 80)*— **Keith Richards,** *(48, 84, 95)*— **Allene Roberts,** *(2, 5, 51)*— **Dan Seymour,** *(8, 13, 17)*— **Phillips Tead,** *(64, 70, 87, 98, 99, 104)*— **Sid Tomack,** *(60, 75, 101)*— **Aline Towne,** *(1, 21, 28)*— **Rick Vallin,** *(64, 71, 86, 101)*— **Phil Van Zandt,** *(24, 33, 65)*— **Herburt Vigran,** *(11, 48, 56, 75, 90, 98)*— **Pierre Watkin,** *(3, 46, 78, 92)*— **Ben Welden,** *(8, 35, 39, 63, 70, 85, 99)*.

Several guest stars appearing in the *Adventures of Superman* may be recognized from some of their performances in other works of television and motion pictures. The following list may not be complete, but it is certainly a beginning. As you watch the Superman episodes on television, you may wish to add to this list of notable guest players.

Claude Akins, *(69)* appears in *Rio Bravo* with John Wayne, *Inherit the Wind* with Spencer Tracy, and numerous television shows and commercials.

Leon Askin, *(33, 65)* appears in *Hogan's Heroes* as General Burkholter.

John Banner, *(84)* appears in *Hogan's Heroes* as Sgt. Schultz.

Hugh Beaumont, *(28)* stars in *Leave It To Beaver* as Ward Cleaver.

Paul Burke, *(41, 56, 77)* appears in the feature film *Valley of the Dolls* (1967) as well as in several TV series roles including *Twelve O'Clock High* and *The Naked City.*

Tristram Coffin, *(3, 4, 60, 91)* appears in many westerns and he took to the air in the serial, *King of the Rocketmen.*

Chuck Connors, *(63)* stars in *The Rifleman* as Lucas McCain, *Branded* as Jason McCord, *The Big Country* and *Soylent Green* with Charlton Heston, and numerous other movies and television shows.

Elisha Cook, *(44)* appears with Humphrey Bogart in *The Maltese Falcon* and *The Big Sleep,* and later went on *Star Trek* to defend Captain James T. Kirk against a charge of treason.

John Doucette, *(7, 49, 60)* appears in *Sons of Katie Elder* with John Wayne, *Patton* with George C. Scott, and dozens of feature westerns.

Jimmy Dodd, *(16)* appears as the leader of *The Mickey Mouse Club.*

Bob Easton, *(17)* often served as a dialect consultant, appears as "Sparks" in *Voyage to the Bottom of the Sea (1961),* and more recently as a Klingon in *Star Trek VI (1991)* and the Mayor in *Beverly Hillbillies (1993).*

Paul Fix, *(22, 44)* appears in *The Rifleman* as Sheriff Micah Torrence, and as the ship's doctor in the Star Trek pilot *Where No Man Has Gone Before.*

Billy Gray, *(31)* stars in *Father Knows Best* as Bud, with Bob Hope in *The Seven Little Foys,* and has a featured role in the science-fiction classic, *The Day the Earth Stood Still.*

Jonathan Hale, *(19, 38)* appears in the *Blondie* series of movies as Dagwood's boss, Mr. Dithers.

Sterling Holloway, *(39, 51, 53)* will be remembered as the voice of Winnie the Pooh.

Russell Johnson, *(17)* is the "Professor" on *Gilligan's Island* and plays Steve Carlson in the sci-fi classic *This Island Earth.*

Robert Lowery, *(76)* starred as *Batman* in the 1949 Columbia serial.

Denver Pyle, *(46)* appears in *The Andy Griffith Show* as Mr. Darling, *The Dukes of Hazzard,* and numerous movies and television shows.

Hayden Rorke, *(36)* appears in *I Dream of Jeannie* as Dr. Bellows.

Victor Sen Yung, *(20)* appears in *Bonanza* as Hop Sing, the cook.

Dan Seymour, *(8, 13, 17)* appears in *Casablanca* with Bogart, *Road to Morocco* with Bob & Bing, and in *Abbott & Costello in the Foreign Legion* and *A&C Meet the Mummy.*

Pierre Watkin, *(3, 46, 78, 92)* was the original Perry White in the Superman serials with Kirk Alyn.

HOME OF SUPERMAN
METROPOLIS, ILLINOIS

IN THE SUMMER OF 1997, VISITORS FROM ALL CORNERS OF THE NATION DESCENDED UPON the city of Metropolis, Illinois to help celebrate the Silver Anniversary of their association with Superman. The city and Superman have both changed quite a bit in those twenty-five years, but one thing has remained constant—Superman is the hometown hero and adopted son of Metropolis, and he will forever stand tall as a symbol for all that is good in the world.

It all started on January 21, 1972, when the city organized a press conference to announce that National Comics had indeed granted them the permission necessary to officially identify Metropolis, Illinois as the *Home of Superman.* Volunteers were commissioned to suit up in the familiar colors of tights and cape to portray the Man of Steel at public funtions. Many celebrations have taken place over the last two and a half decades

Truth—Justice—The American Way The fifteen foot statue guards the entrance to the Massac County Courthouse in Metropolis, Illinois.

that have culled international attention, including the dedication of two Superman statues, the latest of which stands fifteen feet tall and proudly guards the front steps of the Massac County Courthouse.

But it did not happen overnight. It was the work of many local residents of the little city in southern Illinois and a dedicated Chamber of Commerce to continue the efforts of one man with a vision. His name was Bob Westerfield.

Bob Westerfield moved from Owensboro, Kentucky to Metropolis in 1970 and operated a dry cleaning store in the town he had expected to be full of public reminders that he was now living in the Home of Superman. How could such an obvious connection go unnoticed? Westerfield expressed his feelings in an interview with NEWSWEEK in 1972. He had assumed that the people of Metropolis *(the only "Metropolis" in the postal zipcode directory)* would have naturally associated themselves with the hero of the comic books, "but when I got here, you couldn't find hide nor hair of him." Westerfield took it upon himself to change that missed opportunity. He entered the local drug store and bought a copy of a Superman comic book. He was hoping to find within its pages a way in which to contact the publisher. He had an idea he wanted to discuss.

Since the adoption of Superman by his new hometown of Metropolis, Bob Westerfield worked tirelessly for over twenty years for the city and its new identity. He had big dreams and initiated the construction of the *Amazing World of Superman* in May of 1973. The exhibition center included a comic artwork collection, a detailed explanation of how comics are created from pencil sketches into a published magazine, and intricate models of Clark Kent's home and Superman's secret fortress of solitude. The grand opening ceremonies of the exhibit were coordinated with the 35th birthday party for the Superman character, and the event was featured in an oversized comic magazine that collectors still hold today as a cherished item of memorabilia. The exhibition and funhouse was intended to be the first step in an ambitious Disney-like theme park.

However, the planned highway exit at Metropolis from the new Interstate-24 was not completed as scheduled causing tourist access to the attraction to be severely limited. The escalating prices of gasoline and the floods that ravaged the Midwest in 1973 also contributed to a poor season and resulted in the financial collapse of the exhibit. The *Amazing World* closed in the fall of 1973 and never reopened again.

Though it has yet to be constructed, Westerfield never gave up on his dream of a first class theme park, and he was never at a loss for words when it came to discussing his favorite subject. He strived to be the most interviewed man on the topic of Superman, appearing in print and broadcast news stories that attracted attention from all over the world. He was a driving force in the activities of his community right up until the very end of his life.

Bob Westerfield died in November of 1992 at age 64, just days after Superman died in the pages of his comic books. That same week, the city of Metropolis commissioned the construction of the bronze statue that now stands at the county courthouse, their most spectacular attraction to date. Though he never lived to see his dream develop into a theme park, the citizens of Metropolis will always remember Bob Westerfield.

But the story of Metropolis doesn't end with Mr. Westerfield. It continues with Jim Hambrick, owner and curator of the new *Super Museum* presently contained in a 8500-square foot building just across the street from the Superman statue standing at the courthouse steps.

After moving to Metropolis from Fountain Valley, California, Jim Hambrick established the newest home for his collection of Superman memorabilia in 1993. Though it has been expanded several times in the few years since the doors first opened to eager tourists and enthusiastic fans, the material displayed still only represents a fraction of the entire inventory, certainly the largest collection of its kind in the world. In the few short years that it has been opened, the museum has already received the AAA Auto Travel award as the number one small-town tourist attraction in America.

Also housed in the Super Museum building is a store of merchandise offering a wide variety of Superman related collectables and currently licensed products that is sure to satisfy everyone interested in the various forms the character has taken on over the years. The store offers comics, videos both animated and live-action, toys, clothing, radio programs, cards, buttons, candy, stills and statues that are priced to sell and sure to fall within anyone's budget. But most important to the readers of this book, Jim has on display in the museum hall the finest collection of George Reeves material one could imagine. No matter where you live, it would be worth the trip, and I know Jim would love to show you around.

Metropolis, Illinois is a wonderful place to make a stop while on vacation. In addition to the sights of interest to any Superman fan, there are a number of recreational possibilities within the area. If you are planning such a trip, you might wish to contact the Metropolis Area Chamber of Commerce at 1-800-949-5740.

The Episodes in Brief

Here is a list of all 104 episodes in the series. Episodes 53 through 104 usually appear on television in color. The directing and writing credits are noted along with brief descriptions of each storyline.

1: SUPERMAN ON EARTH

Directed by Tommy Carr, written by Richard Fielding. The first show details the origin of Superman from his infant departure of the doomed planet Krypton to the beginning of his career as a reporter for the Metropolis Daily Planet. His first public appearance as Superman is a sweeping rescue of a man hanging on to the mooring line of a dirigible.

2: THE HAUNTED LIGHTHOUSE

Directed by Tommy Carr, written by Eugene Solow. When Jimmy Olsen visits his Aunt Louisa's lighthouse, he soon discovers a smuggling operation. Notable episode for the first display of the springboard takeoff. Superman saves Jimmy from drowning in a cave open to coastal waters and then ties up all the loose ends.

3: THE CASE OF THE TALKATIVE DUMMY

Directed by Tommy Carr, written by Dennis Cooper and Lee Backman. The villains are using a ventriloquist's dummy to relay locations for armored car robberies. Dangerous highlight is Jimmy locked in a safe hanging high above the sidewalk. Notable first appearance in the series by *Pierre Watkin,* the original Perry White of the Superman serials.

4: THE MYSTERY OF THE BROKEN STATUES

Directed by Tommy Carr, written by William Joyce. This episode has Lois curiously chasing down repeated appearances of gang members smashing plaster statues in search of clues to a puzzle that will unlock a post office box full of stolen cash. Clark Kent directs the problem solving process for Lois and Henderson.

5: THE MONKEY MYSTERY

Directed by Tommy Carr, written by Ben Peter Freeman and Doris Gilbert. International intrigue with Superman being assisted by an organ grinder's monkey to retrieve a secret atomic formula from a power in a communist bloc country.

6: NIGHT OF TERROR

Directed by Lee Sholem, written by Ben Peter Freeman. Lois Lane stumbles into murder at the *Restwell Tourist Camp.* A call to Jimmy leads him into a bungled rescue attempt and it takes Superman to arrive just in time to keep both Lois and Jimmy from being silenced by Baby Face Stevens.

7: THE BIRTHDAY LETTER

Directed by Lee Sholem, written by Dennis Cooper. A handicapped little girl wishes a visit from Superman, but after accidently intercepting a message intended for some underworld character, she instead gets a visit from an incredibly absurd imposter with a heavy Bronx accent comically overplayed by veteran actor *John Doucette.*

8: THE MIND MACHINE

Directed by Lee Sholem, written by Dennis Cooper and Lee Backman. Perhaps one of the best shows of the series for high-energy action scenes, it rekindles the fast paced spirit of the serials with an ambitious villain and an incredible machine. Designed by a captured scientist, the machine is used to selectively burn out people's brains. Several well-staged outdoor shots of Superman rushing around to apprehend the bad guys before lovely Lois is victimized makes this a *do not miss* episode.

9: RESCUE

Directed by Tommy Carr, written by Monroe Manning. Most of this episode is used to set the stage for a rapid rescue of Lois who is trapped in a mine shaft explosion.

It seems like it takes forever for Kent to discover that Lois is in need of his super assistance. Provided producers with an opportunity to supplement the stock footage library with outdoor take-offs and landings.

10:   THE SECRET OF SUPERMAN

Directed by Tommy Carr, written by Wells Root. Another sinister man of science attempts to use mind altering drugs to discover the secret of Superman. The irony is that not knowing who his adversary really is forces him to tangle with Clark Kent who ultimately foils the scheme.

11:   NO HOLDS BARRED

Directed by Lee Sholem, written by Peter Dixon. An unscrupulous wrestler is using special tricks he has learned from an intimidated captive from India to paralyze his opponents. When he comes up against a college friend of Lois, Superman lends a hand to prepare him for a fight to expose the wrong doings.

12:   THE DESERTED VILLAGE

Directed by Tommy Carr, written by Dick Hamilton and Ben Peter Freeman. This moody episode has Lois and Kent investigating a reported sea monster story designed to drive away all but a few residents who plan to cash in on the mining deposits of a rare element. Notable for violence, this show contributed to that reputation by allowing the appearance of a dead dog. No question, the bad guys mean business.

13:   THE STOLEN COSTUME

Directed by Lee Sholem, written by Ben Peter Freeman. A small time crook suffering from a bullet wound stumbles into Clark Kent's apartment and uncovers the torso portion of what proves to be the only costume of Superman. When a more ambitious crook named *Ace* gains possession, he tries to make a deal with Superman for its return. Notable scene is Kent, unable to change into proper clothing for flight, crashing through the door of the apartment holding his costume hostage. Ace and his girl friend pay dearly for attempting to blackmail Superman by falling to their death from an Arctic mountain.

14:   MYSTERY IN WAX

Directed by Lee Sholem, written by Ben Peter Freeman. The operator of a wax museum, *Madame Selena,* seems to have a knack for creating life size figures of local notables just before they commit suicide. When Perry White is selected as her next exhibit, Lois is captured while attempting to expose a sinister kidnapping plot, and Superman ultimately finishes the job.

15:   TREASURE OF THE INCAS

Directed by Tommy Carr, written by Howard Green. Lois and Jimmy are in Peru when they stumble into another cave being investigated by a sinister gang. Superman lends a hand while at the same time recovering a lost Inca treasure.

16:   DOUBLE TROUBLE

Directed by Tommy Carr, written by Eugene Solow. Clark Kent thwarts a smuggling scheme where Nazi agents attempt to import a million dollars worth of radium stolen from an Army base hospital in Germany. Watch for the police fingerprint lab worker played by Mousketeer leader *Jimmy Dodd.*

17:   THE RUNAWAY ROBOT

Directed by Tommy Carr, written by Dick Hamilton. Another story of a scientist's invention falling into the hands of the wrong people, this time it's a rather silly looking mechanical man named *Hero.* His appearance probably inspired the manufacture of more homemade robots by kids around the country than did the tin man in *The Wizard of Oz.*

18:   DRUMS OF DEATH

Directed by Lee Sholem, written by Dick Hamilton. Perry White's sister Kate stumbles into a scheme where a voodoo witch doctor is scaring people out of the jungle. Kent arrives to investigate and soon uncovers the deception perpetrated by their jungle guide playing a dual role.

19:   THE EVIL THREE

Directed by Tommy Carr, written by Ben Peter Freeman. Another sinister tale where the villains use fear to keep a secret. When road-weary Perry and Jimmy decide to stop and rest for the night, they fall into a trap. Notably violent episode with one of the bad guys doing his Richard Widmark impersonation by shoving an old lady in a wheelchair down the stairs.

20:   RIDDLE OF THE CHINESE JADE

Directed by Tommy Carr, written by Ben Peter Freeman. This episode takes place in Chinatown of Metropolis, and it revolves around the theft of a family heirloom in the form of a jade figurine. *Bonanza's* Victor Sen Yung falls into the scheme of the crooked art thief, but he later sees the light after Superman rips up the pavement to rescue him and his fiancée from drowning in a tunnel under the street. Lois is held hostage at the end, giving Superman his excuse to fly straight up and down only to slap up the crook and recover the jade statue.

21:   THE HUMAN BOMB

Directed by Lee Sholem, written by Richard Fielding. This low budget episode, confined to even less than the few sets of an average adventure, has Superman up against a bet that he can be immobilized while a museum is being robbed under his nose. However, he manages to slip away using a recording of his voice repeating, "no comment until the time limit is up!"

22: CZAR OF THE UNDERWORLD

Directed by Tommy Carr, written by Eugene Solow. Kent is sent to Hollywood with Henderson to be a consultant on a screen production about a notorious underworld godfather, who in turn is attempting to thwart the exposure of his dirty laundry in public. The fictional movie director is played by *Steve Carr,* the real episode director's brother.

23: THE GHOST WOLF

Dirceted by Lee Sholem, written by Dick Hamilton. This story has Lois hot on the heels of another mystery in timberland. Notable scenes include Superman rushing to rescue a train headed for destruction when he supports a collapsing tressel, and Superman's take-off from the forest which had George Reeves crashing to the stage floor after one of his wires broke loose.

24: CRIME WAVE

Directed by Tommy Carr, written by Ben Peter Freeman. Superman wages war on crime with most of the first half of the show being edited action clips from several earlier episodes. Superman is lured into a trap up on Dover's Cliff where he is subjected to a silly display of electrical fireworks and fakes his demise long enough to learn the true identity of the ringleader.

25: THE UNKNOWN PEOPLE
Part One

Directed by Lee Sholem, written by Richard Fielding. Kent and Lois are the only series regulars appearing in this two part episode. They are sent to Silsby to investigate why the world's deepest oil well is being shut down. Superman soon discovers that visitors from an underground world have come up to find out why there is a big hole in their ceiling. Feared to be radioactive, the town mob sets out to destroy the visitors.

26: THE UNKNOWN PEOPLE
Part Two

Directed by Lee Sholem, written by Richard Fielding. Superman manages to save the Unknown People and assist their escape back down to their own world. I remember watching this episode as a kid and noticing with amazement that the ray gun of the miniature creatures looked remarkably like my mother's electrolux vacuum cleaner with a special kitchen funnel attachment.

This two part episode is actually an edited version of what was the mostly forgotten first Superman feature film production entitled *Superman and the Mole Men,* released in 1951 by Lippert Pictures, Inc.

27: FIVE MINUTES TO DOOM

Directed by Tommy Carr, written by Monroe Manning. This show marks the return of Noel Neill from the Superman serials as *Lois Lane.* Superman manages to crash through a prison wall just in time to prevent the execution of an innocent man. A notable scene is when Kent jumps from a moving car driven by Lois, with a bomb that blasts part of his clothing off to reveal his true identity.

28: THE BIG SQUEEZE

Directed by Tommy Carr, written by David Chantler. Actor *Hugh Beaumont,* later to become the father of Wally and Beaver, appears as a rehabilitated criminal who is being squeezed back toward the wrong side of the law by an old partner in crime. Beaumont's wife is played by *Aline Towne,* her third appearance in the series.

29: THE MAN WHO COULD READ MINDS

Directed by Tommy Carr, written by Roy Hamilton. In this episode, *Lawrence Dobkin* portrays a swami with apparent powers as the title describes and becomes involved with Lois and Jimmy. Not long after, Dobkin would turn up on the VistaVision movie screen as one of Moses' associates in *Cecil B. DeMilles'* blockbuster production of *The Ten Commandments,* and later into a film director himself.

30: JET ACE

Directed by Tommy Carr, written by David Chantler. Cowboy actor *Lane Bradford* makes his first appearance in the series as a jet pilot who falls into a scheme designed by some not so sinister foreign agents that prove no match for Superman.

31: SHOT IN THE DARK

Directed by George Blair, written by David Chantler. The title refers to a photograph taken by *Billy Gray* that shows Superman changing into Clark Kent. The photo falls into the hands of a criminal who apparently faked his own death and was also photographed by Billy. Kent must capture the criminal without exposing his true identity.

32: THE DEFEAT OF SUPERMAN

Directed by Tommy Carr, written by Jackson Gillis. Using Lois to lure Superman into a basement trap, with Jimmy dragged along for good measure, Kryptonite is used to defeat the Man of Steel. Jimmy's quick thinking puts the deadly rock in a lead pipe, and the rejuvenated Superman decides it is better off hurled into the ocean where it will never threaten him again. The second and last time villains pay for opposing Superman with their lives.

33: SUPERMAN IN EXILE

Directed by Tommy Carr, written by Jackson Gillis. Preventing an early version of *The China Syndrome* forces a radioactive Superman into a self-imposed exile on a mountain top for the good of the citizens of

Metropolis. A publicity agent played by *Leon Askin*, decides to become a jewel thief and take advantage of Superman's absence.

34: A GHOST FOR SCOTLAND YARD

Directed by Tommy Carr, written by Jackson Gillis. Kent and Jimmy are in England when they get involved with a friend of Perry White who is being threatened by the predicted reappearance of a dead magician. When the magician turns out to be alive and holding Jimmy captive with threats to explode a bomb, Superman intervenes just in time.

35: THE DOG WHO KNEW SUPERMAN

Directed by Tommy Carr, written by David Chantler. A rather weak premise has a gangster discovering that his dog has snatched a glove that belongs to whoever is really Superman. Kidnapping Olsen to set a trap, the crook has the little pooch lead him to who he hopes will be the secret identity, but instead runs directly into Superman. There is an attempt to draw tears from the viewers as Kent explains to the little dog why he can't keep him.

36: THE FACE AND THE VOICE

Directed by George Blair, written by Jackson Gillis. The title refers to a Superman look-alike who is coached by a master criminal into impersonating the real Superman to execute crimes in order to discredit our hero. Even Superman begins to question his own sanity until the imposter goofs by being sighted at the same time Superman is chasing a confused Henderson around his office.

37: THE MAN IN THE LEAD MASK

Directed by George Blair, written by Leroy H. Zehren and Roy Hamilton. This episode unfolds a scheme where crooks attempt to do a number on other crooks. The man in the lead mask is a phoney demonstration that an unscrupulous surgeon is able to alter the finger prints and facial appearance of any wanted criminal who is willing to pay his price. In spite of the visual handicap, Superman manages to see through the operation.

38: PANIC IN THE SKY

Directed by Tommy Carr, written by Jackson Gillis. Reputed to be, if not the best, certainly the most popular episode of the series. Superman is forced to test the very limits of his power when he squares off with a meteor rapidly approaching a collision with Earth. His first attempt merely slows it down and causes him a loss of memory. Only in the last moment does he recover in time to finish off the invading rock with a strategically placed explosive.

39: MACHINE THAT COULD PLOT CRIMES

Directed by Tommy Carr, written by Jackson Gillis. Once again, a scientific invention is put to use by the criminal element, this time it is a room full of computer power used to plot a series of bank robberies. But even in the end, after apprehending the crooks, the machine is too smart to give away Superman's secret identity.

40: JUNGLE DEVIL

Directed by Tommy Carr, written by Peter Dixon. Clark Kent sheds his double breasted suit for a Jungle Jim outfit in this safari encounter with a wild gorilla and spear carrying natives. memorable scene is Superman appearing in a puff of magic smoke to a crowd of bewildered natives and the creation of a replacement diamond by squeezing a hunk of coal in his hand.

41: MY FRIEND SUPERMAN

Directed by Tommy Carr, written by David Chantler. A restaurant owner is being pressured by the local mob that collects protection payments in exchange for a guarantee that no accidental damage will befall his property. Claiming to be Superman's best friend, the food king refuses to buckle under the pressure. Luckily, the Daily Planet reporters frequent the establishment and Kent finds out in time to call in Superman after an uncommon pie fight.

42: THE CLOWN WHO CRIED

Directed by George Blair, written by David Chantler. A charity telethon in the Jerry Lewis tradition is a target for a robbery scheme with a crook impersonating one of the entertaining clowns in the show. When the bad clown is chased to the top of a building by the good clown, they both struggle and fall. Superman manages to save the hero, the bad guy is the clown who cried.

43: THE BOY WHO HATED SUPERMAN

Directed by George Blair, written by David Chantler. A classic case of misguided hero worship with a young man's admiration directed toward a common criminal. When Kent is discovered to be responsible for putting the criminal away, the young man uses Jimmy to get even. But when both are kidnapped by the crooks, it takes Superman to set the record straight on who are the good guys and who are the bad guys, which was Jimmy's plan all along.

44: SEMI-PRIVATE EYE

Directed by George Blair, written by David Chantler. A shining example of *Jack Larson's* gift for character development. The story is simple, Jimmy witnesses the kidnapping of Lois and a private eye. He decides to assume the identity of a 'Sam Spade' type character complete with narrating his own investigation in a great parody of Humphrey Bogart. Superman steps up just in time to inhale a room full of poison gas.

45: PERRY WHITE'S SCOOP

Directed by George Blair, written by Roy Hamilton. A dead man found in a diving suit is the beginning of a mystery story that Perry White wants to solve himself. With the assistance of Kent at a dangerous health club and Olsen inside an almost empty water tank, the clues lead to a railroad yard where the solution is found to be a boxcar full of paper used for counterfeit cash. Perry gets the scoop and Superman saves the day.

46: BEWARE THE WRECKER

Directed by George Blair, written by Royal Cole. A story similar to the first season's *CRIME WAVE*, the terrorist villain turns out to be a leading citizen seeking not to make a political statement, but rather phoney claims for insurance money. Watch for another appearance by *Pierre Watkin* and also a young *Denver Pyle*, who later led the Darling clan from the hills of Mayberry.

47: THE GOLDEN VULTURE

Directed by Tommy Carr, written by Jackson Gillis. A salvage vessel docked in the harbor is the target of a Lois and Jimmy investigation after Jimmy finds a note washed ashore in a bottle. They become unwilling guests of the pirate captain. When Kent arrives, has an incredible fight with half a dozen sailors, is forced to walk the plank, and then finally gets to become Superman for the final resolution. Especially memorable for its eerie night scenes and lots of great second season background music.

48: JIMMY OLSEN, BOY EDITOR

Directed by Tommy Carr, written by David Chantler. Jimmy Olsen abuses his temporary power when he becomes editor of the Daily Planet on Youth Day. He intentionally plants a false story in the newspaper to draw an underworld thug out in the open. The plan backfires, but Superman intervenes just in time to ensure everyone's safety.

49: LADY IN BLACK

Directed by Tommy Carr, written by Jackson Gillis. A classic tale of the boy who cried wolf when Jimmy falls victim to several false scare episodes designed by his landlord to convince Superman that Jimmy is only hallucinating. Sure that Superman will not return, the crooked landlord and his band of thieves proceed to empty an art gallery vault through a hole in the basement wall.

50: STAR OF FATE

Directed by Tommy Carr, written by Roy Hamilton. Superman is called to action when Lois Lane becomes a victim to an ancient curse placed on a sacred jewel. Superman declares his devotion to the lady reporter by flying to Egypt where he must retrieve the antidote by lifting a great pyramid for a rare plant leaf.

51: THE WHISTLING BIRD

Directed by Tommy Carr, written by David Chantler. The title bird belongs to the returning Uncle Oscar *(Sterling Holloway)* and is instrumental in completing a secret formula he has invented for an explosive compound. Foreign agents get wind of the new invention, but Superman manages to round them up without letting the bird give away his secret identity.

52: AROUND THE WORLD

Directed by Tommy Carr, written by Jackson Gillis. When the Daily Planet sponsors children's 'Round the World with Superman contest, a young blind girl wins and insists that her mother be allowed to claim the prize. Before the show is over, Superman reunites the girl's parents, who have been separated by a misunderstanding, assists in a surgical operation to restore the girl's sight, and then flies her around the world to fulfill the contest obligation.

53: THROUGH THE TIME BARRIER

Directed by Harry Gerstad, written by David Chantler. First of the color episodes has Sterling Holloway as the inventor of a time machine that lands himself, Lois, Jimmy, Clark, and Perry back in prehistoric Metropolis along with a silly criminal named Turk. What could have been great science fiction drama becomes instead a mindless excuse for a series of play on word jokes.

54: THE TALKING CLUE

Directed by Harry Gerstad, written by David Chantler. The son of Inspector Henderson accidently records the sound of the tumblers on his father's safe that holds evidence against a criminal who ultimately buys the tape. When the kid later turns up missing, Kent solves the puzzle by splicing two pieces of sound effects tape intentionally left behind by young Henderson.

55: THE LUCKY CAT

Directed by Harry Gerstad, written by Jackson Gillis. Superman finds himself up against an anti-superstition club. Lots of nonsense involving black cats and walking under ladders. Not one of the best.

56: SUPERMAN WEEK

Directed by Harry Gerstad, written by Peggy Chantler. Metropolis is preparing to celebrate Superman Week and a couple of villains are planning a reception of their own. They recover the lost Kryptonite rock from the earlier show entitled *The Defeat of Superman*. Superman protects his secret identity by arranging an interview with a plaster bust filling in for Clark Kent. Very weak.

57: GREAT CAESAR'S GHOST

Directed by Harry Gerstad, written by Jackson Gillis. The favorite phrase of editor Perry White conjures up the image of Caesar himself. Actually, it's a clever plot to make Perry look crazy and destroy his credibility as a jury witness. Superman, of course, does not believe in ghosts and ultimately convinces Perry of the same.

58: TEST OF A WARRIOR

Directed by George Blair, written by Leroy H. Zehren. Good excuse to go west, this time to an indian village to take part in a tribal ritual that challenges strength and courage, but the old chief being tested can hardly stand up. To stall for time, Jimmy fills in until Superman arrives and exposes the nonsense.

59: OLSEN'S MILLIONS

Directed by George Blair, written by David Chantler. Jimmy gets a reward when Superman saves a lady's cat that has been accidently locked inside a safe. Crooks get wind of his new fortune and plant an unscrupulous butler in Jimmy's service. Some of his money goes up in smoke as a signal to bring Superman to the rescue.

60: CLARK KENT, OUTLAW

Directed by George Blair, written by Leroy H. Zehren. Kent goes undercover as an outlaw to bring a notorious crook out of hiding. He is taken in by the gang after demonstrating his uncanny talent for opening a combination safe with his finger tips. After faking the fiery deaths of Lois and Jimmy, and having his cover blown by Perry White, Superman steps in and saves the day.

61: THE MAGIC NECKLACE

Directed by George Blair, written by Jackson Gillis. A crafty archaeologist creates a hoax concerning an alleged charm necklace that makes whoever is wearing it invulnerable, only to raise money for future expeditions. When crooks become the target for his scheme, it takes Superman to set everything straight.

62: THE BULLY OF DRY GULCH

Directed by George Blair, written by David Chantler. On a road trip, Lois and Jimmy stop off in Dry Gulch to discover a town bully that pays his henchmen to make him look notorious. Jimmy is threatened and thrown in jail, but it's the bully flirting with Lois that brings Superman rushing to the scene to expose this phoney gunslinger and teach us all a lesson in honesty.

63: FLIGHT TO THE NORTH

Directed by George Blair, written by David Chantler. Rifleman *Chuck Connors* teams up with a non-speaking relative of Francis the mule. Claiming to be Superman, he takes on an assignment to deliver a home baked pie to a lady's fiancé working in Alaska, but some crooks have designs on the same pie as the subject of a $25,000 wager. The real Superman makes all things right.

64: THE SEVEN SOUVENIRS

Directed by George Blair, written by Jackson Gillis. A better than average episode involving a contrived mystery over a series of knives that are claimed to have been disfigured by a spy attempting to stab Superman. The ringleader of the scheme is hoping for Superman to examine the knives with his x-ray vision and chemically alter their composition into pure radium. Superman figures it all out in the end.

65: KING FOR A DAY

Directed by George Blair, written by Dwight Babcock. A case of mistaken identity with Jimmy Olsen filling in as a prince of a foreign country where several of its leaders wish to assassinate him. With Kent keeping an eye on things, Jimmy remains safe while the real prince is free to work on bringing the bad politicians to justice, with the welcome assistance of the American Superman.

66: JOEY

Directed by Harry Gerstad, written by David Chantler. This time, the crooks are involved in race track corruption that involves an innocent young lady's horse. Lots of stock footage of *Hollywood Park* raceway before Superman steps in to make necessary corrections.

67: THE UNLUCKY NUMBER

Directed by Harry Gerstad, written by David Chantler. Kent accurately guessing the quantity of jelly beans in a jar allowing the landlady of a racketeer to win a contest that his gang has sponsored and rigged. The gang gets upset, attempts to shoot the racketeer, sporting a bullet-proof vest, with the landlady's grandson witnessing the affair and mistakenly assuming the racketeer is really Superman.

68: THE BIG FREEZE

Directed by Harry Gerstad, written by David Chantler. It is election time and an unscrupulous politician executes a plan to lure Superman into a specially designed refrigerator. Superman spends a portion of the show as a walking iceman, using makeup found in Lois' desk to appear as a normal Clark Kent, and proclaiming that the vote of the people is more powerful than any superman.

69: PERIL BY SEA

Directed by Harry Gerstad, written by David Chantler. Perry White, apparently a scientific mind before becoming editor, has been instrumental in developing a secret formula for getting uranium out of sea water. When Jimmy publishes Perry's exploits, the villains steal the formula, attempt to destroy the inventor, and escape in a submarine. Watch for Claude Akins as the leader of the gang.

70: TOPSY TURVEY

Directed by Harry Gerstad, written by David Chantler. This episode is more humorous than suspenseful as crazy Professor Pepperwinkle invents a gadget that disorients people in the immediate area. Crooks decide to make use of it in order to facilitate bank robberies.

71: JIMMY THE KID

Directed by Phil Ford, written by Leroy H. Zehren. A villain who is a Jimmy Olsen look-alike kidnaps the real Jimmy in order to assume his identity as a Daily Planet reporter. His intent is to thwart an investigation being conducted by Clark Kent, and when he breaks into Kent's apartment, he steals a Superman costume. When he is ultimately captured, Kent is once again faced with the task of explaining why he cannot be Superman.

72: THE GIRL WHO HIRED SUPERMAN

Directed by Phil Ford, written by David Chantler. A rich socialite is tricked into convincing Superman to unknowingly do a little smuggling by air. Our young reporters get themselves trapped in a bomb shelter with Kent who redirects lightning into a dead radio.

73: THE WEDDING OF SUPERMAN

Directed by Phil Ford, written by Jackson Gillis. Lois becomes a love interest for Superman. A courtship develops that makes Henderson jealous and Kent nervous because he is asked to become the best man. The doorbell rings to wake Lois up from a dream.

74: DAGGER ISLAND

Directed by Phil Ford, written by Robert Leslie Bellem. A treasure hunt on Dagger Island has a dead man's relatives competing for his estate. Lois and Jimmy end up in danger, and Superman manages to expose the estate owner as still being alive as well as keep the two reporters from becoming dead, all without ever showing his face.

75: BLACKMAIL

Directed by Harry Gerstad, written by Oliver Drake and David Chantler. A gang of silly villains attempt to use a new weapon on Superman. They also set out to plant some stolen money on the good Inspector Henderson to discredit his position on the police force. Superman once again proves that no invention of man will harm him.

76: THE DEADLY ROCK

Directed by Harry Gerstad, written by Jackson Gillis. Jimmy sees a government agent react to Kryptonite like Superman after being exposed to radiation from an exploding meteor *(Panic in the Sky)*. A scientist has recovered a fragment of the deadly meteor and offers to flush out the Man of Steel for any criminal willing to pay his price.

77: THE PHANTOM RING

Directed by Phil Ford, written by David Chantler. Each member of a gang carries a special coin that renders him invisible. When Kent refuses to join the gang, he is thrown out of an airplane. Free to act now as Superman, he gains possession of a special ring to become invisible for a climactic fight scene when he makes a surprise visit to the other very visible gang members.

78: THE JOLLY ROGER

Directed by Phil Ford, written by David Chantler. Kent, Lois, and Jimmy go to sea to witness a demonstration of Navy power. They are captured by a band of time-lost pirates who cannot be convinced that their island hideaway is about to become history when Navy weaponry is turned loose. Superman proceeds to intercept every shot fired by the Navy guns to save his friends.

79: PERIL IN PARIS

Directed by George Blair, written by David Chantler. While in France, Superman unknowingly becomes a jewel smuggler to assist an actress who wishes to flee a communist country. Jimmy provides the humor posing as an American jewel expert until Superman crashes through a wall to tie up the loose ends. Robert Shayne plays a French Police Inspector.

80: TIN HERO

Directed by George Blair, written by Wilton Schiller. A very thin plot has a meek bookkeeper accidently trapping an escaping criminal. He is hired by Perry White as a crime-solving consultant. Gangsters plan to trap him, but instead capture Jimmy. Superman's appearance saves the day before the final fade out. A boring affair at best.

81: MONEY TO BURN

Directed by Harry Gerstad, written by David Chantler. In this episode, villains pose as food service workers that appear on the scene of large warehouse fires to provide coffee and donuts to the firemen. They use the opportunity to rob safes by sneaking into the burned out buildings before the police arrive. Perry White figures out their activities after he is framed by the villains as a suspect in an insurance fraud.

82: THE TOWN THAT WASN'T

Directed by Harry Gerstad, written by Wilton Schiller. The villains have a clever set-up where they literally move a phoney town around on the interstate and collect cash in a phoney traffic court from unsuspecting travellers. When Jimmy is duped while off on vacation and returns to the office with his story, Lois and Kent get involved and Superman ends up solving the mystery.

83: THE TOMB OF ZAHARAN

Directed by George Blair, written by David Chantler. Lois Lane is mistaken for an ancient princess by two visiting dignitaries from an Egyptian-like country. She is invited to visit to do a story. Jimmy tags along only to find that they are being sealed away in a tomb to fulfill a prophecy. Kent senses danger and as Superman, goes to the Middle-Eastern tourist attraction to free his friends.

84: MAN WHO MADE DREAMS COME TRUE

Directed by George Blair, written by David Chantler. A clever crook convinces an aging monarch that he has the power to make things happen. The king has a superstitious nature that the con artist plans to use to his advantage until Superman intercedes.   Watch for John Banner who later appeared on *Hogan's Heroes.*

85: DISAPPEARING LOIS

Directed by Harry Gerstad, written by David Chantler and Peggy Chantler. Lois wants to scoop Kent on a story by pretending to vanish from her apartment to confuse him while she manages to enter the hotel suite of a gangster for an exclusive interview. Lois and Jimmy accidently discover they are hiding stolen cash and get themselves kidnapped.

86: CLOSE SHAVE

Directed by Harry Gerstad, written by Steven Post and Ben Crocker. Waiting to get a haircut, Jimmy overhears the barber trying to convince an old gangster friend to turn himself in and go straight, but the gangster's accomplices do not share his wish. Jimmy and the barber get caught in an explosive situation.

87: THE PHONEY ALIBI

Directed by George Blair, written by Peggy Chantler. A gang of crooks get hold of a new invention that allows them to commit crimes and then transport themselves through the telephone lines to a far away place to establish an alibi. When Lois and Jimmy are shipped off to the frozen North, Superman intercepts the call and captures the bad guys before the final fade out.

88: THE PRINCE ALBERT COAT

Directed by Harry Gerstad, written by Leroy H. Zehren. Superman is recuited by a young boy who has accidently given away to charity the old coat containing his great grandfather's life savings. He also manages to prevent a flood and save Lois and Jimmy at the same time.

89: THE STOLEN ELEPHANT

Directed by Harry Gerstad, written by David Chantler. With the series fast approaching the depths of mediocrity, this mindless story revolves around a missing circus elephant. A farm boy finds the animal in his barn where it has been stashed by the thieves, he tells Kent, and Superman catches the crooks.

90: MR. ZERO

Directed by Harry Gerstad, written by Peggy Chantler. Superman has his only close encounter with alien beings when he meets Billy Curtis portraying a green man from Mars with an incredible talent for immobilizing humans with a point of his finger. If only he had used it on the writer and director.

91: WHATEVER GOES UP

Directed by Harry Gerstad, written by Wilton Schiller. This time, it's Jimmy Olsen who accidently invents a new formula that defies gravity. As usual, this tired plot involves unscrupulous crooks who want to make a quick dollar on the work of someone else. Superman makes everything right and another season comes to a close.

92: THE LAST KNIGHT

Directed by Tommy Carr, written by David Chantler. The only color show directed by Tommy Carr has Lois and Jimmy quickly kidnapped by a secret order for the preservation of Knighthood. Kent soon learns of the plot to dupe an insurance company and steps in to save the day as Superman dressed in a suit of armor.

93: THE MAGIC SECRET

Directed by Phil Ford, written by Robert Leslie Bellem and Whitney Ellsworth. The newest dastardly criminal of Metropolis enlists a scientist with a theory to build a Kryptonite ray gun. Jimmy and Lois are used to lure Superman into yet another trap where the walls are closing in on the helpless hero. Superman manages to levitate Lois into a horizontal position to keep the walls from moving while Jimmy climbs to safety and redirects the deadly ray.

94: DIVIDE AND CONQUER

Directed by Phil Ford, written by Robert Leslie Bellem and Whitney Ellsworth. Lois, Kent, and Perry White are visiting a banana republic when Superman saves the life of a threatened political leader. The opposition uses a law to force Superman into jail to eliminate his interference in their next assassination attempt. Superman pushes a molecular division theory to the limit and becomes two supermen. One stays in jail while the other attempts to keep order.

95: THE MYSTERIOUS CUBE

Directed by George Blair, written by Robert Leslie Bellem and Whitney Ellsworth. An interesting premise has a notorious criminal attempting to beat the statute of limitations on crimes committed by remaining out of site within a cubed enclosure made up of some strange concrete material. Superman steps in at the very last moment to trick the gangster into making an exit just a little too soon. Another theory tested when Superman attempts to move his excited molecules through the solid walls of the cube.

96: THE ATOMIC CAPTIVE

Directed by George Blair, written by Robert Leslie Bellem and Whitney Ellsworth. A nuclear physicist has become contaminated by radiation and is in exile. Lois and Jimmy want an interview and foreign agents force a kidnapping, all ignoring the dangers of exposure as well as the desert test of a new warhead. Superman saves the day by flying around the mushroom cloud, driving the deadly explosion back into the ground.

97: THE SUPERMAN SILVER MINE

Directed by George Blair, written by Peggy Chantler. A rich Texan donates a silver mine to a children's charity fund, his devious double kidnaps him and assumes his identity, and Lois and Jimmy are thrown into the trap for good measure. Superman saves the day by capturing the bad guy with a super powered magnet aimed at the metal plate in the imposter's head.

98: THE BIG FORGET

Directed by George Blair, written by David Chantler. The tinkering Professor Pepperwinkle develops an aerosol spray that causes anyone who inhales it to forget the last fifteen minutes. Clark Kent puts it to good use when he is forced to expose his secret identity to save the day. Just think, two whiffs of this spray and we could forget the entire half hour episode.

99: THE GENTLE MONSTER

Directed by Howard Bretherton, written by David Chantler. Another invention of Professor Pepperwinkle, this time it is a mechanical man that is powered by a chunk of Kryptonite, causing the Man of Steel some temporary discomfort.

100: SUPERMAN'S WIFE

Directed by Lew Landers, written by Robert Leslie Bellem and Whitney Ellsworth. Lovely Joi Lansing portrays a policewoman who is assigned to go undercover *(not under cover)* as Superman's wife to help flush out some law breakers. Nice water scenes with our heroes trapped in a diving-bell.

101: THREE IN ONE

Directed by Lew Landers, written by Wilton Schiller and Whitney Ellsworth. Two unscrupulous circus performers, *The Human Fly* and *The Escape Artist*, team up with the *Strong Man* to execute crimes that appear to have been perpetrated by Superman.

102: THE BRAINY BURRO

Directed by George Reeves, written by David Chantler. Superman goes south of the border. Reeves teams up with his real-life friend *Natividad Vacio* and a non-speaking relative of *Francis, the Mule*. The mule has a gift for reading minds. Harmless and cute.

103: THE PERILS OF SUPERMAN

Directed by George Reeves, written by Robert Leslie Bellem and Whitney Ellsworth. This episode is an attempt to emulate the exciting cliff-hanger suspense of the serials of a by-gone era when Superman saves Perry from a buzz saw, Lois from a railroad train, and Jimmy from a runaway automobile.

104: ALL THAT GLITTERS

Directed by George Reeves, written by Robert Leslie Bellem and Whitney Ellsworth. This story revolves around a new invention to turn lead into gold, but is mostly made up of a dream sequence where Jimmy imagines that he and Lois have acquired the powers of Superman.

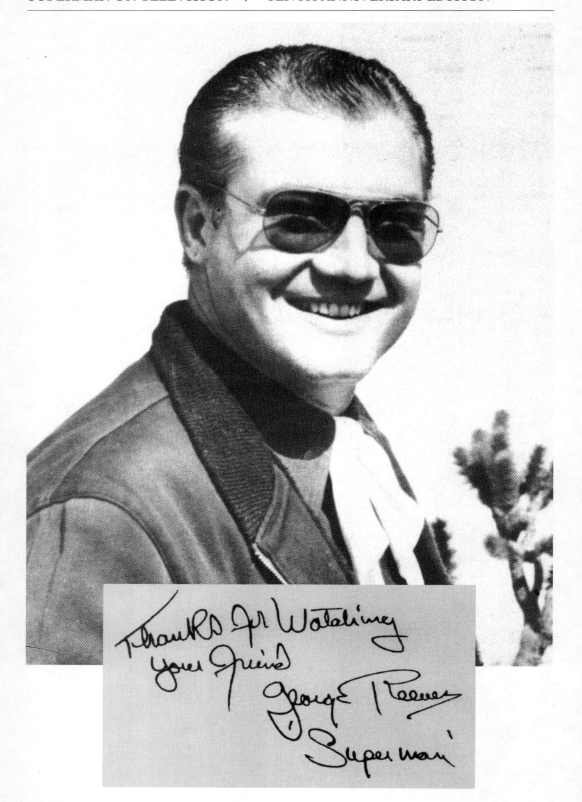

020911